PROMISED LANDS

CINEMA, GEOGRAPHY, MODERNISM

Sam Rohdie

'Is this all?' he said spontaneously.

He saw regret in her face – but there was a flick of the lip, also, a bending of the smile towards some indirection, a momentary dropping and lifting of a curtain over a forbidden passage.

F. Scott Fitzgerald

 Publishing

First published in 2001 by the
British Film Institute
21 Stephen Street, London W1P 2LN

The British Film Institute promotes greater understanding of,
and access to, film and moving image culture in the UK.

Cover design: Paul Wright/Cube
Cover images: (front) *The Geographer*, c. 1668–9, Johannes Vermeer (Städelsches Kunstinstitute,
Frankfurt am Main), *Sideways jump*, 1890–1, Eadweard Muybridge (Cinémathèque Francaise);
(back) *Mounting*, 1891, Eadweard Muybridge (Collège de France), *Walk with bent knees*, 1884,
Eadweard Muybridge (Collège de France).

Set in Italian Garamond by Alden Bookset, Oxford
Printed in England by The Cromwell Press, Trowbridge

British Library Cataloguing-in-Publication Data
A catalogue record for this book is available from the British Library
ISBN 0 85170 853-6 pbk
ISBN 0 85170 854-4 hbk

Contents

FOR AH FOON

'The history of the thing might amuse you,' he said. ' When I first became one of the New Anarchists I tried all kinds of respectable disguises. I dressed up as a bishop. I read up all about bishops in our anarchist pamphlets, in *Superstition the Vampire* and *Beasts of Prey.* I certainly understood from them that bishops are strange and terrible old men keeping a cruel secret from mankind. I was misinformed. When on my first appearing in episcopal gaiters in a drawing-room I cried out in a voice of thunder "Down! Down! presumptuous human reason!" they found out in some way that I was not a bishop at all. I was nabbed at once. Then I made up as a millionaire; but I defended Capital with so much intelligence that a fool could see that I was quite poor. Then I tried being a major ... I threw myself into the major. I drew my sword and waved it constantly. I called out "Blood!" abstractedly, like a man calling for wine. I often said, "Let the weak perish; it is the Law." Well, well, it seems majors don't do this. I was nabbed again. At last I went in despair to the President of the Central Anarchist Council, who is the greatest man in Europe.

'... He looked at me with his large but indecipherable face. "You want a safe disguise, do you? You want a dress which will guarantee you harmless; a dress in which no one would ever look for a bomb?" I nodded. He suddenly lifted his lion's voice. "Why, then, dress up as an *anarchist* you fool!" he roared so that the room shook. "Nobody will ever expect you to be dangerous then."'

G. K. Chesterton

Preface

I projected you into a future made of my present, helping you over streams and muddied banks, holding your hand on the cliffs of an Irish bay, strolling with you by a Belfast towpath, waking with you in my morning fantasies and playing with you in daytime dreams, and watching you in them, movements repeated but never the same. You accompanied me everywhere. Now, abruptly, having taken away your future presence, the present presence left of you is fading. Without a future reality, there is no remembering forwards, no fantasy, to look towards, no imagined place for taking place.

You were gone completely having been overwhelmingly here.

No more remembering, I said.

The nothing of images is made of something which if gone, nullifies the image, blankens it, empties it of everything save absence.

Nothing in the writing of this book, nor in my search for its subject, has been exterior to me. It has not been motivated by scholarly issues, something not yet known, a contribution to learning, the acquittal of a responsibility. Such motives left me cold. I have pursued the writing for no ambition, no good cause, nor duty, but for its pleasure and compulsion.

It is difficult to say what the pleasure or compulsion specifically are. The book is the search for them and their exemplification, the reason and the practice.

> – Qu'est-ce que vous allez chercher là-bas?
> – J'attends d'être là-bas pour le savoir.[1]

The book is vagrant.

It is made up of encounters and disappearances, the movement of words and their unravelling. It is not a report or a record, but a procedure. It begins in writing, its comings and goings, returns, hesitations, pauses, vaguenesses, disconnections, doubts, disappointments, obsessions, fatigue, misunderstandings and happiness.

There is no anterior, no before to this book, of which the writing is the after. Its tense is the present no matter how far back it goes into the past of myself or of history, of events or feelings, sayings or ideas, of what I read or thought, whenever by whomever, and no matter how often the writing has been drafted, rewritten, expanded, overwritten, crossed out. If something is recalled, it is now, as with a revision. And if I, from time to time, write in the past tense or make nominations which presume an earlier state, these are inexactitudes, fictions of tense and nomination.

What motivates the writing are suggestions, analogies, things that arrived without my calling, that I noticed or that intrigued me or that simply forced themselves upon me, paths that seemed possible and interesting, and which you can find only when you are upon them, at a crossroads or from a cliff top. By then you have already travelled some way. In any case, these encounters were unforeseen. There were occasions when I was taken by surprise. At times, a promising road became a dead end. This too said something. I have sought not to deny them, just in case.

Notes

1   – What are you looking for over there?

    – I will know when I get there.

Introduction

Le petit déclara soudain que ce qu'il aimait mieux c'était 'la géographie'.
Je soupçonnai que derrière cet amour se dissimulait un instinct de
vagabondage.[1]

André Gide, *Les Faux-Monnayeurs*

One

In April 1995, by chance, without definite intention or particular interest,
I wandered into a preview screening at the Hong Kong Film Festival of
early films made by travellers to China in the first three decades of the century. I wandered into the theatre as one might into a square, palace, church,
museum, small temple or park in a city one was visiting, or simply might
pause before a particular sight, even the most banal, of children with their
balloons, an ice-cream vendor, a pond with model sailboats, a fountain with
horses and nymphs spurting water, or where others might pass, like myself.
Not quite a *flâneur,* an almost impossible occupation in Hong Kong, a city
which scurries; nevertheless, in that spirit of openness and relaxed, attentive curiosity.

The films I saw that morning in Hong Kong were newsreels, familiar and
impersonal. One struck me. It was *The Chinese Revolution* made in 1912.
Prisoners are judged, then executed, in a terrifying, casual, offhand,
bureaucratic sorting of lives, almost inattentive, amid laughter, anecdotes
perhaps of some women the night before. The prisoners are blindfolded
as you might tie a shoe, then murdered as you might break a twig, the
everyday banal, hardly a ceremony or the usual *coup de théâtre* of execu-
tions, certainly for a camera.

One film caught my attention most of all, then absorbed me. I felt I had found something new and wonderful. It was a compilation film made by the Musée Albert Kahn in Boulogne-Billancourt with footage from a journey to China by Albert Kahn in 1909. Kahn was a merchant banker and a Jew. He was accompanied to China by his chauffeur, Alfred Dutertre. Kahn had substantial investments in Japan and China. He was fond of Japan, where development occurred within the order and structures of stable traditions and institutions. Investments were safer there.

Before the trip, Kahn encouraged Dutertre to learn to use a film camera, a still camera, and the techniques of stereoscopy, colour, panorama and sound recording. The images in the compilation film were Dutertre's.

Dutertre kept a written diary of the journey to China which the Hong Kong Festival reproduced as programme notes. The diary is plain and matter-of-fact, concerned with modes of transport, schedules, sardines in tins, the anxiety of arrivals. It is in the manner of Jules Verne. Realistic details catalogued and amassed.

Might Dutertre have felt himself to be Passepartout, acting out the role, doubling himself?

Two

At the time, I was working on a book on the films of Federico Fellini, a book not yet written. It has not yet been written for reasons to do with my wandering into the screening in Hong Kong. The book was to be concerned with Fellini's spectacularisation of forms of popular entertainment and his doubling and mirroring, often vertiginous, of objects, persons, incidents. His film *Lo sceicco bianco*, for example, set in the world of photo-romances, is as false (or as true) as the photo-romance it describes, yet the distortion, the mirror, provides its truth because the double is the key to a difference. The film is the shadow-clouded mirror image of the projected images and fantasies within the film and of the characters.

In *La dolce vita*, the Via Veneto was reconstructed by Fellini. So too was memory and hence self. These are reflections, and reflections of reflections, receding towards no centre or place where they might come to rest because they generate further likenesses. Memory is presented as a silhouette. The borders between fiction and fact, invention and reality, projection and document, dream and memory, are permeable.

The characters inhabit worlds of popular spectacle – variety, opera, television, the fairground – worlds enmeshed in fantasies and projections. Characters flow between realities, like Cabiria in *Le notti di Cabiria*, thus they are easily duped, taking a reflection for an object, an image for a fact. Entrances and exits proliferate.

The films are prismatic, faceted, like a gemstone, without a privileged surface. And all surfaces falsely reflective.

Gilles Deleuze's work on the cinema was then current. Deleuze was a Bergsonian. As a consequence, I read Henri Bergson for the first time. I was delighted by Bergson, what he said about memory and time, a playfulness that cut the ground from surety, an elegance and lucidity of writing.

Bergson helped me to approach Fellini. He also took me away from Fellini (the better to return). He suggested a wide field that I had not imagined of movement, philosophy, structures of thought ('thought is a movement'), photography, painting and the cinema.

The birth of the cinema was contemporary with Bergson's philosophy. Both are essays on time and the subject.

The history of the cinema belongs to modernism and the history of modernism is shaped by philosophical concepts of time, memory, desire, the unconscious: areas of uncertainty and instability. A history of the cinema needs to take this philosophical/ideological context into an account of the origins that made the cinema not only likely and possible, but necessary.

Three

Eric Rohmer narrates philosophical tales. In these, he obsessively records characters speaking: dialogues at dinner parties, over lunch, at breakfast, in cafés, at cocktails, on walks, in gardens, in cars, on balconies, in restaurants, in flats, on the beach, at receptions. It is what his films principally *show*, words spoken. The words adhere to images, or try to, as characters seek to understand what they see. Their sight, however, is clouded and distorted by desire, as in Hitchcock.

A discrepancy opens up in Rohmer's films between what is seen by the characters and what they believe they see, what they say they see, between what is and what is imagined. Their attempts to interpret lead to misunderstanding, inconclusiveness, falsity. They invent fictions for themselves as truths. Signifying is elusive, often absurdly, mockingly so. In Rohmer, we are only a step away from Hitchcock and the terrors of misunderstandings.

The elusiveness of understanding, the trap of surety, are problems not only for the characters but for the audience who observe but do not always see.

Rohmer's characters vainly seek to create sure realities from realities that are blank, ambiguous, mute, if not unsignified, open nevertheless to multiple significations. Every fiction, every interpretation, every certainty in Rohmer's films is shadowed by an alternative that unsettles them.

No image, no voice, no line is singular or secure.

Rohmer stages intersections at which characters and their words, interpretations, fictions, dreams and projections meet and criss-cross at odds with each other, a passing by, a touching and glancing, seldom cohering; as each tries to unify and assert their own reality each speaks for the other as for themselves, with the result that realities multiply and identities are confounded. The images they seek to secure exist in a reality that shifts with each perspective placed over it.

The desires of Rohmer's characters to understand never *settle*. The discrepancies and imbalances between images and words are the motors of his films. Each attempt to line these up, misaligns them further. Despite the long takes of interminable dialogue going nowhere, the films are never stationary, nor are we.

Bergson, interested in time passing, in the openness of thought, in the provisional nature of significance, sensitised me to Rohmer and to the films I saw that morning in Hong Kong. His writing flows. As it flows, it creates streams and rivulets. These grow, a writing that expands. You literally see the expansion, the openings, feel it as you become the wave of your thoughts in a current of words which 'takes' you with it.

As you read, surfaces extend, depths intensify, and with a resonance, as with music and poetry.

Bergson's writing exemplifies the thoughts he has of time passing and thoughts passing in time. His words permeate, leave ripples, traces like the traces of light, vibrations and tails of movements. His writing is crisp and sensual like Antonioni's images, clear, unstable, impermanent. You watch the image and the objects in it being transformed, fading in, becoming other. Bergson thought the movement of thought with a writing that moved accordingly.

It has the qualities of Proust and Kafka and Joseph Roth.

Four

Verne wrote *Le Rayon vert*, which is also the title of a Rohmer film. The *rayon vert* is the colour of the last rays of the sun as it sinks below the horizon, but which only occurs in exceptional atmospheric conditions. Rohmer uses the phenomenon to play with his character Delphine's (Marie Rivière) search for a rare, unique, equally exceptional romantic encounter, an almost impossible one, a love invented, projected, a wish-come-true-as-illusion, an alternative story to the one Delphine has been living of loneliness and dissatisfaction that we have been watching, and hoping, as she does, for it to be transformed, for the unlikely/impossible to happen and the wish to come true, as it can in the cinema.

Unbelievably, it does.

But does it?

As she sits with a man she wants to be her lover waiting for the *rayon vert*, does the green ray actually appear?

And do we in fact see it?

Or do we imagine we see it out of our (her) desire?

Do we too invent a story of something out of nothing?

The *rayon vert* is, and the wished-for lover is, like the unexpected discovery of the murderer in a detective story when you have thought, have been (mis)led to think, it was someone else as if you had been thinking yourself in one story then encountering another one, the 'true' story in which perhaps you were but never realised.

Rohmer plays on the ambiguity between stories imagined and stories taking place. The principal events of his films record these imaginings, the 'other' narrative, there but unnoticed. These tales, imagined and real, shadow one another, like an absent lover shadows present ones, as nuance, tone, motive and threat.

All true loves are triangular.

In Rohmer's *Le Beau mariage*, Sabine (Béatrice Romand), frustrated in the triangle of affairs with married men, wilfully decides to take a husband.

She assumes that someone who is not interested in her (the lawyer Dussollier who is determined not to get married) is interested in her, and wants to marry her without even knowing it. She is the romantic heroine of her own story which possesses her.

Five

Bergson, when a student at the Sorbonne, had been employed by Albert Kahn as his private tutor. Kahn moved up the hierarchy of a Jewish merchant bank in Paris, the Goudchoux Bank. He made shrewd investments in South African gold and eventually came to control the bank that had hired him as a clerk. Kahn became one of the wealthiest men in France.

The head of the bank was a Jew from Alsace. Alsace had been ceded along with Lorraine to Germany after the French defeat in the 1870 Franco-Prussian war. The defeat encouraged the reform and modernisation of French institutions, particularly educational ones, on grounds of 'national' necessity. It gave an impetus to geographical studies (military uses), and movement studies (physical fitness, physically efficient soldiers, efficient workers, streamlined assembly lines). Both these studies used photography, the one to measure and map geograpical details of terrain, the other to measure muscular structures in movement and under stress (as in the work of Étienne-Jules Marey).

Kahn was the son of a cattle dealer, a traditional Jewish occupation since the 1400s. He had no formal higher education.

Bergson, the tutor-to-become-philosopher, and Kahn, the banker, became friends. Bergson's efforts to bring the United States into the war with Germany (he travelled to Washington to try to persuade Woodrow Wilson) and his later involvement in the formation of the League of Nations were connected to Kahn's philanthropic activities before the First World War which Kahn initiated immediately on his return from China: travel scholarships, a geographical photographic archive, a Chair in Geography, international affairs institutes, publications and foundations to better understand the mechanisms of the new world being formed.

French Jews particularly associated themselves with the universalist values of French republicanism, its secularism, modernism, liberalism, rationalism and education, a reason for the virulence of French anti-Semitism, part of a wider traditionalism feeling itself under threat. The Jews identified with with the French state. Some in France, including the church, felt that the state had betrayed them. They associated the state with modernism and the Jews as the instrument of modernism.

Kahn and Bergson were liberal internationalists.

The film material in the Dutertre–Kahn film was like the films of the Lumières, part tourism, part a fascination with the exotic, part an interest in the mundane and the everyday. The film displayed the capacities of new technology to facilitate travel and to record: the railway/steamship/motor car and the camera. It features monuments (the walls of Beijing), urban intersections (a bridge across a river), ports, economic activities (discharging cargo, street sellers, caravans), transport (railway lines carved through mountain passes), local customs (a tea ceremony).

Some sequences, shot from the back of moving trains, moving ships and automobiles, as with the earliest films, broke from the immobility and fixity of the camera. These were images in time recording time.

The recording and representation of movement were among the signs of modernism. It could be enchanting: the serpentine dances of Loïe Fuller, registered by Lumière, attended by Rodin.

The dancer, the horse, poised motion and unusual poses, dramatic instants, were late nineteenth-century obsessions.

They are present in Degas, for example.

Eroticism, for Rodin, belonged to a becoming, a restless, a flowing mobility. His sculpting was fluid, tentative like a caress, or a glance, feeling its way in material, along surfaces. Rodin did not like photography. In it nothing moved, he said.

His erotic watercolours of women are beautiful. A grazing brushstroke, a seeping stain of colour beyond definition of line, the rapidity of line and its nervousness, the quivering, seeking of a caress, gesture more than representation.

The making of a mark is the subject of the mark made, like the women caressing themselves as he caressed them in a stroke of the brush, a glancing and seeking of the instant and its passing trace, the strokes accompanying each other, two realities shifting place.

The film material I saw in the Kahn film I had wandered into in Hong Kong had the indefinite sense of responding to what came its way, unlike the newsreels I had seen which insidiously filmed their spectacles of death. The Kahn material had a personal aspect, a sense of the diary, the subjective which made the objective clearer, placed it for me more sharply into focus.

In *The Birth of a Nation* actions are either motivated by the emotional/psychological needs of characters or are presented in order to provoke emotional/psychological reactions. It makes of us a subject in relation to the object-film, a subject desirous, fearful, investing ourselves in the object.

The characters mirror us and we mirror the characters.

It was the perfection of the devices of cinema to convey this subject/object relation and to see the subject as the motive of the narrative and at the intersection of narratives (other characters, other possibilities, the Klansmen would arrive or not arrive, for example, or the gun butt fall or not, innocence be rescued or not, the threat therefore of another 'story', a threat codified in parallel editing, in the chase, in the coming-to-the-rescue-of-the-lady-in-distress). That was Griffith's gift and his modernity.

There were sequences in the Dutertre–Kahn film that recalled familiar Lumière genres: arrivals and departures from stations, ports, quaysides; an obsession with launchings, passers-by, the milling of crowds. The sequences compressed in them notions of progress (modes of transport, port installations), movement, modernity, activity, commerce, associating these and verifying them by the actuality of having-been-there, a truthfulness connected to travel, as true as the snapshot of tourists posing before the Sphinx, attesting to presence.

Witnessing had most to do with the photograph, the sensation of having-been-there. The Lumière films, without a future of an as-yet-to-be cinema to which it might belong, belongs to a past of photography and its witnessings of place and to a future/present in which the past passes in the moment of the fading of the present.

The cinema's tense is a present one, an illusionary being-there where truth (authenticity) is less a factor than it is in the photograph. The cinema invites you to enter an experience that is occurring, that includes you, the dizzying track, for example.

One of the most engaging sequences in the Dutertre–Kahn film, in the sense of physical, kinetic engagement, is of a train leaving Beijing. As it goes forward, the walls of the city pass by, retreat backwards and disappear. The rapidity of the temporal flow is stunning. The acceleration gives a sense of force, of power. Objects and monuments are caught up then flung aside to vanish, dissolved by the movement that seized them.

The most solid things and the most ancient appear fugitive, transitory.

Six

When Kahn returned from Japan and China, he established a geographical archive of photographs (*autochromes*) and films, *Les Archives de la planète*, a vast record of the world (72,000 *autochromes*, 180,000 metres of film), the necessity for which Kahn insisted upon because the world was disappearing, and disappearing in the instant it was being photographed as a consequence of technologies to which photography belonged.

Photography witnessed transformations and destructions in which it was included and of which it was in part the instrument. The social sciences, like geography and anthropology, documented and recorded what science was effacing, transforming, making obsolete, sometimes whole peoples, regions, continents such as Africa. The social sciences were in a similar position to photography, recording the passage of what it was implicated in causing to pass. Photography was the favoured documentary/research tool of the social sciences, as it was the principal instrument for the Kahn *Archives*.

The technology of modernity had made travel, like Kahn's journey, more possible, and more comfortable. It was fitting then that the *Archives* were geographical, dependent on the technology of travel and the photographic recording of the effects of technology (the transformation of the world). The dominant category of films until 1914 was 'geographical'. Comings and goings, arrivals and departures, were their principal subjects.

Neither Kahn, nor the *Archives* director, Jean Brunhes, ever spoke of the *autochromes* that constituted the collection as 'representation'. To them these images were not 'views', but reality.

The archive, the collection are the inclusion and ordering of what is identifiable, solid, factual, real. Social science disciplines, like geography and anthropology, and also history, all of them marked by evolutionism, were disciplines which amassed evidence as collected facts within evolutionary structures. The structures were structures of facts and were the means for defining what fact, document and reality were.

In these structures, there was a vertical evolutionary hierarchy (stages of development) and a horizontal evolutionary line (the line of progress). Different levels of development, coexisting at the same historical time, were made part of a universal narrative advancing toward higher stages of development which referred back to vertical structures of an evolution.

The evolution and the facts it contained were equally deemed to be true (positive).

The collection was reality plus objective science.

Facts were sculpted as objects, immobilised in structures, then brought into a movement of time.

Facts (realities) literally fell into place.

Places were reserved for realities by the collection, the catalogue, the archive, the museum as remains in a mausoleum.

Seven

In *The Great Train Robbery* of 1903, made by Edwin S. Porter, the forms of a linear film narrative are already in place and with it the hysteria of parallel editing, the hallmark of early American films, and especially of Griffith's films. (Parallelism is there too in a compressed space in the tenements in Eisenstein's *Strike* and in the Odessa Steps sequence of his *Potemkin*.)

Porter displays a mastery in the organisation of time as at once progressive and simultaneous, advance and overlap. He uses it to dramatic/emotional effect, not simply to tell a story but to involve the viewer.

At the end of *The Great Train Robbery*, one of the cowboy characters, in close-up, faces the camera (the audience), draws his six-shooter, and fires.

This film-shot/gun-shot at the beginnings of cinema is emblematic of its modernity. The image faces in two directions. It is presence and absence, similitude and illusion, a something because of resemblance, a nothing because it is only an image. The figure in close-up defies perspective and distance. It overturns balances, within the frame and within the fiction, exploding beyond these directly towards us.

It is a new kind of involvement.

It creates a new position, a new subjectivity.

The attempt to render movements of the horse posed an unresolved conflict between the objective accuracy of the depiction of movement and the depiction of the sense of movement interior to subjective perception. The horse belonged to an outdated and superseded world, just as the primitive did, and like the primitive, and the passing world, it was a subject central to modern preoccupations with perception and perception of objects passing through time and of time passing.

The photographed real, the actual natural, seemed unnatural in the photograph (Degas's horses and his dancers), while what seemed natural, in contrast, was the effect of an illusion, of misperceptions, an inability to see the way things really were in objective realitiy as science defined them to be. Objective reality in movement, often imperceptible to the eye, was perceptible to the machine, to lenses and the camera, or could be tracked by a machine-engine.

The interest in the gait of the horse belonged to a reassessment not simply of movement, but of perception.

In the paintings of Delacroix, which prefigure Impressionism, desire and passion destabilise the canvas and the figures in it. The reality of Delacroix's feelings distort a neoclassical, harmonious, symetrical ideal and a positivist scientific one because it introduces into the painting the subject who sees and who paints.

In the paintings of Degas, the instantaneous, photographic sight, the objective/subjective impression, makes all ideals strange.

The work of Eadweard Muybridge on the horse's gait at a gallop and the zoological photographic analyses of movement by Marey need to be situated in the vector of interests in movement and perception. Muybridge was so caught in the dilemma of the natural and the illusory, the objective and the subjective, that many of his studies of movement fake continuities in order to make them appear more pleasing and more acceptable, by giving them a fluidity they lacked in fact but were sought for in conformity with ideas of the natural. Muybridge was a showman.

He was not principally a scientist belonging to the prehistory of the cinema and technologies related to the analysis and freezing of movement in time. He was one of the first illusionists of the early cinema.

His studies are studies of narrative continuity. The impulse was not as it was with Marey, to analyse movement, but a desire to astonish and to please even at the expense of 'truth'.

Muybridge's work on the horse at gallop was financed by the owner of a California railroad, Leland Stanford, whose passion was racehorses. Stanford wanted to settle a bet on the actual placement of the hooves of the horse at gallop.

The track (rail) back in *The Birth of a Nation* of the ride forward of the Ku Klux Klansmen is exhilarating. These mythic racist monsters on horseback ride against the modernity that would suppress and overwhelm them, and with a fervour and energy that only modernity could represent. The physical excitement of the ride exacerbates the emotion that motivates it. The movement of the horse is aligned with a movement of emotion in the spectator organised in a pursuit-chase shaped by parallel cutting, a narrative of time made urgent, compressed, the hysteria of which is the consequence of technologies that could virtualise and fictionalise time. Science served spectacle and brought subjectivity, impression, desire, into the soul of the image.

The cinema is linked, like Impressionism, to the modern sciences, but not in the obvious way, by technology, but by the inclusion of the subject as a constituent of the image and of what can be seen, a new optics that touched on psychologies of sight and thereby upon desire.

The steamship that brought Kahn to Shanghai and the railways in China and Japan in which he had invested were altering the social and physical landscape that the photographs and his films recorded. Kahn was an agent of that passing. The technological transformation of the past was a source of pride to those promoting it, to industrialists, colonialists, bankers like Kahn, but also a source of doubt to them, even of regret, as it was for Griffith and later for John Ford. Ford mourned the past and the loneliness its passing brought.

Mourning is a condition of modernism.

The *Archives* belong to the triumph and optimism of progress and to the nostalgia for what progress was causing to be lost. The Western, the *Archives*, the ride of the Klansmen in *The Birth of a Nation*, share a history and an ideology that regretted a fading out, was uncertain of the fading in, and was complicit in both. These practices were driven by the gap, by irreconciliability.

The photograph by its form and its relation to time, and by its relation to progress, condensed contradictory sentiments.

It immobilised time, events without movement, no longer existent or soon to be extinguished, passing at the moment the photograph was being taken, thereby initiating its loss. The favourite subjects of early photography were the portrait, the family (posed), the exotic. The exotic (and the traditional as exotic) – the subjects of the *Archives* – had been opened up by the technology of which photography was a product, and by the demand for markets and materials of which colonialism was a consequence.

One often forgets, particularly with the concentration on studies of representation and because of the immense capital investments in the cinema, that photography was a vast mass-consumption industry in the 19th century. The cinema, which was heir to photography, was organised by the Lumières on the industrial lines of their photographic enterprises, that is globally, to capture and secure markets and to forestall competition.

It was fitting that on his journey to Japan and China, Kahn brought with him his chauffeur, Dutertre, trained in the technologies of visual recording that the Lumières had invented. They, like Kahn, were entrepreneurs on a global scale. They sold the new machinery of representation (Kahn and the Lumières would have thought of it as recording) on world markets. Kahn archived what he recorded as he exploited markets, central to the liberal faith of spreading progress: reaping profits and modernising over the seas.

The object immobilised in time in the photograph was, more so than the photograph, subject to time. Immobility was a means of taking possession of movement, stopping it down, seizing hold of it, arresting time in the pregnant moment. The cinema reinscribes movement in the object and thus an order of time that destabilises the object by returning it to the flow of time, thereby combining presence (object, document) with disappearance, certainty with instability (passing) and taking the subject along with it within time.

Eight

Godard remarked that the cinema resembles sculpture and music. In it appearances are solid, like statues. The statues however are not still. They are, like music, passing and unpossessable. Cinema is not one thing nor the other but the movement between.

For Godard, the passing of appearances is caught in a generation of likenesses and resemblances, mirrors that move and shift likenesses forward and backward like reflections inflecting each other as they are translated into a difference to reflect then go beyond their sameness. The movement is a translation, a metaphor, each thing defined by an other which it is not that it resembles or is made to resemble.

For example, in *Vivre sa vie*, the title suggests an unattainable likeness because it can only be realised by a comparative otherness. Nana (Anna Karina) sits in the cinema crying at the tears of Jeanne d'Arc who hears her sentence of death in the Dreyer film – the sentence is addressed to Jeanne in the one film and Nana in the other and Anna Karina outside of both; the story of Porthos, who died at the moment he reached consciousness, is told to Nana by the philosopher Brice Parain who brings her to language and consciousness as the Inquisitor (Antonin Artaud) brings Jeanne to her consciousness of death; the quote from Edgar Allan Poe's *The Oval Portrait*, the story of a young woman posing for her portrait by her husband, progressively drained of life as her portrait takes colour, is read by the young man to Nana in Godard's voice. Godard is like the artist in the Poe story painting the portrait not only of Nana (Anna) but of his wife Anna (Nana). Nana's death at the close of the film is a death dictated by the gangster film which encloses *Vivre sa vie* and by the other associations. Finally, there is the pair Nana/Anna and the simultaneity/overlap of character and actress, fiction and the real, a double portrait within the fiction which contains the film and is the outside of the film, the film and its enunciation, at once, side by side.

There is no centre in a Godard film.
Every appearance is associated with another analogous to it.
These associations are neither linear nor directional but plural and reversible. Cited texts by Godard of literature, painting, the cinema generate other texts to form series and circles of texts, overlaps, webbings of textual similitudes as in *Vivre sa vie*.
In the stream of associations – the link of one thing resembling another – there is neither original nor copy. No position is fixed, or direction secure. Links are not explanations. The metaphor is a play of meanings, dreams of meanings, possibilities of meaning without settling ever into the stability of meaning.

A text cited is a locus which shifts as new texts proliferate as if from within it. This is not displacement, nor addition, but approximation. The metaphor causes you to see what you had seen a moment before as different from what it now appears to be. You will see that difference again differently in the course of further seeing, another perspective without cancelling or limiting others as in a Cubist painting or the swirls of Soutine which 'take up' vision, hurl it into space, Soutine approaching Pollock.

In *Le Mépris*, Homer's *Odyssey*, Rossellini's *Viaggio in Italia* and Lang's *Die Nibelungen* invoke each other, like rhymes and distant echoes. What is seen, more precisely felt, is a movement of metaphor/analogy/translation/association, a movement between appearances, in space.
Godard liberates texts into a vast space where they float, combine, coalesce, disjoin, find each other. In so doing the unaccustomed, unexpected, unaccounted for are generated, made possible and encountered.

In *Le Mépris*, the Greek statues are also those that Ingrid Bergman gazes at in the museum in *Viaggio in Italia*, are the gods of Langian fatalism, are the excavations of Schliemann at Troy, are the doubled objects of the film of a film that includes the film Godard is making whose fictional director is Lang and the one Godard is making within the fiction as Lang's fictional assistant.

Godard and Lang are the enunciated of one film and the enunciators of others. The shifts are caused by mirrors. They recall Velazquez in the mirroring of doubles and the reflected presence of the artist in the canvas and Velazquez again in the nudity of Brigitte Bardot as statue, model, painting and historical reference as in Velazquez's *Odalisque*.

The film, by virtue of the streams and meanderings of language and images, opens them towards an unknown, to the mad and incomprehensible, the criminal and scandalous. It violates grammar, confounds good sense, disrupts decorum, skews reasonableness, liberates significance.

The statues in *Le Mépris* move within a stillness of space that whirls around them.

The *Archives* are photographic (the *autochrome*). Its 'record' of geographical objects, infinite and exhaustive, with the indiscriminateness of the collection (roofs, horses, rivers, bridges, irrigation systems, toyshops, temples, ruins, waterfalls, cultivated fields, outdoor restaurants), proposed itself as scientific: objective documents for a geography of place and people as they were. Photography, declared Jean Brunhes, was '*the* scientific method' of the science of geography. Geography was photographic (visual) and photography was geographical (objective).

To Brunhes there was no ambiguity in the photographic image, no illusionism. It was simply, irrefutably 'true', not a verisimilitude, not a fictional truth-seeming, not a representation, not a 'view'.

It was fact.

Scientific progress created the need for the document (on which science based itself and could proceed) and the catalogue as inventory and material for progress. The document was also a motive for progress. It presented sights of backwardness to be conquered, of an exotic to be tamed, of a bizarre normalised in the name of the benefits (and self-evident necessity) of the civilised modern, of areas to exploit.

Jean Brunhes was a theorist of *la géographie humaine.* He had been a student of Paul Vidal de la Blache, the founder of French modern geography.
Brunhes's brother worked in thermodynamics. Brunhes was devoted to science and progress. He was also a spiritualist Catholic concerned with
interiority, tradition and faith that he felt to be threatened by science and
modernity. Brunhes's personal position informed his geography which was
intent to find certainties (truths, facts) in the face of the uncertainties of
time, change and the unreliability of observation.

Human geography studied human traces on the physical surface of the
earth. In part, this involved adaptation, linked to biology, to Darwinism and
Lamarck (*the* most revolutionary scientific achievement of the 19th century). In part, this involved transformation, linked to engineering, energy,
thermodynamics: the digging of canals, of tunnels, the laying of cables, the
expansion of rail, mechanically power-driven machines and transport, the
building of bridges; nature spanned, shifted, diverted, disembowelled,
reconfigured, reformed, rebuilt and encompassed. These two aspects – one
conservative, regionalist, adaptive, gradualist, and the other radical,
nationalist, transformative, rapid, man-made and global – were compressed
in the structures of *la géographie humaine* and were at the heart of it as if
in dialogue and debate with itself.

In this manner and by these means geography and photography were
connected. Photography provided the evidence for change, the documents
of it, the now and the later, the backward and the yet to be, the worm of
progress at the centre of the image, and the nostalgia for what was changing, including a nostalgia for the permanent and the objective recorded in
the shifting and the unstable.

Such ambiguity was a source of internal conflict in the new discipline of
geography. Colonial geography, for example, was modernist, expansive,
aggressive, transformative. Bring the modern to the colonies, it argued,
shift people to new places, overturn nature, create lakes, build dams.

The geography of Vidal, centred on France and to which Brunhes was
heir, was conservative and conservationist. It wanted to preserve landscape
and region, and ways of living (*genres de vie*) considered adaptive, natural.
Of course, there had to be change. Development was needed for progress,

but based not on a machine model but on a biological one of adjustments, the human not unduly disrupted, the social not radically overturned, nature developed but by degrees.

The adaptive conservative aspects of *la géographie humaine* were in line with a liberal ideology of gradualism informed by fears of the social consequences of rapid change (revolution, upheaval). It was a central assumption in the great philanthropic efforts of nineteenth-century industrialists, financiers and bankers like Kahn whose fortune was made in colonial investments.

It was an enlightened, productive charity.

Nine

Reasons come after as rationalisations ('She had green eyes' – *le Rayon vert*).

Pursuit is not of the object but of your attachment to it, of you in the object, and is therefore a pursuit of self, the object figured and drawn by your desires.

The magic of the phenomenon of *le Rayon vert* is that it is supposed to offer, in the split second of its appearance, and for that split second only, an understanding, an illumination. The observer/subject and the external world are fused in the moment of the green ray, an incandescent enlightenment. You need to be patient and fortunate enough to be there in the instant it appears and which endures only in the instantaneous.

'... en portant la subjectivité à son comble qu'on atteint l'objectivité ...'

'Le sociologue et le psychologue ont beau serrer de plus en plus leurs réseaux de connaissances, toucher de plus en plus près à l'*objectivité*, ils seront toujours des observateurs, c'est-à-dire situés en pleine *subjectivité*. Tous les savants en sont là.'[2]

Ten

In Jean Rouch's cinema, there is a double interrogation propelled by the question, formulated variously as, 'How do you live?'. The response to the question is inevitably some kind of representation, some kind of story which includes the self as subject and as storyteller. It is the beginning of Rouch's narrative and of his documentary, a narrative founded on the problem of how to film the response to the question. It involves the creation of a narrative by the characters (usually a journey), in action or words. The films are documentaries in so far as all answers, all tales, all stories, all sketches, no matter how fantastic, how contrived, how silly, belong to ethnography.

The characters become their own storytellers, their own invented characters, which is their truth and which Rouch 'objectively' and affectionately records. Like his characters, he too is a storyteller and he too is within his stories.

Because Rouch's fictions arise from the everyday document, and because the document resides in the manner and performance of fiction, Rouch displays an essential truth about ethnography, which is its fictionality. Fiction is a means to ethnographic truth for Rouch, and a truth about the cinema. What brings the cinema and ethnography together in his work is this will to fiction and the fact of it. His documentaries are the means to find the truth of cinema and of ethnography, partners in fabulation, in invention, projection, of narration in images, the pleasure of telling stories, of arranging myths, of making precious nothing (rien) *out of something* (quelque chose), *creating resemblances in images.*

The dimension of play and awareness, of losing and finding yourself and to become lost again in illusions and denials and in fictions, and yet never completely, is at the heart of the pleasures of the cinema. The acknowledged 'father' of the French nouvelle vague *was Jean Rouch.*

In Rouch's film Cocorico *the main character, M. Poulet (Mr. Chicken), travels in the West African bush in his ramshackle Citroën to buy chickens for sale in town. He returns with a few mangy specimens. Along the way he finds witches, liars, inventors, charlatans and bricoleurs like himself. He fords rivers on rafts, picks up hitch-hikers, dismantles his car, experiences magic, makes friends, listens to stories and sleeps under the stars. Like many of Rouch's films, this is a road movie.*

I want to travel like M. Poulet, even to accepting some of the discomforts. I have tried to design locations with as many entrances as possible for things to pass through and, fleetingly, take place, encountering each other, overlapping, encouraging opportunities for surprise, the delight of chance meetings and unexpected similitudes, as you might find at a party.

Sometimes, I am sure, I shall be forced to disassemble everything, cross where there are no bridges, and reassemble what is left on the other side, even to stealing what I don't have, but need, or inventing and making do, like M. Poulet and, like him, taking, if necessary, an illogical leap.

Notes

1 'The youngster suddenly announced that what he preferred was 'geography'. I suspected that what lay behind this love was an instinct for wandering.'

2 '... by taking subjectivity to its limits one arrives at objectivity ...' 'Even if the sociologist and the psychologist bring together their networks of knowledge, coming closer and closer to *objectivity*, they will never cease being observers, that is to say, completely situated in *subjectivity*. All scholars are like that.'

Chapter One
Italy

Her ego began blooming like a great rich rose as she scrambled back along the labyrinths in which she had wandered for years ...

'Why, I'm almost complete,' She thought. 'I'm practically standing alone, without him.'

Tangled with love in the moonlight she welcomed the anarchy of her lover.

F. Scott Fitzgerald

One

I trained as a historian, later as an anthropologist. For a time, I was a historian of modern West Africa. I came to study film relatively late in my life. I began to see films in an organised way only in the mid-1960s in Ghana.

The Americans had dumped US film production of the 40s and 50s on Africa. In Ghana I saw the films of Minnelli, Hawks, Ford, Boetticher, the Westerns of Lesley Selander, Jerry Lewis–Frank Tashlin comedies, the films of Jacques Tourneur. I discovered Nicholas Ray's Johnny Guitar *and I discovered Anthony Mann and the late films of Fritz Lang.*

Most of my work on film centred on Italy, a place I always come back to. Italy became an adopted home. A part of me became an adopted son of fathers I loved: Antonioni, Pasolini, Rossellini, Visconti, later, Bertolucci.

My father was hard for me to believe.

My wanderings from New York, where I was born, from a Jewish-American culture I rejected, parents I loathed, a past fictionalised and never reconciled, caused me to search for home, home never feeling like home, and not anywhere feeling like it ever. It seemed my childhood had never been, that I grew without growing up.

I invented everything, including myself. The search for home projected itself on to persons and places, films and books.

What if, this is my father, that I was born here, that I will live there. It was a hope that in fictions I would find a centre to return to, call a halt to the weariness of looking, of dispersion, loneliness, lostness. In the fictional, in performance, I might, at last, live in the real.

Italy was the nearest thing to home. It was where I could be who I was though I knew the belonging was invented.

I am dark, olive-skinned. It was easy to go in disguise.

I was most myself when I was at a distance, a stranger, and a stranger to myself, a condition of travelling which is a displacement. I travelled alone to guarantee displacement and better permit an unchallenged make-believe. Bringing someone with you might contradict you with their presence, with facts. 'Do you love me?' 'What shall we do today?' 'Did that really happen?'...

I could find no one to share make-believe. No love. R sometimes, and that could be terror. I acted, I lied, I was false, I conceived myself other than I was, insisting on it. I became what I was not and was not what I became.

The best films take deceit as their theme and deceive their audiences for the pleasure.

The Dutertre–Kahn film material was strange and familiar to me. It was like a going back to familiar places, as when you return home to find you are a stranger to the place you once belonged and a stranger to yourself who had been there. The strangeness recalls to you a familiarity that you can't reach. It happens when you return in memory to your childhood and return to childhood places that cause you to remember.

The mirror is terrible.

It happened with R. I lost boundaries and lived in reflections.

One day I returned to where I had lived as a child. There is an eighteenth-century Dutch church at a corner from before the British. Across the street is a Jewish delicatessen, sharp yellow mustard that made your eyes water. That day was grey, the street grimy, there was plastic and paper in the wind.

The Dutertre–Kahn film involved a return. It must have been so since the film was too slight otherwise to justify my enthusiasms. It evoked other journeys, my life of journeys, which perhaps, in the period I saw the Dutertre–Kahn film, I felt I had to renegotiate. I shifted the renegotiation in my life to the film. It was as if to find its significances would allow me to find something of myself, make up for losses, recover things.

There was the history and anthropology I once studied, wanderings taken (to nowhere), my time in Africa, Kahn, the Jew. There were old photographs in an album of Uncle Joe who I loved more than anything, records of his travels and his women. Kahn and Joe, I suppose, merged for me into a fictitious Jewish father I could trust.

Kahn's home in Alsace was taken from him by the Germans in 1870. I wondered what that meant. I wondered too at his choice to belong to France and in so doing to embrace republican ideals, modernity, progress, the accumulation of wealth, the Jewish skill to allay Jewish insecurities.

Joe had wandered for years without a home. In Basle he learned to play the piano. In Vienna he trained to sing opera. He was my hero. He was a character of dreams and my longings, from a novel.

The journey of the book begins with the Dutertre–Kahn film and its implications as I fashioned an understanding of it. Nothing in the film nor in the Archives corresponded to what I knew or what I had been trained for. I had to start at a beginning, make a new beginning and remake myself. The memories evoked as I proceeded and the experiences retraced and imagined have been the instruments to make connections and help me to see.

Two

Most journeys end where they begin, coming home. You can sense Dutertre's relief in his diary when he and Kahn arrive back in Paris, as when the characters in Verne's novels come home after a journey round the world, or from under the sea, or across Africa in a balloon.

The adventure is exciting, but it is fine to return home.

Three

At the gate she kissed him an almost automatic goodbye. The sound of her feet on the walk was changed, the night noises of the garden were suddenly in the past, but she was glad, none the less, to be back.

Four

When you travel imaginatively, returns are frequent. Wherever you go, when you pause, and however compelling the pause may be, it reflects on where you had come from at the outset, where you had been yesterday and the day before, the encounters of those days, and a dream about where you might go.

Such itineraries are flexible.

The variants of the Amazon Indian myths studied by Claude Lévi-Strauss alter the other myths previously encountered in the group of myths. The first myth changes as you find the second, and so on. The myths are not variations of an original one, but episodes in a corpus, like all the films of a film director, each film is a moment of one single film.

In a journey, returns, repetitions, overlaps intersect with desires and the crucial components of journeys, disappointments, despair. Going forward colours every destination previously traversed. It alters at each return and at every intersection the place of origin where the journey commenced, not only home, but identity and self. Every arrival, every stage is an opportunity to reconstitute the journey, to narrate it as opportunity.

One consequence of the journey is to reveal the falsity of origins. As you progress, you find other origins, more hidden ones, secret ones. There is no end to such encounters, the infinite hiding and invention.

The multiplicity of surfaces unfixes everything. You ask questions to discover exactly where you are. The responses are interpretations, stories, speculations, new imaginings which you tell yourself as if they are reasons and make sense, as if they are purposes known in advance, goals. But they are only afterthoughts, hindsights of cohesion.

I prefer fictions which begin with home and lose their way, as in Welles's *Citizen Kane*, or those which seek home as a new place, a promised land, whose promise is lost and irrecoverable, like a dream, a sad myth.

In Ford's *The Searchers*, everyone but Ethan Edwards (John Wayne) returns home. Ethan brings back those who strayed or were taken, makes home safe, reconstitutes the community, restores Debbie (Natalie Wood) who had been abducted, restores the rocking chair to old Mose, restores lovers to each other, then resumes his wandering, like the Indian whose eyes he had shot out.

They are doomed together to wander for eternity.

The Ford hero has no heaven nor home. I am in Ireland now. I want to see the poignancy of Ford's *The Informer* again, resee the *The Quiet Man* where home is a myth attained and where the Irish think it an Irish film.

In Rohmer's films home is temporary, a place where people camp, migrating from one location to another as in their relations. On return, the petals of flowers left in a vase have wilted.

The search for home provokes stories. Roads not taken, places not reached, absences not filled, are the interesting things in journeys. Arrival is a conclusion.

Better unhappiness.

Not to reach your destination impels writing. *Lord Jim* is a fine example.

Jim is in geographical flight from a self who always accompanies him. When there is a risk that the self he thought he left behind will be discovered, forcing him to face himself, it causes him to flee elsewhere.

Elsewhere is nowhere. It is where he is. Jim is this flight, this gap within himself.

Conrad's *Heart of Darkness* is a journey to one hardly knows where. The journey is murky and grows murkier.

Marlowe losing himself with each step forward into the heart of things. In Michel Leiris's journey across Africa, Leiris wanted to be Lord Jim. In his diary, he discusses Sartrian bad faith, *bovaryisme*, possession rituals in Ethiopia. Possession is theatre, impersonation, mask, deception, the uncertainties of identity in fiction, the present threats to oneself, the thread of life.

Is possession real or is it an act?, Leiris asked.

André Gide's *Voyage au Congo* was dedicated to Joseph Conrad. *Heart of Darkness* is Gide's model. It is the writing he travels with, retraces, rewrites, and fictionally, improbably, what he becomes.

The 19th century closes with the invention of the cinema, which places the spectator in the flux of movement, thereby in doubt. The hysteria of parallel cutting and the last-minute rescue is that doubt and deception.

The image hides awful truths, terrible ends.

Time, memory, movement, multiple perspectives gnaw at the security of the observer, compromise the outlines of the object, point to the limits of the senses and the incapacities of language.

The popular heros of the 19th century were explorers, travel adventurers, missionaries. They were men like Livingstone, and like the yellow-journalist showman, Stanley, who found Livingstone. These men were idolised and fêted. Their exploits helped to make new industries flourish like the penny newspapers, illustrated postcards, magic lantern entertainments.

The *autochromes*, the basic material of the *Archives*, were the principal source of images in popular magic lantern shows, a path to the mysterious.

For a precious moment in the mid-19th century the exotic was thought to embody classicism, a lost antique ideal, and also primitivism, a lost innocence. These were the imaginary prizes explorers brought back with them as they took possession of strange places and planted flags on beaches and hilltops. The imaginary was unsettling. It decentred a European world by positing other worlds even if initially the otherness was accounted for in an evolutionary frame. The primitive was the past to overcome. Going back to it, however, was irresistible, even against our will.

These journeys were interior explorations, Mr Hyde mirrored in Dr Jekyll, the dark places of Romantic imaginings, Dracula and Frankenstein, the other sides of reason.

Five

The Napoleonic expedition to Egypt in 1798 was as much a revolution in European culture as the French Revolution. It helped to abolish a geographical/cultural sense based on classicism and Holy Scripture, on Delphi and Jerusalem, the cradles of Europe and the West. Egypt was 'before'. It predated Christianity and the classical world, and, it seemed to be out of conceptual reach, completely other, as indecipherable as hieroglyphics.

Jean-François Champollion, who had found the key to Egyptian hieroglyphics by grasping the significance of the Rosetta Stone, opened the possibility of knowledge about Egypt. He was instrumental in organising the transport of a huge obelisk from Upper Egypt (Luxor) to the Place de la Concorde, though he died in 1832, a year before its installation.

Champollion had been appointed director of the Egyptian section of the Louvre. On the engraving on the obelisk, Champollion's name is absent. Instead, beside the name of Louis-Philippe, is M. Lebas, the engineer who organised the transportation of the 233-tonne object, a journey of three years and a remarkable engineering feat. Technology overshadowed Egyptology. The obelisk was the background to engineering, not the object for which it was the instrument.

In this instance Egypt had not conceptually decentred the West. The West triumphantly took possession of Egypt, looted it, displayed booty in the city square, applauded the technology that had done so.

The mysterious was still lurking there in the Louvre and would have its day as would Champollion.

Six

In so far as journeys to the exotic were journeys to cultures back in time on a scale of civility, though coexisting with a progressive present, the coexistence of times, their overlaps and interpenetrations suggested that the exotic had once been the ancient time of us all, a savagery lurking within respectability, compromising reason and civility, which were only a part of our substance, and not even its most true aspect, but rather a veneer.

Freud took up the theme. He associated classicism and antiquity with a primordial psychological condition, the problems of Oedipus, of symbolic (and false) mothers and (fictitious) fathers. Oedipus travels back in time where he encounters himself, a lost true identity and with awful consequences. These consequences confronted Lord Jim and Nostromo. Going forward was a terrifying return.

The past in the present, savagery in civility, had a negative, critical edge. Freud was fascinated with Egypt.

Delacroix was fascinated with barbarism, the 'other' side interior to ourselves, at a boundary. Delacroix played this other side against the idealisations of neoclassicism. He substituted volumes, planes and colour for neoclassical line and form. Neoclassical line held objects in place. Delacroix, interested in emotion, in self, dispersed these lines, blurred boundaries, overlapped them with a sense of movement in colour.

Albert Londe, Marey's assistant, worked for Charcot at the hospital of Salpêtrière. Londe compiled a photographic encyclopedia of nearly twenty volumes cataloguing the gestures of mental illness: psychosis, catatonia, seizures, hysteria. These were images of unreason, its ticks, horrors, the bizarre, the freak. At Salpêtrière, the movements of madness were exhaustively documented, an encyclopedic record in images like the volumes of motion by Muybridge and the chronographs of movement by Marey, but in Londe's case it was a record of the aberrant and insane.

Madness and its sources pointed to a fissure within reason that could not be contained, a limit of the image, invisible and terrible.

Marey ended by compromising his own tenets, revealing what could not be measured. The frenzy to seize what seemed out of reach to justify its objectivity and the force of science which could objectify were the signs of a new science, not against uncertainty, but embracing it, assuming uncertainty as its principle, its very motive and celebrating it. These were the foundations of relativity and quantum physics.

The will to collect, classify, list, sort, nominate within the confines of the cabinet and in a single room, the universe compressed into boxes, stored on shelves, the world given a new dimension so that it might be collected and literally housed, was an obsession, a craze.

There were the *Archives de la planète*; Marey's chronographic catalogues of movement of every kind, every species, every posture, his invention of elaborate, extraordinary devices to measure these and make them visually manifest; the Muybridge volumes of animal and human locomotion; Atget's photographs of Paris, its courtyards, doors, windows, streetscapes; photograph albums from ethnographic, geographical, archaeological expeditions; the catalogues of the Lumières and of Pathé and Gaumont; zoological and biological gardens; glasshouses to cultivate the exotic; the novels of Verne, a positivist science-fiction fantasy in 101 volumes of all things terrestrial, celestial, aquatic and igneous; *la Comédie humaine* of Balzac; Zola's encyclopedic naturalism; the culture of museums; the rich collector, his home a museum, a showcase less of taste than of accumulation; the world in dioramas under glass, miniaturised and displayed, a scaled exactitude.

The mad at Salpêtrière, catalogued on the basis of a classification of symptoms were not dissimilar to other photographic/encyclopedic collections of monuments, tribes, plants, animals, the shapes of skulls, temples, native dances.

Because of Charcot's work on hysteria in Paris, Freud went to Paris to study with him. It was the beginning of Freud's psychoanalytic work. Freud helps to usher in a world in which the catalogue is made obsolete. He reveals another field of fascination, what the catalogue and exhibit could not encompass, the invisible, the unconscious, desire.

Freud, in his journey to the unconscious, transformed all journeys. He found new boundaries, invented, then explored, new territories.

Seven

The Dutertre–Kahn film images appeared freer and more suggestive than those of the Lumières, not because they were so different, but because they did not belong to, nor had been appropriated by, a history of the cinema. The images related to travel and tourism, but served the purposes of geography. Their likeness to the Lumière images and their difference of context made the similar different.

The same thing newly recontextualised was a new object.

Lumière films belong to the history of the cinema. No matter what else the films may suggest, the history of the cinema repossesses such suggestions. What the cinema would become is an inescapable presence in studies of what it once was. Such a history ignores what images became in geography or anatomy, for example, or at Salpêtrière. The history of the cinema may belong to a wider history of images.

Since histories of photography have been primarily aesthetic, or documentary without serving science, the 72,000 *autochromes* of the *Archive* collection are seldom if ever referred to except in very specialised histories of photography, and those almost exclusively French.

The *Archives* are excluded from histories of cinema and histories of photography.

In film histories, the intersection of other histories are refashioned to become subordinate to the history of the cinema. For example, the significance of Marey becomes nothing more than a precursor to the Lumières, which belittles an achievement and impoverishes the history of the cinema.

Film history can have a repressive, exclusive function, causing other relations and other histories to fade or disappear. Histories, in the case of Marey, of anatomy, mechanics, language, the factory system, the assembly line, thermodynamics, the collection, the encyclopedia, positivism, physical fitness, the avant-garde. Marey's involvement in film may be his least significant activity and film history his least interesting context. Might this also not be the case for the Lumières?

The relative historical poverty of the Dutertre–Kahn images made them seem rich to me. Richness was not inherent in the images, but in their lack of a definite context, even the geographical one seemed wanting. The *Archives* have been a resource for museum exhibitions and as a result the images have been contextually left undisturbed, not possessed anywhere in particular by any discipline in particular and thus free to float and attach themselves to a variety of practices.

The *Archives* belong to a geography of the past. It is not considered by geography except in geographical historical studies. It certainly does not seem relevant to modern geography. The *Archives* have no written documentation. It is an archive of images only, and these images, relatively unmoored and unlocated, and without texts, lack significance.

Where do the *Archives* belong?

The not-belonging of the *Archives* made of it a multiple object through which multiple histories might pass. It suggested that perhaps film history ought to be similarly thought. With the *Archives* I could move back to Marey, Regnault, Delacroix, Gautier, Flaubert, Daguerre, Degas. I could move forward to Leiris, Rouch, Godard, Rohmer, *King Kong*. I could move to the side, to geography, anthropology, sociology, philosophy, science, photography, medicine, disease. These were not linear precursors. They were contemporaneous relationships, a now for me, which leapt time and consequence. The *Archives* were the present.

'Lumière, mon frère,' said Godard.

No single history or time was privileged. The *Archives* gathered times and objects and what they gathered became dense.

It may very well be – in fact, it makes sense for it to be – that the early cinema belongs as much to geography as it does to 'cinema', an institution yet to be, 'without a future', as the Lumières said. Notions of significance and relatedness assumed for the early cinema may not hold. If the objects that constitute a history of the cinema are dislodged from that history and the history itself fragmented and dispersed among other histories, new significances and possibilities for understanding the cinema might occur, even if, or precisely because, they are more open, migratory, less conclusive.

The Lumières become interesting when they exceed the history of the cinema. The cinema becomes interesting when it exceeds itself.

I found it difficult to limit the boundaries of this study as I proceeded or to impose upon it consistency. The multiplicity of histories and their turnings, retracings, intersections, created gaps, absences, unlooked-for directions. I found differences I could not smooth over, encountered analogies in unexpected places, over great distances. New relations formed, old ones dissolved.

This experience became a method.

Eight

How do you organise such material? How do you write it? This book is the response to these questions.

Each section is titled by place names. The places, distant in space and time, form affinities, without limiting what these might be. The names describe an itinerary without fixing details or directions. Something may catch your eye or you arrive and find the place to be empty of interest or discover the urge to be somewhere else. At times, it is possible to rest and let your mind wander and digress.

The book has three subjects: French modernism, geography, the cinema. These subjects, however, are not exactly studied. They are traversed.

Chapter Two
Boulogne-Billancourt/Delft

Sans doute, au fond de mon oeil, se peint le tableau. Le tableau, certes, est dans mon oeil. Mais moi, je suis dans le tableau.[1]

Jacques Lacan

One

I guided a blind man at dusk to the train station. What could I say? As we walked, I described the coming of darkness, the elephants and giraffes carved from hedges in the park. I wanted to be his eye. He wanted to know how many steps we had to descend. Was the pavement steep? Would we turn right or left? Where was the pillar? Could I stop the traffic? I wanted to say more than that, to describe the world, because he was blind and I could see. But my words seemed banal. The more I sought colour, the more pale did everything seem. The more I strived for detail and shape, the more did everything become blurred and flat. Language was worse than inadequate. It was draining the world. Sight seemed an irrelevance. I simply could not find the right words. I too began to count the steps, feel their texture, while the blind man, tentatively, felt his way.

Bergson said that an artist sees reality best because he is most divorced from it.

Two

'Nuovo del paese, sono ancora nella fase in cui tutto quel che vedo ha un valore proprio perché non so quale valore dargli.' '… è solo col progresso delle esplorazioni che l'inesplorato acquista diritto di cittadinanza sulla carta. Prima ciò che non si vedeva non esisteva' (Italo Calvino).[2]

Three

Psychoanalysis is a science of the invisible. Freud imagined the unconscious, then drew a map of it. Before that it had not been seen, nor could it have been. He charted it out of words, like a novelist. Theologians have mapped hell and purgatory.

Freud's geography was a geography of desire. It was like the invisible cities (*Le città invisibili*) that Calvino's Marco Polo invented for Kublai Khan in order that the great Khan might *see* his empire, encompassing it without ever moving. The cities had names of women. They defined an erotic space like the urban cartography of the surrealists. The body of a city was a space to be explored, as with a caress. Marco Polo's descriptions made visible the invisible of his desires.

'Forse un Nuovo Mondo ci si apre tutti i giorni, e noi non lo vediamo.'[3]

Four

Do you remember Fellini's Roma? *The ancient Roman frescoes that fade and disappear the moment they come to light? And the brother and sister in* Otto e mezzo *chasing the vision of the Madonna, rushing here, there? Then the arc lights are blown by a storm and the hope of vision extinguished. And* E la nave va, *a film built on nothing? Where memory is invented and absence never had a prior presence? And absence is invented along with the memory of it, a memory only of what is imagined? And the characters in mourning for a non-existent being with a disembodied voice, as at a séance? And reality, only one among other dreams?*

I wonder where you are.

Five

As you write, writing opens up a gap, a sense of absence, a disconnection, also new horizons, glimpsed as you go along, tempting you by the something else of your direction, the something sensed just beyond your sight line, an elsewhere that you feel you need to reach and touch with your eye. I am not tempted to fill the gap, but to enter the divide as a girl did through the looking glass. As she saw her reflection, and fell into the abyss of herself, she found the fall exhilarating. It provided images of her desires so that she might know them. She had never seen such things before.

The Cheshire cat smiles then disappears.

But the smile remains.

The central image of Luis Buñuel and Salvador Dali's Un Chien Andalou *is the slicing of the eye from which the images of the film proliferate as ants propagate from within an invisible gash in the palm of the character's hand.*

Six

Bergson was a member of the founding committee of the *Archives*. Bergson, who had been refused a post at the Sorbonne on political grounds, was made a professor at the Collège de France. His public lectures at the Collège, in which he sketched out his philosophy of time, were extremely popular. Bergson was instrumental in persuading Kahn to urge Brunhes's appointment in 1912 as Professor of Geography for the Chair in Geography at the Collège which Kahn endowed for thirty years. In the same year, Kahn appointed Brunhes director of the *Archives*. The Collège de France administered Kahn's travel scholarships – *bourses autour du monde* – that he founded in 1898. Placing a professor at the head of the *Archives* and assigning the Collège the responsibility for the *bourses* gave both the Kahn projects academic/scientific status. Kahn's philanthropic work was associated either with the Collège or with the University of Paris.

Bergson is the great French philosopher of modernism. The relation of geography to modernism, and of Brunhes and Kahn to modernism, however, was ambivalent. Bergson developed a philosophy of uncertainty, indetermination, temporal flow, that challenged the sureties of positivism. The work of the *Archives* was to conserve, number, catalogue, collect. It converted time into measure, space, classification. The concepts of Brunhes's *géographie humaine*, which informed the *Archives* project, related to the positivism that Bergson's philosophy undermined.

What Bergson, Brunhes and Kahn had in common, however, was a faith in progress and in education as its instrument, particularly of social elites.

They shared republican, conservative values centred on education, reason, social order. They were egalitarians, but of an equality tempered by social constraints to be administered by the privileged. They wanted change that was cohesive, not disruptive. It was a species of Saint-Simonism, much of it evident in the sociology of Durkheim. This political/ideological orientation had excluded Bergson from the more radical Sorbonne.

The first edition of Brunhes's *La Géographie humaine* was published in 1910. It went through a number of subsequent editions. The full title was *La Géographie humaine: essai de classification positive*. The title was abbreviated to *La Géographie humaine* in the third edition of 1925. In 1921, Brunhes, with Camille Vallaux, published *La Géographie de l'histoire: géographie de la paix et de la guerre sur terre et sur mer*. The later work is significantly different than the earlier one. The first sketches the foundations of the discipline. It reflects nineteenth-century positivist assumptions: facts exist outside the discourse about them; the observer is external to the reality observed; facts can be directly observed and classified.

La Géographie humaine is a classification system of physical facts. The facts classified are the visual, physical traces left by human beings on the surface of the earth, a shifting, moving reality, which Brunhes immobilised in categories, emptying the world and its contents into a filing cabinet. It was encyclopedism. He described the *Archives de la planète* as an 'encyclopédie du réel'. The certainties present in *La Géographie* are less sure in *La Géographie de l'histoire*. By then the war had intervened, and with it the intrusion of history into geography.

The *Archives de la planète* belong to the initial, positivist phase of Brunhes's *géographie humaine*.

Paul Vidal de la Blache was the author/founder of the French school of modern geography. Vidal had been a historian. It was he who named the subject *géographie humaine*, influenced by German geography, in particular, by Frederic Rätzel's '*anthropogéographie*'. There was considerable admiration in France for Germany after the 1870 French defeat. The French ascribed cultural and intellectual factors to German military superiority. The defeat gave a spur to educational reform in France, and within education it helped to promote the study of geography which, among other things, was considered a military science.

Brunhes had been Vidal's pupil. Vidal, with Marcel Dubois, founded the *Annales de géographie* in 1891. Vidal concentrated primarily on the geography of the French regions. The reason for this concentration was a mixture of experimentation (the regions constituted a self-contained observable field) and social conservatism (the regions preserved traditional ways of life, *genres de vie*).

The regions provided a theoretical model for the concepts of *géographie humaine*. For Vidal they had a natural unity, though a unity socially imposed, the consequence not of nature but culture, not physical geography but historical geography, that is, *géographie humaine*. Human activity had created the region, albeit with what nature offered. Nature was only a guide, a field for human choice, not a determinant: 'la nature n'agit que comme conseillière.' 'Les nécessités nulle part, des possibilités partout.' '... la nature a déposé le germe, mais dont l'emploi dépend de l'homme.'[4]

Human society had produced from natural circumstances what Vidal named *genres de vie*. His geography combined Lamarckian–Darwinian elements of physical determination with notions of cultural adaptation, a libertarian structure that overcame the limits of the merely physical and of a deterministic positivism. Man was free to act, to transform, to bend nature to his will, but within 'reasonable', sustainable limits. Almost certainly, this was a point of contact between Bergson and the new geography and constituted the most modern elements in Vidal's thought.

Forms of human adaptation to nature became autonomous, shaped an environment, used it as one would a tool to progressively free human beings from the domination of nature. This mix of restraint and freedom was at the ideological heart of Vidal's *genres de vie*. The stress was not on the struggle for existence (a vulgar social Darwinism), but on man-made social harmony exemplified in an idealised French region, where adaptation was gradual, relations of culture to nature negotiated, and social relations peaceful. It was a world where progress was governable. It seemed to prove in practice the justness of Vidal's *géographie humaine* and the theoretical rightness of his concept of *genres de vie*.

Vidalian geography, while recognising an expanding technological, scientific and industrial progress, also recognised the political and social disruption that progress might entail. The work of Karl Marx was a reference point for most social thinking in the late 19th century. Socialism and a French revolutionary tradition were an uncomfortable presence for the mainstream of a conservative French republicanism post-1870. The ideological centre of Vidalian geography was to preserve social arrangements from a too rapid transformation by the contrary gravitational force of the French regions, nature, traditional social institutions, above all, by 'natural' processes of adaptation. There is little genuine reference to historical forces, social conflict, political upheaval. Scientific progress, though it promised enormous benefits, could threaten those benefits by a tearing of the social fabric, which republicanism, with its experience of the Paris Commune, and a century of French revolutions, was aware of and committed to avoid, ideologically, politically and in its social policies.

Regionalism had a peasant, rural base. Much of the ideology of republicanism rested on the social foundations of small-scale agriculture and small-scale industry. A mass of *petit bourgeois* under the direction of the *grand bourgeois*.

As late as 1896, 83 per cent of French industrial establishments employed less than five workers and only 1.3 per cent employed fifty or more.

The Lumière factory in Lyon, with its output of nearly 7,000 photographic plates per day, was a major industry. The Lumières employed just under 500 workers. The Lumière enterprise was an exception to the general pattern of industrialisation *à la française*, which combined the artisanal, often rural workshop, with the factory, quite different from the more concentrated and urban pattern of industrialisation in Germany and Great Britain.

This was not a defect of French industrialisation or a sign of backwardness. The small, rural-based enterprise was an adaptation to French conditions: a shortage of investment capital for manufacturing credits (at least until mid-century with the reform of the banks) and an abundance of rural labour in the countryside. It was often the case in France that rather than the peasant being forced to come to the city, the factory came to the country with its source of abundant, cheap labour. Despite considerable liquidity in the French economy, particularly after 1870, investments tended to go overseas (Russia principally), and into state bonds, where capital returns were generous and secure, rather than into French industry where returns were modest.

In Renoir's *French Cancan*, bankers are behind Danglard (Jean Gabin). When the Moulin Rouge opens, thanks to them, 'La Belle Abbesse' (Maria Félix), who belly-danced to the delight of bankers in the 'Oriental' erotic spectacle which opens the film, plays 'Catherine La Grande' in the Moulin Rouge, bending cossacks to her will, making them serve her desires. In the audience, the Russian mariners who are present are wildly applauded by the French. The enthusiasm represented the newly concluded Franco-Russian alliance. It was a hurrah for finance capital and the particular investment patterns then current in the exceedingly prosperous French Republic of *la belle époque*.

The French state used investment as a political instrument. It negotiated military/political alliances with Russia and Italy on the coat-tails of bank investments and bond issues that the French state underwrote.

Overseas rather than national investment was the field of French merchant bank activity. Kahn made his fortune in investments abroad. It was the pattern of investment of the Goudchoux Bank. Kahn's philanthropy was financed by his overseas investments, investments in the French colonial empire and in the British empire, including South Africa. Investments, like philanthropy, were instruments of progress. Philanthropy was not the alibi of investment, but its partner. Investment could be considered a form of philanthropic enterprise: liberalism certainly; at the very least, social engineering. It bettered the world and it built Danglard's Moulin Rouge.

However modernist Vidal's geography was, with its emphasis on human activity and change rather than physical determinations, its political disposition was conservative: to preserve and sustain. Hence, though this was a 'human', not a physical geography, it reinscribed a naturalism by recourse to biological notions of adaptation, though less about man adapting to nature than nature being adapted by man and the human reordering of the natural environment. This reordering in Vidal's framework was to be harmonious and peaceful, not disruptive, or it ought not to be.

Man, a cultural entity, and admittedly so in Vidal's *géographie humaine*, was biologically conceived, that is, a creature whose nature and thus culture was based on adaptation. Vidal evacuated from *géographie humaine* discourses on social relations, social class, capitalism, colonialism, history. Its concentration on the French hexagon, and within it on the regions and the peasantry, while not outside history, was not wholly within it either. It was a geography without cities, workers, conflict, or politics.

Though Vidal recognised change, his geography was permeated by a nostalgia for what was being changed and lost to change. The areas he focused on, the regions, were gradually being developed and were points of resistance to rapid change. They were socially stable, able to integrate new institutions and processes within established social forms. The regions were midway between conservation and progress. They had a theoretical value for *géographie humaine* as exemplifying a cultural transformation of nature, and a political value in reinforcing a politics sustained by traditional class relations and a faith in the reason, skills and good intentions of a social elite, exactly the ideological position enunciated by Kahn, the force and motive of his philanthropy, and his initial interest in promoting geographical studies.

Bergson ideologically belonged to this social/political framework.

Seven

Vidal believed in the benefits of colonialism.

Colonialism belonged to progress. The *Annales* never wavered from a pro-colonial position. But Vidal's colonialism was less practical and militant than it was theoretical. He was not interested in the colonial enterprise, but in the implications of a primitivism encountered in the colonies for the structures and thought of his geography. What he found in the colonies conformed to his concepts of *géographie humaine*, or more precisely, this-other-than-Europe was made to conform to his progressist ideology.

Primitivism was a cornerstone of the idea of progress from the 18th century onwards with its obsessions with reason and unreason, reason and religion, and the attempt to find a reasonable theology.

Vidal's interest in exotic places was an interest in their theoretical structural status as primitive forms of more advanced states, thus forms of degrees of enslavement to nature (physical geography), and, from a reverse perspective, of lesser degrees of freedom from nature. *Géographie humaine*, with its emphasis on shaping the environment, on freedom defined as freedom from physical necessity, the freedom of culture, was at the apex of a conceptionalisation of the world as fundamentally advancing, of an ideology of progress, liberalism and optimism.

Géographie humaine was a history of the liberation of man from physical and environmental determinations, towards freedom by means of science, technology, education, the central features of post-1870 French republicanism. The historical framework is neither political nor social, but biological derived from evolutionism.

Géographie humaine expelled nature from one door (it was no longer a determinant), to have it re-enter by another (it was the principal context for human activity). The colonies, for Vidal, were historical/theoretical evidence for the conceptual correctness of *géographie humaine*, a laboratory for it and its progressist underpinnings. Primitive forms coexisted with advanced ones, as in Darwinian evolution, at once chronological (things evolved) and synchronic (things remained, older forms endured). The primitive was a living fossil, a layer in evolution.

'D'un côté les civilisations franchement autonomes; de l'autre des civilisations où le milieu ne se distingue qu'à travers les complications d'éléments hétérogènes. Il semble qu'il y ait un abîme entre ces rudiments de culture, expression de milieux locaux, et ces résultats de progrès accumulés dont vivent nos civilisations supérieures.'[5]

These notions could be, and were, rationales for French colonialism, justifications for the expansion (advance) of civilisation, bringing progress (light, enlightenment to souls lost in darkness) through manufacture and trade, even if forcefully imposed, as in China and Indo-China, and more violently in Africa. While Vidal used the example of primitivism as a theoretical model, he shied away from the ideas of a colonial geography in practice (to radically alter environments), that is, its contrary theoretical implications for *géographie humaine*. Colonial geography was not a conservative one.

It could endanger Vidalien positions.

Eight

Marcel Dubois, who developed and theorised a colonial geography, and had jointly founded the *Annales* with Vidal, in time became isolated and his colonial geography marginalised. A hexagonal, Vidalien geography became *the* geography of French universities, actively supported by Kahn through Jean Brunhes and the *Archives* and Kahn's *bourses autour du monde*. The problem posed for Vidal by Dubois's colonial geography was that the gap in power and economic intention between rural, primitive, non-industrial societies and industrial, colonial, capitalist ones was immense and unbridgeable. The colonisers took possession of the colonised and of their societies. Social and political transformations were radical, destructive, disruptive, aggressive and violent.

Colonialism did not preserve ways of traditional life; it abolished them and imposed others. It shattered an evolutionary framework by bringing together, at once and unmediated, extreme poles of societies still in nature and societies that dominated nature by technology and science, replacing the structures of the one society by the mechanisms of the new, more dynamic one. The rural idyll of Vidal's regionalism and of his geography could not be sustained outside the boundaries of industrial societies where gradual change was a possibility, and particularly within the boundaries of France and capitalism *à la française*, the mixture of the strong political state, elite education, social control, technological advance, rural industrialisation and regional integrity.

It was not the welfare of the colonised that concern Vidal or Brunhes, but the welfare of their geography faced with colonial practices, and perhaps, more importantly for Vidal, faced with the colonial geography of Dubois. The adaptation/biological heart of *géographie humaine* would have been torn from it, theoretically at least, by colonial practices that were modern and developmental in the extreme, with little concern for traditional cultures or native sensibilities. Colonialism transformed entire cultures, destroyed peoples, rearranged demography, altered environments, drew political boundaries, redirected rivers, connected continents, irrigated deserts, literally and radically changed the face of the earth. This transformational activity was at the centre of Dubois's geography (and of modernity). Adaptation was not in the colonial lexicon, nor part of the colonial experience nor in the theoretical vocabulary of Dubois. Positions taken by Dubois eliminated the need for adaptation.

Changes introduced by colonialism were not gradual, but immediate and shattering. Centuries of social and cultural adjustments and their political forms were forcibly eliminated in the name of progress. Even entire empires could disappear (China). If republicanism could justify colonialism by a progressist ideology, colonialism, in theory at least, threatened the social/political assumptions on which a conservative republicanism was based, and the politics, education and philanthropy derived from it. It was this threat that caused the concerted and unpleasant suppression of Dubois's colonial geography by the school of Vidal. Colonial geography brought with it uncertainty and instability.

The issue was not for or against colonialism. Both Vidal and Dubois were committed to it and regarded colonialism as a benefit and a progress. The issue was over methods and theory, and beyond these a politics that related to metropolitan France, not the colonies of the French empire.

For nearly the whole of the period between the wars, the French government rigorously excluded *savants* and intellectuals from journeying to the colonies. When an obscure Catholic priest, Père Aupiais, tried to suggest a gradual syncretic blend of Catholicism and paganism in what was then

Dahomey (Benin), the Vatican shunted him away for ever in a small parish in the depths of the Landes, one of the most backward and rural of the French regions.

The *Archives* collected photographs from around the world. The images were already of an immobile yesterday. Images from Vietnam, Cambodia, China, Afghanistan, however different because of the local colour and local costumes, resembled the images of rural France in the *Archives* (the greatest number) and a backward Ireland. The subjects were bullocks hitched to carts filled with hay, women weaving cloth, a thatched cottage, the picturesque poor, the costumed 'native', a still life of a village at dusk, a rice harvest, fishing with nets.

   These were pictures of tranquility from which time had been expelled. There was no disturbance.

Nine

'Ma inutilmente mi sono messo in viaggio per visitare la città: obbligata a restare immobile e uguale a se stessa per essere meglio ricordata, Zora languì, si disfece e scomparve. La Terra l'ha dimenticata' (Calvino).[6]

For Jules Michelet, geography was the anchor of history. 'Sans une base géographique ... le peuple, l'acteur historique, semble marcher en l'air, comme dans ces peintures chinoises où le sol manque.'[7]

   Brunhes and Vidal quoted Michelet with approval. Geography for them was like a photographic fixative. Its historical dimension was faked.

Ten

Jean Renoir and later Jean-Luc Godard, who, with Jean Rouch, are Renoir's successors, introduced play into acting and play into narration. Renoir opened a gap that classical films had kept rigorously closed. I am not talking about depth of field, though that is part of it, rather a flexibility in the image, a return of ambiguity to it, as Bazin marked out, so that, whatever place the image was in, it was clear that another place and other possibilities not only could have existed but still did exist, as if relations of substitution and paradigm were not simply implied in the image but were co-present within it.

It returned to the cinema its ability to make metaphors of reality as a principal activity and an area of pleasure.

Ferdinand (Jean-Paul Belmondo), in *Pierrot le fou*, is Ferdinand Céline, and a character in Nicholas Ray's *Party Girl*, and in Sam Fuller's *House of Bamboo*, and Michel Simon in Renoir's *La Chienne*, and 'Pierrot', of the *commedia dell'arte*. It is the name Marianne (Renoir!) gives him, to which he replies, 'Je m'appelle Ferdinand.'[8] His name is no more true than her name, Marianne Renoir. He is also Ferdinand playing Ferdinand in *Pierrot le fou*. There is no depth here, no profundity, nor a surface linearity of one identity succeeding another. The character is all the identities at once, superimpositions, but without levels, including being Belmondo with his wacky cool. It is not addition, nor accumulation, nor substitution; it is simultaneity, shiftings, seepages, suggestions, insecurities. The image is permeable to other images.

Every image is destabilised by being multiple, and by being destabilised it is given the capacity to migrate, to combine with other images, to form other stories, logically, or to form analogies with things, analogically, or to function as memories, real and literary, painterly and filmic, personal and not.

Pierrot le fou opens with wisps of cloud and a literary reference to the paintings of Velazquez (a contemporary of Jan Vermeer), the blurring of boundaries, the ability of the image to re-form, recolour, discolour, reshape like clouds and the sky, become abstract, or nearly so, hence the porosity of Velazquez and Renoir, Renoir *père*, the painter, and Renoir *fils*, the filmmaker, adult and child, and the porosity between document and fiction, and between fictions, and between cinema and writing, images and sounds, and between film-maker and film, not a film from which the author is expelled or remains exterior, where he 'writes' from above, fixed in a superior position, but a film which includes him, in which he is written, which he enters as a subject in multiple perspectives in space and of time, feeling his way.

Because of this mobility, return and memory are qualities present in Godard's images. To watch a Godard film is to attend the birth of the cinema at each moment, in each image, historical moments which Godard repeats not as reference, but as practice, concretely, and which he frequently recalls: 'Lumière, mon frère!'[9]

His narratives, whose temporal narrative line is their weakest attribute, need to be weak in order not to unduly fix the image. In unfixity, Godard allows the image its variety, its movement, its ability to combine, its freedom and possibility.

'Ce n'est pas une image juste. C'est juste une image.'[10]

I remember the first films I saw of Godard and the sense I had after each of them of exhilaration. Anything, simply anything could be done. The cinema was liberation. I could return to childhood, to play the lost serious play of childhood where representation was an activity, not a substance, and thus it made me free to imagine. To imagine was always to imagine freedom.

The adult world required of me a different, paler reality, where only a single dimension was permissible, for safety's sake. It made me unhappy. It was not that I was given stories by Godard that made sense. They seldom did. I was given language, the means to make things, like an engine or a tool, for the luxury of play without the constraint of significance.

'Godard, mon frère.'[11]

What occurs in a Godard film is not determined from an exterior, given its cue by a rule (of reality, for example), but is generated at an interior, from within the image, suggestions and movements that belong to the ambiguity and richness of an image, or a sound, or a gesture, or a line, so that nothing is ever straightforward.

It is the strategy for Godard's *Histoire(s) du cinéma*, history without chronology, history as intersecting multiplicities, history truly in time, thus reversible, overlapping, simultaneous, superimposed.

Eleven

Do you remember, darling Brigid, it was your birthday? You were twenty-one. You were going to a party. You wore a bright-red dress. Your lips were red, like the dress. You sparkled, wiggled with excitement. 'Do you like it?' your green eyes said. You picked up the front of your dress. I was charmed by the sight and the scent of you. But it was the gesture, the dressing up, the invitation to play that mattered, the redness of the dress, like the blood of red paint in Pierrot le fou *when a spy-dwarf, knifed in the neck, keeps talking and bleeding with every gurgle, or a finger-painting. I liked that.*

I would give anything to play with you again. To see you whirl and make things go topsy-turvy.

Twelve

One of the loveliest books I know is *Grammatica della fantasia: Introduzione all'arte di inventare storie* by Gianni Rodari. Rodari was a school teacher and columnist for the Italian Communist Party national daily, *L'Unità*. *Grammatica della fantasia* is a primer for teachers to nourish the fantasies of the children they teach.

Rodari also wrote books for children. It was through his children's books that I found at a friend's house in Rome that I was introduced to Rodari. The first book I read was *C'era due volte il barone Lamberto, ovvero I misteri dell'isola di San Giulio*.[12] It is the story of a rich baron, old, peeling, dried out, near death, almost a ghost, who hires a team of people to repeat his name without pause. As one speaker tires, another takes over, and so on, seamlessly. As the baron's name is repeated, *'Barone Lamberto'*, the baron becomes rejuvenated, each day of utterances restoring him, in a regressive progress, to his youth.

One day the reiteration team goes on strike over pay and conditions of work. They do not, as you might suppose, stop repeating his name, but instead, repeat it at breakneck speed, causing the baron to rapidly return to childhood, then infancy. At this point he gives in to their demands.

After this first book, I read all his books.

The subject of his books is the same – to invent stories and to see thereby the power of words as the power to generate words, and the power of stories to generate stories, and thus the power of both to create reality, to imagine impossible worlds, and to make the impossible and the imaginary real, literally grammar for the creation of fantasies, grammar as production and generation.

The impossible real is an absolute pleasure because it is made safe from constraints and likelihood. It was not for that fact unlikely. It is only unlikely in reality. It is perfectly likely in language.

Language can exceed the world and transform it. It has the capacity to create numerous realities in accord with what we might imagine and beyond that to be the very source through which we imagine, not to constrain language, but to liberate it and accompany that liberation.

All words and all stories, for Rodari, were open and multiple. Rather than fixing them, he unleashed them.

In the films of the *nouvelle vague*, and particularly those by Godard, grammatical instances are brought to the surface. It is as if the films of Hitchcock or Hawks were turned inside out (as Rohmer and Rivette did) causing you to see the turnings and mechanisms and take pleasure in them, playing more with the doing of film than with its done.

The long tracking shot emblematic of the *nouvelle vague* was often only that, a shot without a referent, what it depicted the measure of the distance traversed by the shot, turning representation into background shifting representing to the fore.

Rather than things taking place within a space, space was flattened by the shot, made into a surface of play of the shot rather than only a place for a drama. In a Godard or Rohmer film, dramatic instances appear equally as formal attributes, the activity of bringing the scene into being is co-present with the scene, constituting the scene and its performance, each signified a signifier and not either one or the other as if the sign has been riven and the film the play of division in that fissured gap.

Thirteen

The 72,000 *autochromes* in the *Archives de la planète* are views taken in forty-eight countries. The *autochrome* is the earliest colour photographic process, invented by the Lumière brothers and commercialised by them in 1907.

The *autochrome* image is produced on a glass plate coated with three-coloured, chemically treated minute potato granules which register a colour image when exposed to light through a camera lens. The Lumières spent more effort developing the *autochrome* than they did the cinematograph, which, relatively speaking, was a simpler process and less central to their entrepreneurial interests than was the *autochrome*.

The *autochrome* is meant to be projected on a screen by a magic lantern projector which is like a slide projector. The colour plate is placed on a movable sliding mechanism which can hold two colour plates. The plate is set in front of a light source and behind the lens through which the image is projected.

The *autochrome* image, because it is on glass, is not reproducible like a photographic image. The image is unique. The *autochrome* was most often used for illustrated lectures, particularly of travel to exotic places like the 'Orient'. The illustrated lecture exploited a popular enthusiasm for geography in the widest sense of geography: science, travel, the exotic, exploration.

At the first film show in Paris in 1895, the exhibition of an early form of the *autochrome* was exhibited by the Lumières. For them, it was the centrepiece of the exhibition.

From 1870, when geography began to be established as an academic discipline in France, the projection of photographic images by a magic lantern was standard practice in the geography lecture theatre. The use of *autochromes* after 1907 belonged to an established tradition of illustrated talks.

The *autochrome* was marketed by the Lumières a decade after the invention of the cinema. By then, the cinema was no longer a simple record of reality, but had become narrative and spectacle. The film image was manipulated by editing procedures and positional camera changes and focus, and not simply a reproduction of an object or scene. Changes in scale, rhythm, time, perspective, depth and a dramatically defined order of succession, hierarchy and significance gave an emotional range and subjective substance to the film image. It brought the subject within the image. It thereby introduced an uncertain play between object and subject, between the real and the fantastic, the true and the projected, the sure and the imagined.

The colour *autochrome* image, no more than the photograph, was not simply a realistic, objective reproduction of objects or perfect rendering of real colour. The *autochrome* reproduced the sensation of colour, not the objective referent, but perception and the emotions of perception.

The first time I saw *autochrome* images, they were projected in Pordenone in an auditorium by a magic lantern. The hall was filled. I felt I was at a magical show in fairyland. There were scenic staged effects, puffs of smoke, thunder, clattering of hooves, as Proust's Marcel had heard in his bedroom late at night. The colours were luscious. Each change of image made me gasp in astonishment. No ordinary photographic image, nor the cinema at its most spectacular, has had such an effect upon me. No visual experience I had had seemed to enclose me and address me so directly or transport me into another universe so real-seeming and so without substance.

It was as close as possible to love.

The cinema and the *autochrome* bring to visual representation feelings and sensation, that is, subjectivity. The image is not ruled by objective structures, but by orders of emotion. The colour model for the *autochrome* is Impressionism, which is embedded in the same visual/perceptual revolution as is the cinema and *autochrome* photography. With these techniques the image is not determined by a reality that it accurately renders divorced from perception and its drama.

Reality now lacked consensus. It became multiple and negotiable.

Movement and colour were two of the main interests of sensory physiology in the 19th century and its specialism, physiological optics. Physiology was mechanist and positivist. It sought the chemical and physical laws gov-

erning 'sensation' and perception, which it was convinced could be
mechanically measured and understood. Despite what would become of
Mareyian science, Marey's work on movement was in a positivist–physiological tradition. The most important work in sensory physiology in the 19th
century was by Hermann Ludwig Ferdinand von Helmholtz. Between 1856
and 1867, he published his three-volume *Physiological Optics,* which revo-
lutionised the field of colour perception.

Movement and colour presented a problem for representation made
more acute with the invention of photography. It was one thing to observe
a static object, quite another a moving one, since the eye could not perceive rapid movement and colour was difficult to determine objectively.
The shift from trying to describe the object to the attempt to understand
the perception of it moved the viewing subject, and perception, into the
centre of the understanding of the constituents of the object, that is, the
object was no longer conceived as exterior to perception and the observer,
but object and subject were brought together within a viewing situation.

Whatever was the positivist scientific impulse to measure and objectify
perception, this bringing of perception and the viewing subject into the
field of the object and the understanding that the object was formed as
much by itself in nature as by the perception of it in culture brought to positivist science, by way of chemistry, physics and physiology, a problem that
would throw doubt upon positivist assumptions and its presumed objectivity, and the associated idea that the real was singular and homogeneous,
only needing to be observed and, once observed, catalogued and measured.

In the cinema, the image, by ceasing to be simply photographic/reproduc-
tive, the just image of the real, *une image juste*, became only an image, *juste
une image*, and thereby entered a system of language. Narrative, like the
autochrome, was realism and objectivity *and* perception and manipulation.
Just as physiological optics and the movement studies of Marey in anatomy
tried to secure perception within the measurable and the mechanical, so
film narrative, which stressed the image quality of the film image, also
sought, if not objectivity, at least the illusion of objectivity, the illusion of
reality. Narrative film naturalised the image.

The position of an image within a narrative assigned it a fixed sense which appeared as right and natural and thus necessitous.

If narrative gave birth to *juste une image* by revealing the arbitrary nature of the image stream and its emotional/perceptual determinants, even if grounded in an external real referent, narrative also gave birth to the idea of the correct image, *une image juste*, because it aligned the image with a natural sense, as if it were objective and true.

The pull between these poles, not simply between object and subject, reality and perception, the real and the dramatic, but between the demands of a reality cinema and the possibility of a formal or language cinema, define the historical movement of the institutionalisation of the cinema. One path leads to the liberation of the image from the confines of narrative and from an illusionist function to create realistic images. The other leads towards securing the image by narrative and dramatic/emotional force, editing images into a meaningful series with a scenic, internal reality whose function is to mimic a hypothetical external reality, the real.

In practice, the border between these territories has been open, porous and shared. Classical narrative is filled with exceptions, and the experimental and avant-garde are not free from classical conventions.

All of the cinema belongs to modernity.

Fourteen

Godard's contrast, *juste une image/une image juste* is a Bazinian inheritance.

Bazin wanted to convey the image towards an openness, an inherent ambiguity, the reason why he and the *nouvelle vague* critic–directors so admired Renoir. Renoir's characters inhabit different worlds and realities. As a result, they are deceived by what they see and what takes place. Renoir's films are dramas of misconceptions, misreadings, skewed perceptions by the fact of images not being signified, or not unduly. When Christine looks through a lens and spies her husband, the marquis, embracing Geneviève, she takes the embrace to be an infidelity when in fact it is the contrary, an intention to be faithful. From this error and projection within the limited field of the lens comes many of the confusions in *La Règle du jeu* and the attendant tragedy, a tragedy also of misperception and mistaking blurred by desire: Schumacher mistakes Christine for his wife Lisette and André Jurieu for Octave, whom he kills as one might a rabbit.

It is the signification of images and costume (Christine is wearing a cape given to her by Lisette which Schumacher had earlier given to her) rendered by characters in the films that lead to error, confusions and tragedy. Not to weight an image is to open it up to ambiguity and to see illusion there by as the productive condition of the cinema, its capacity as language and fantasy, and not as an end to be achieved.

La Grande illusion and *La Règle du jeu* play in the gap between a real and the projections upon it, between reality and its illusions, between reality and film.

It was not documentarism that interested Bazin, in the sense of limiting the image to a referent, but rather allowing all manner of references to invade the image against classical narrative procedures that had limited the referent and its range and, with it, limited meaning.

No cinematic image, by 1907, certainly by the early 1950s when Bazin wrote, could be returned to photography and taken out of narrative. No one, least of all Bazin, had that intention. To free the image from the constraints of narrative was not to free it from narrative, but to reveal these constraints, and thereby open the image to a multiplicity of possibilities and possible narratives. Classical editing, as Bazin understood it (Griffith, for example, thought this editing in a wide sense could include the Soviet experience of montage), had immobilised, fixed the image by fixing a sense upon it. It mattered less to Bazin if a falsification by editing was naturalised as in a tradition derived from Griffith or denaturalised in a Soviet tradition, for example, as in the rising up of the lions in Eisenstein's *Potemkin* (1925), than the fact that in both cases a singularised meaning was imposed.

It was the imposition and immobility, hence impoverishment, for Bazin which marked the classical (and Soviet) tradition, and which he wanted to change. Hence, his positive response to Italian neo-realism and to De Sica and Rossellini.

'Reality is there,' Rossellini said, 'why manipulate it?' It is more than questionable that such a cinema would be more true or realistic than the classical cinema, as Bazin claimed it to be.

The stage is littered with exceptions.

Pasolini sketched out a 'natural' semiotics in which reality was thought to be a language and such language was, or could be, the language of the cinema, the cinema as a language that spoke with reality. Such views, not unrelated to Bazin's phenomenological reality, were essentially theological, even if Pasolini's intention was to use his idealised notion of the language of reality against the false languages and false realism of the prevailing tradition of cinema. The ideas were provocative, as were Bazin's, because they restored to the image, hence to the cinema, its polysemy, hence its modernity and productivity.

Conventional realism in the cinema is scenic. Everything belonging to the scene coheres to provide a consistency and seamlessness perceived as continuous and integrated. Nothing should appear to disrupt the scene and thus reveal its truth as scene and its falsity as reality – a turning to the audience, for example, outside the fiction, or an unnatural cut or angle where angularity or disjoin brings one to the act that enunciated it, away from the act it is meant to denote.

A non-illusionist realism is tied directly to a consciousness of language, not because language is the reality that constructs illusions but because any image of the real has to be seen as a linguistic element. This is the sense of *juste une image*. The image is language because it is only an image, and it is that with which you write cinema.

In the notion *une image juste*, the image is not linguistic. It is the illustration of a meaning elsewhere, externally determined and in such a way as to mask the linguistic activity, the enunciation of a narrative by images. To openly acknowledge enunciation compromises the force of the illusion by returning it to language. On the other hand, it heightens the game, increases the stakes.

Vittorio De Sica, who Bazin championed as emblematic of Italian neo-realism, is now out of favour as being conventional, a charlatan even, and his cinema of only superficial interest. In De Sica's *Ladri di biciclette*, though in all his early neo-realist films the drama is between hope and despair, each sharing elements of the real and of the fantasies of projection and desire.

Will Antonio get the job or not? Redeem the bicycle or not? Will he find the stolen bicycle or not? The game to which the characters are subject, and which they play out and mark, is a game between reality that is mute yet full of power, and desire that is voluble and desperate, trying to resignify the real and make dreams come true.

Bazin identified the image with reality and reality with ambiguity. To institute a cinema of reality required new procedures to reaffirm the force of the image in the cinema, precisely in its potential as ambiguity (reality), a force diminished, he felt, in classical films.

But what is this ambiguity?

It is certainly not reality. It is the realisation of the linguistic aspect of the image as a signifier without a fixed sense and the construction of a spectator as within the film where subjectivity and projection are openly acknowledged elements in image production. An image points to something, but what that something means is not given objectively by an image. In a film, narrative predominantly provides images with sense. The problem in restoring reality (ambiguity) to the cinematic image required one, it was believed, to find narrative means that were, relatively speaking, blank, dedramatised, not interpreted, or not narrowly so.

Bazin appreciated Renoir and Rossellini because they presented an image of reality without oversignifying it, or allowed the reality they presented its (inherent) multiplicity, variety and misapprehension. Are not the dramas of Renoir and Rossellini the dramas of overlapping, contiguous, mutually opaque realities? In their films, there is no definite sense of what characters do until they do it, and no inevitability, even after they act. Not only are motives unclear, hence significance unsettled, but consequences are obscure. Either characters make up stories (interpretations) for what occurs (they often lie, more often are mistaken), which invades the image with an excess of meaning, or the film refuses to reach a conclusion, which empties the image of definite sense.

Actions are rarely conclusive, and they seem to suggest the possibility that every action could have been other than it was even after it has been accomplished. And, once accomplished, it is not clear what exactly has been signified. Action does not clarify. It restores ambiguity. It confounds certainty. It multiplies realities.

Bresson's method was to minimise action to the point of blankness. In so doing, he maximised meanings. Less, opened the film to more. And more, introduced alternatives, choice. Bresson was a Catholic (Jansenist). God and the world may be given to you, but you have to choose Him and accept the world and your place. The choice given to you is to choose in the full sense of knowing that you cannot refuse, no matter how awful the choice. Bresson's Catholicism renders in theological terms, and restores by filmic ones, the mystery and sacredness of being. It requires the imperfect image to retain this mystery, the openness and the acceptance. The Bressonian image is pared down, emptied of significance. Each of his characters, including the donkey Balthasar, faced this emptiness and desolation and act within it as they must, as a choice and a realisation.

Is not the choice made by Mouchette and Balthasar the choice made by Edmund in Rossellini's *Germania, anno zero* when he leaps to his death?

Bazin and the directors of the *nouvelle vague* especially appreciated the films of Hitchcock. Hitchcock turned everything seen into not what it appeared to be, thus giving the lie to the sufficiency of sight (*Rear Window*). Whatever is seen is open to a range of understandings, hence of fictions. The narrative which the characters give to what they see, and the narrative audiences give to what they see, are determined by desire, that is, by fictions. The film projected on a screen constitutes a screen for projections of self. It is we who give films their fiction.

This is a crucial break with a scientific realism of perspective and objective registration of objects and events and a realism that is perceptual and subjective. Bazin was sometimes caught between these positions and he

often confused them. His confusions have led to confusion in the understanding of his writings and to the troubled term 'realism'.

Images in Hitchcock's films are neither full with meaning nor emptied of
it. They are somewhere in between, like a hesitation. Each image is thereby
filled with possibilities of being true and not. It is this gap or tear which
allows the fiction to take place; more precisely, it allows the characters to
enter the fiction, their fiction, their fantasies, as Alice does through the
looking glass. The possibilities are the stories that characters invent and
pursue to fill the lure of reality and the drive of desire, self-serving stories
of fear and illusions, and which we watch, and are equally subject to.

The Birds is a multiple series of overlapped projections which includes
those of the audience.

Into an apparently perfect, symmetrical, harmonic and normal order, a
gull slashes through the order to wound Melanie (Tippi Hedren), and when
it does, all the characters, and the entire film, rush into a void of chaos and
terror, as do we, as reality unravels and we become the projector.

Hitchcock understood, as Bazin did not always, that there is literally a
world between the image the camera registers and the image projected on
the screen. This world, virtually infinite, is the film.

It is not difficult to understand how Pasolini came to the position he did.
If reality were ambiguous, and if the image could duplicate that reality in
its ambiguity, then the complex of reality–image–ambiguity belonged
equally to reality *and* to language. Language was the consciousness of
reality. Both shared the nature of the other.

Language is a reality and reality is only perceptible in language.

To return the cinema to the real was to return it to language and to the
paradox of their relation, hence to what cannot be resolved, only negotiated. Irresolution is the source of Bazin's theory, the sign of his modernity
and the reason his writing, at its best, is as beautiful as it is.

Fifteen

There are no illusions, no illusionism in Godard's *Pierrot le fou*.

When the American cinema became in the practices of the *nouvelle vague* a celebratory citation, it was a moment of recognition of the linguistic example of that cinema, not its adaptation or mirroring. The American cinema was cited, not duplicated. The *nouvelle vague*, by converting an entire tradition into a signifier and into language and grammar, allowed one to fully see the nature and achievement of that tradition, and allowed one to see Hitchcock properly, and Hawks, and Fuller and Ray.

It permitted Anna Karina to be Cyd Charisse, Belmondo to be Gene Kelly, and both to turn to the audience for applause.

Sixteen

Brunhes insisted that the documentation of the *Archives* be photographic and, with few exceptions, in colour. The reason for his insistence on colour was the same that had led to the invention of the *autochrome*, namely, the desire to be true to nature. Like the cinematograph which reproduced movement, stereoscopy which reproduced depth, and the panorama which reproduced breadth, the *autochrome* reproduced 'couleurs vraies', 'enregistrement fidèle à la verité'.[13] This objective, documentary truth made the *autochrome*, for Bruhnes, a perfect replica of reality and thus the perfect instrument of the *Archives*, a collection of reality in miniatures.

The subjects and compositions of the *autochrome* and of many of the Lumière films are direct copies of Impressionist paintings. The copy was not intended to be equated with the original painting, any more than the lithograph was. Rather, it was a demonstration of the capacity to reproduce images by mechanical reproduction cheaply and in series, not unlike posters and postcard reproductions of gallery masterpieces.

Godard referred to Lumière as 'le dernier peintre Impressioniste'.[14] One way of seeing this relation is in the common quest for realism by scientific, industrial and artistic cultures, including literary. What makes an *autochrome* formally Impressionist, or the Lumière films Impressionist, is the quest for lifelikeness, a bourgeois realism. Thus, what was imitated was not simply (in instances the subject) of an Impressionist painting, but its realistic manner.

There are contradictory aspects to this realism, especially true in the use of colour and rendering of movement, because it introduces the subjectivity of the observer to an objective scene. Colour and movement were impressions. They were emotional, perceptual phenomena caught in memory and in the flux of time. If it can be said that such impressions were realistic, the realism was unnerving because it decentred the viewer and the object, presenting not an ideal perspective, but a multiple and subjective one.

Photographic exactitude in the photograph and in painting, thought of as exact because it captured the instant, involved a perceptual subjectivity and multiplicity that shattered certainties. Photography, rather than ensuring truth against subjectivity, to the contrary, affirmed such subjectivity in the concern with the perceptual instant, made possible towards the end of the century by developments in lenses and emulsions (the snapshot).

Impressionist painting includes in the sight seen, the seeing of what is seen. Its realistic ambitions linked it to the science of optics and the physiology of perception. The fascination of Impressionist paintings is the relation between the object seen and the subject who sees, which extends to the viewer taken into the picture and presented, upon entry, with the distorting mirror of his or her perceptions.

In a Degas, where the viewing situation is emphasised, exteriority is virtually eliminated. There is no outside to the view in his paintings. The apprehending of a scene is situated interior to it. The ballet dancer in the wings, horses at the races, are points of convergence between their reality and the observation of it and these points are various and not fixed. They are vectors.

Degas took care to indicate, with references to the Japanese woodcut, the perceptual oddity of what is seen, and that the real is not an independent entity exterior to us but perceptually constituted. Without the element of perception, realism was only a form of idealism, reality desired.

With Impressionism, painting becomes interiorised, self-sufficient, not specified by its objects nor dependent upon them. By pointing to perception and emotion as constituents of the image, painting opened the way to compositional patterns that could openly be marked as interpretative, exactly what perception is, not sight as duplication, but sight as interpretation and reconstitution. The introduction of the subject to painting is a revolution that dispenses with the need for accuracy and thus makes possible a pure painting where the forms of painting can become for the first time the object. It was not photography that freed painting from realistic pursuits, but the invention of a new viewing subject and its relativity and engagement with reality.

It is unlikely that the first audiences thought the train in Lumière's *L'Arrivée d'un train en gare à la Ciotat* (1895)[15] would arrive in their laps. They knew it would not. Rather, it was the feeling that it would, the perceptual sensation, that was the thrill, and the game of an illusion, seeming true and not being so.

Movement highlighted two related incapacities: the immeasurability of time (how to quantify what was passing) and the subjectivity of sight (how to measure a sensation). Both were part of every visual perceptual situation. Marey tried to take the measure with instruments of what the eye could not see, nor the mind possess; the Impressionists tried to reproduce the viewing situation, to render time and sight as an impression, that is, imaginatively. The cinema used these incapacities in the subject and the will to realism to create the elaborate game of make-believe, in which an audience is complicit in the knowing play of fantasy and reality.

Time is by definition movement, a passing.

Impressionism is the high point and culmination of realism, as Mareyian science and the sensory physiology of Helmholtz are the culminations of positivism in the fields of anatomy and physics. Impressionism and these sciences helped to undermine the positivist realism to which they were in part subject and which they pursued. The pursuit of objectivity and the philosophical and technical conditions that made a realism of direct observation possible ended by unravelling the certainties objectivity promised and seemed at first to have delivered.

Marey had a background in anatomy, Helmholtz a background in medicine. Helmholtz applied chemistry and thermodynamics to physiology. Both scientists applied physics to their work. The object of their studies was human physiology linked to an interest in the sensations. They attempted to make the human condition, with its vagaries and particularities, a field of objective measurement.

The scientism of Jean Brunhes, and his devotion to the objectivity of vision, of which the *autochrome* became his primary, indeed exclusive instrument, is revealing. He too pursued a positivist programme but by means that compromised it. The *autochrome* existed in a perceptual field developed by a physiology of optics that compromised the objectivity of the *autochrome* image upon which Brunhes based the documentary objectivity and scientificity of his *géographie humaine*.

The fifteen volumes that constitute Eadweard Muybridge's photographic studies of animal and human locomotion were marketed to artists, academies and schools. Anatomy was considered a central part of an artist's training. Professorial chairs in anatomy were normal in art schools in France. The function of the photograph in anatomy was to provide an accurate, realistic model of the human body to supplement anatomical studies that were traditionally drawn. The photograph became particularly important when the issue at stake was movement that the eye was incapable of grasping.

The photograph provided the artist with exactitude and objectivity and served as an *aide-mémoire*. Though it could be argued that there was art in photography, or that photographs represented artistic intentions, the context in which most photographs circulated was as document and record. The urge was encyclopedic, scientific, not artistic. Muybridge's studies are an exhaustive catalogue of human and animal movement. The photograph was the perfect instrument for such encyclopedism, as in the recording of the geography and peoples of the entire world in the *Archives de la planète*.

The frequent confusions in the aims and purposes of painting and pho-

tography were owing to the fact that both practices shared a scientific culture and a common interest in the exactitude of reproduction. As painting
moved towards the directions indicated by physiologists such as Helmholtz,
that is, towards the perceptual situation in which the object was constituted
within observation, photography moved in a similar direction, making the
issue of personal expression in photography more pronounced and casting
doubt on the scientific grounds of photography. The photograph was
equally evidence of a perceptual vision and could no longer be thought of
as the unmediated inscription of reality.

From the middle of the 19th century works appeared on optics and painting that sought to link the object seen with the viewing subject. They sought
out means for the objective representation of subjectively perceived
phenomena, that is, the objectivity of the subject and of sensations.
Helmholtz and his work on colour were the high point of these general
investigations: '... il faut ... que des phénomènes subjectifs de l'oeil soient
reproduits objectivement sur le tableau ...'.[16]

The *autochrome* was a finer instrument than painting for objectively
reproducing not the object, but vision. The colour plate had the advantage
and virtue of being perceptually true: '... il ne faut pas oublier que ce que
nous demandons à l'autochrome est de nous rendre aussi exactement que
possible *l'impression physiologique* que nous avons ressentie en regardant le
sujet';[17] 'En photographie des couleurs, il convient en effet de distinguer
deux éléments: la couleur physique, objective des objets, et la sensation col-
orée ou couleur subjective. La première est définie intrinsèquement par les
radiations émises par l'objet, lorsque la seconde résulte de la synthèse subjective des radiations perçues par l'oeil. ... La plaque autochrome permet
d'enregistrer ces deux constituents de la couleur.'[18]

Such intentions are central in the history of the cinema and the debates
in that history surrounding the issue of realism: a documentary realism
based on the scientific registration of the object and a projected realistic
image on the screen that exists within a perceptual field and is organised
to be so projected and perceived; that is, the image as registration and the
image as structured perception.

Bazinian realism tries to negotiate, and not always satisfactorily, these two dependent yet opposed positions.

Seventeen

Among the most beautiful and compelling *autochromes* in the *Archives* collection are the *autochromes* taken by Léon Busy in Vietnam between 1914 and 1916 and in Cambodia between 1918 and 1921 (both formerly French Indochina). Busy was a French colonial officer serving in Vietnam. There are a number of reasons perhaps for the loveliness of these *autochromes*: Busy's evident love and attachment to Vietnam and its peoples, his inherent good taste and skill, and a pictorialist ambition to produce a beautiful photograph to be regarded not simply as a geographical record of a monument, an agricultural process, or a typical habitation, but as a pleasing, expressive and personal statement. There is a halo to his photographs of love, nostalgia, timelessness and sensuous beauty.

Busy is an exceptional case of a more general fact about the *Archives'* *autochromes* – their pictorial beauty. It is in this period, during and just after the First World War, that pictorialism in photography, and the claim to photography as an art and not only as a document, began to be voiced and to be institutionalised in photographic movements, exhibitions, albums, criticism. Looking at many of Busy's *autochromes*, especially of Vietnamese girls and women, it is difficult to see their documentary, scientific function for the presence in them of sensuality and eroticism, that is, of desire, emotion, response, feeling and the care that was exercised to these ends in lighting, framing and posing. Some of his images duplicate paintings or are unashamedly painterly and expressive. The best are very beautiful, the worst, merely vulgar.

These images exceed the *Archives* and the encyclopedia.

Eighteen

In May 1921, seventeen months before he died, Marcel Proust went to the Musée du Jeu de Paume in Paris to attend an exhibition of paintings by Jan Vermeer. More than 250 years separated writer and painter. The art critic Jean-Louis Vaudoyer, had introduced Proust to Vermeer. The two men went to the exhibition together. While looking at *View of Delft* (1660–1), Proust fainted. The incident is fictionalised in *La Prisonnière*, the first part of *Sodome et Gomorrhe III*. The character Bergotte, an aesthete whom Marcel, the narrator, admires, becomes ill as he looks at *View of Delft*, 'the most beautiful painting in the world'. Struck by its care for detail, its delicacy and precision, Bergotte feels he has at last understood the true essence of painting, an essence he had sought, unsuccessfully, in his own work. At that moment, Bergotte dies.

Jan Blaeu published his Grand Atlas in 1663 in Amsterdam. He was contemporary with Vermeer. Vermeer painted *The Astronomer* and *The Geographer* in 1668 and 1669, some years after the *View of Delft*. The model for the astronomer and the geographer was the same person. There have been various suggestions as to who this was: Vermeer (painter), Antony van Leeuwenhoek (anatomist), Baruch de Spinoza (philosopher). The exact identity of the model is not important. It is the substitutive overlaps that are interesting.

The objects in the paintings include a celestial globe of 1600 of Hondius, his later terrestrial globe, an astrolabe invented by Metius and his manual on astronomy and geography from 1621, a compass, a marine map of Europe, a nautical map, a device for measuring the elevation of the sun and the stars, an optical square. Blaeu explained to Louis XIV that geography was 'the eye and light of history' ... 'maps enable us to contemplate at home and right before our eyes things that are farthest away'.

The globe and the map miniaturise the world and at the same time bring it closer. It allows you to see what you normally could not. Cartography is a type of optic, and the globe a telescopic view bringing the far near. The microscope had the same function by the enlargement of the very small.

This represents an important revolution not only because it displaces verbal testimony and speculation with the visual and the concrete, but that in doing so it alters perspectives. In enlarging the distant and the microscopic, it places alongside what is near, what is far away, thus not only changing relations of space but multiplying and equalising views. The lens, and later photography and cinema, shattered the rules and order of classical perspectives. The telescope eliminates the far, introduces more than a single view and changes the relation of time in space.

Blaeu refers to history in speaking of the map and optical changes. Certainly, the new optics suggested the need for a history that would be empirical and visual, a history based on evidence and irrefutable document. But the optical had a more far-reaching consequence in shattering the time structure of history, not as linear and consequential, that is, belonging to the orders of classical perspective, but a history where the past could be enlarged to exist by the side of the present.

This is a major change. History was a narrative. It created a simulacrum of the real by means of a story with its illusions of continuity and consequence. The past, because shaded from view, was necessarily created. The eye, on the contrary, presented the real in a map, not a tale, empirical evidence, not verbal interpretation.

Brunhes's geography is more thoroughly visual, not the illumination of history through sight but its displacement. The observed, he believed, was more solid than the merely reported, hence more objective, less refutable, more true. It was, like most extreme positions of realism, paranoid.

Besides, the present could be seen, whereas the historian, inevitably, had to imagine and invent a past from documents that he only witnessed, reported, interpreted. Geography's claim to be science was that it was visual. The claim of the *Archives* to be considered scientific rested in its collection and classification of the irrefutable visual of the *autochrome*.

'Avant d'interpréter sur la foi de témoignages plus ou moins discutables les faits du passé, on s'efface d'observer, de groupes, et enfin, si possible, de classer les faits du présent. C'est là une méthode qui a un vrai caractère positif et scientifique.'[19]

The *View of Delft* is a painting, not a map of the city. While optical problems were problems to be solved and to be applied to the making of lenses and the navigation of the seas, they were not problems of the same order for a painter, but formed instead the subject of his paintings, which was vision and the play of it in representing. The fact of painting, of visualising, not through instruments but through the eye and the hand, was if anything a more modern activity than the then current empiricism. Leeuwenhoek, through his microscope, was able to describe the movement of blood, and exactly how things are in the world. The scientific view was a view from an exterior.

Vermeer, as a painter, was in a different position. He had a place in constituting what he saw. He was never not within his own vision and line of sight. That is to say, the scientific fact of being able to bring the far near and yet to maintain it hypothetically in its place was also an emotional fact, so that this nearness of the far away, kept at its proper distance in a classical perspective, was reordered by Vermeer to an emotional one. Yet that possibility of realignment and declassification had been offered to him as a real possibility by a current empiricism and its optical revolution.

Vermeer used the *camera obscura* to render the geography of Delft. With its help he produced his *View of Delft*. But Vermeer was too fine a painter to be a perfect empirical scientist. What the *camera obscura* revealed to him, and by the fact of that revelation, he readjusted.

Vermeer was largely ignored and unknown in the 18th century. It was not until the mid-19th century that his works began to be appreciated. A number of writers, such as Proust and Théophile Gautier, came under his spell. It was only in the century of Delacroix and later of Manet, the Impressionists and Proust that Vermeer's modernity had a place.

The first catalogue of his work appeared in 1866 in an article by Étienne Joseph Théophile Thoré-Berger written for *La Gazette des Beaux-Arts*. Thoré-Berger's comments on Vermeer, and particularly on the *View of Delft,* offer a key to some of the reasons for the revival of interest in him and his new-found eminence as one of the world's master painters.

What Thoré-Berger noticed was the luminosity of Vermeer's paintings, the contrasts of light and the intensity of colour, to enforce, indeed create, a sense of reality, most strong in his exteriors such as the *View of Delft* and the *Little Street* (1657–8). The effect of realism was achieved not by line principally, but by light and colour that traced contours and forms. 'Le dessin peut ainsi être remplacé par des touches de couleur juxtaposées qui rendent l'impression lumineuse perceptible.'[20]

In the *View of Delft*, it is light that creates the composition and its geometry. They become effects of a discontinuity of light and colour patches. The idealisation of figures in the 18th century and the emphasis in neo-classicism on line, as if the painting was an ideal illustration (as it often was), explain in part the neglect and lack of recognition of Vermeer, a painter of the everyday suffused in a light that seemed not only to abolish line, but, because of the nature of light, to shift emphasis not exactly away from the object (he was an empiricist too), but towards the perception of it. Light was dynamic, shifting, unstable. In the *View of Delft*, Vermeer concentrated on the shape of clouds, the shimmering of the river, reflections of boats and towers in water, splashed illuminations, uneven perspectives.

The foreground is deep in shadow. The bright sun invades the deeper interior of the city and of the painting.

As the eye wanders along the panorama of Delft, it finds analogous effects that tend to overlap, forcing a return. Once the process begins, fixed points are hard to come by and stability is lost. The Renaissance had established, by means of fixed perspective, a viewing order that spatialised time. The spatialisation of time secularised painting in that all subjects, including religious ones, were placed within an ordered history and narrative, no longer paintings to be worshipped as sacred objects but scenes to be observed, even read; in short, representations, and therefore desacralised.

Though paintings can be apprehended all at once, while the words of a novel need to be successively read, fixed perspective proposes an order of viewing, leading your eye in accord with a determined itinerary. The *View of Delft*, primarily horizontal and panoramic, rather than marking a depth, proposes recurrences instead.

It functions like a track or pan to flatten depth, a favoured gesture by the directors of the *nouvelle vague* who spoke of the ethics of the tracking shot.

Classical perspective, the fixed view, everything in its place, the surface as the field for a receding line into the world of the painting, all this is disturbed by Vermeer and his astonishing *View of Delft*.

In Proust's *À la recherche du temps perdu*, exteriority and objectivity are compromised by the presence of the writer/subject in the novel, the character Marcel who narrates and remembers. Neither the narrator nor the events he writes about are fixed points in time, nor are they successive. Events return, and the writer retraces, cancels, repeats, forgets, invents, rewrites.

The novel is narrated by the fictitious writer who writes it, but is not the source of the writing. Instead, he is its effect. It is difficult in the flow of time, and of identities and positions, which was also a flow of memory in the novel, to arrive at a fixed order. Time has no spatial equivalents, or if it is made to have, as Bergson pointed out, it is then no longer time, but space.

In the Proust novel, space is abolished, eroded, not filled by time.

Time, in which perception and writing (and painting) occur, creates unstable contours, not fixed spaces, forms that move by being out of balance, as in the compositions of Degas, or Vermeer's altered cityscape, for example. In the new novel, the writing is analogous to new forms of painting that privileged light and perception in a temporal, that is, fluid, rather than spatially fixed setting. Proust's writing is layered by time, composed of different levels of consistency, clarity, evenness. The layering is a layering of identity, including that of the subject.

Many of Busy's *autochromes* reminded me of Vermeer. In part, it was because of the diffusion of light and the seepage of colour characteristic of the *autochrome*, its subtlety of tones, like the contrast Thoré-Berger noticed between luminous and sombre tones in Vermeer, their modulation, elegance and sweetness. Perhaps, because Busy was in love with Vietnam, regretting its passing as he lovingly caressed its momentary present, he was able to bring out the inherent qualities of the *autochrome*, more so than those in the *Archives* made by others – or at least his were the most consistent in this regard.

In Vermeer's interiors, where the light is diffuse, unlike the intensity of light in his exteriors, as in the *View of Delft*, his subjects are often women, illuminated by the light from a window, playing the lute, pouring milk, reading a letter, writing.

Busy has a series of *autochromes* that describe the process of opium use from its planting to processing to the ultimate pleasures of its consumption. It is a scientific series. Within it, there is a grouping of *autochromes* of a young woman, elegant and languorous, smoking, reclined on an opium couch. The light is soft, dispersed, melancholy. The scene is scented and coloured by the opium, by her, by the dream, by a sensuality and eroticism. Women are the subjects of many of his *autochromes*.

One of these exactly recalls Vermeer's *Portrait of a Young Girl* (1665–6).

Notes

1 'Without doubt, within my eye, the painting is painted. The painting, certainly, is in my eye. But I, I am in the painting.'

2 'New to the country, I am still at the stage in which everything I see has a value precisely because I don't know what value to give it.' '... only in the course of explorations does the undiscovered acquire the right of belonging on the map. Before it was seen it did not exist.'

3 'Perhaps a new world opens every day and we don't see it.'

4 '... nature only acts as an adviser.' 'Necessity nowhere, possibility everywhere.' '... nature plants the seed, but man makes use of it.'

5 'On the one hand there are civilisations that are truly autonomous; on the other hand, there are the civilisations where milieu can only be distinguished in the midst of complex, diverse elements. It seems that there is an abyss that separates these rudiments of culture which are the expressions of local milieux and the results of the accumulated progress in higher civilisations.'

6 'Uselessly, I set out to visit the city: it was obliged to remain immobilised and the same as itself in order to be better remembered. Zora languished, crumbling and disappearing. The world forgot it.'

7 'Without a geographical foundation ... the people, the actors of history, seem to walk on thin air, as in those Chinese paintings without firm ground.'

8 'My name is Ferdinand.'

9 'Lumière, my brother!'

10 'It is not the right (just) image. It is just an image.'

11 'Godard, my brother.'

12 *Twice Upon a Time Baron Lamberto, or the Mysteries of the Island of San Giulio*

13 'true colours', 'recording faithful to the truth'.

14 'the last of the Impressionists'.

15 *The Arrival of a Train at Ciotat Station*

16 '... it is essential ... that these subjective phenomena of the eye be objectively reproduced on a photographic plate ...'

17 '... one must not forget that what we require of the *autochrome* is to render as accurately as possible *the physiological impression* we have when we look at something.'

18 'In colour photography two elements need to be distinguished: the physical colour, the objectvity of objects, and the colour of sensation or subjective colour. The first is defined intrinsically by the radiation emitted by the object, while the second is the result of a subjective synthesis of the radiations perceived by the eye ... . The *autochrome* plate enables us to register both these constituents of colour.'

19 'Instead of interpreting the facts of the past based on the testimony of more or less unreliable witnesses, one tries to observe, group, and finally, if possible, classify. This method has a true positive and scientific character.'

20 'The drawing can be replaced by touches of juxtaposed colour that make perceptible the impression of light.'

Chapter Three
Tahiti

Les phénomènes qui sont pour les autres des déviations constituaient
pour moi les données qui déterminent ma route – Je base mes calculs sur
les différentielles du temps qui, chez les autres, perturbent les 'grandes
lignes' de la recherche.[1]

Walter Benjamin

One

*The stick of the blind man was a probe to help him visualise, like the stroke of
a brush on a canvas, opening up a sight. I imagined that the journey each day
to the train station was for him a different one. For me, it was the same.*

Two

*When I was an undergraduate, I took a course in English lyric poetry and one
on the plays of Shakespeare, both taught by the same lecturer. He was the lecturer I remember most from university. His name was J.V. Cunningham, an
American poet, an epigramist. He was an alcoholic, often drunk at his lessons.*

*He coughed a lot and said little. His comments on my essays were laconic
and never complimentary. 'Not much.' 'All wrong.' 'You are too young to read
this poem.' (The poem was 'Dover Beach' by Matthew Arnold. I doubt if Cunningham liked the poem.)*

Cunningham did not teach in the way that teaching is today valued.

*His seminars on lyric poetry had few students. He engaged with one student
at each lesson. He often seemed cruel. He began the lesson by reading the poem*

for the week. He read it without stress, almost a drone, but it was clear. He read without interpretation. There was no drama, no rhetorical trick. The only presence was the words.

When he read, I heard, as if for the first time, the sound and texture of words and their relations. All my senses were activated and condensed. By not interpreting, he gave words life and opened poetry to a universe inside me.

After a reading, there was silence. He sustained the silence to the point of unbearability. Then, exactly when it was about to be too much, he called on someone and asked, tonelessly, 'What do you think of the poem?', or, 'Is the poem any good?', or 'Is The Winter's Tale *any good?' He kept at you. He reminded you of the poem (or the play), each detail of it, forced you to measure your words, not cheapen them carelessly.*

I don't remember that he ever smiled or showed emotion of any kind. He questioned you with the same flatness with which he had read the poem. He offered you nothing. No analysis, no information, no explanation, no guidance, no view, no perspective, nor comfort, nor encouragement, nor the lack of it. Instead, a neutral detachment.

You and the poem were brought face to face. He wore away at you, at any superfluity or inexactness. You had to find your way, without a path before you. No landmarks or milestones, no map.

Cunningham, I think, had been educated by the Jesuits.

I know this sounds extreme, but I only felt the same sense of nudity, exposure, unease before La Passion de Jeanne d'Arc *of Carl Theodor Dreyer. It was as if I was made to face the film as Jeanne had to face her existence, realising that to speak the truth was to go to her death, but that saving herself by saying what she knew was not true was not worth doing. Denial only had worth in the world of men, but not before God. The precision, the rightness of her decision matched the order of the film.*

To do justice to Jeanne, Dreyer had to act similarly.

Dreyer possessed perfect exactness. In his films, a transition never comes too early nor too late. Each shot, when it arrives, is in the precise place, from the precise perspective, as it needs to be, meticulously framed. This exactitude is a surprise when you watch the film, as if it was Dreyer, as well as Jeanne, who was blessed. The precision seemed unplanned. It was more arrived at, and you arrive with it, at entirely the right moment. It had about it a feeling of mystery. Jeanne said 'no' because it would have been wrong to have said 'yes'. It was that simple.

Renoir, Bresson, and perhaps Rossellini, had the same sensibility of rightness without rhetoric.

Three

Behind what you write, there is something unnameable, unknown, that the writing exposes. You write, I think, not to say something, but to discover (reveal?) what you cannot say, and perhaps never say. With each phrase, the extent of the unspeakable becomes greater. Each mark made is also an erasure or hiding. It is difficult not to cover up and to admit to what you are not saying and not facing.

This play is at the heart of Rossellini's Viaggio in Italia. *At every moment in the film Katherine (Ingrid Bergman) and Alex (George Sanders) encounter unknown parts of themselves, but unconsciously. She wanders alone through tourist sights in Naples. He seeks romance on Capri. Their impressions – completely diverse – accumulate until a point, at the end of the film, when they seem to find themselves and each other in mutual recognition. It comes as a revelation, suddenly, miraculously, to them and to us.*

The revelation is without clear motive or preparation, yet when it occurs, and though a surprise, it occurs exactly when and as it should. The rightness is retrospective. Nothing prepares you or them for it. The revelation is an insight and an understanding, internal, though manifest in a gesture. It is like Edmund's suicide in Germania, anno zero, *an action and decision he encounters at the moment he enacts it. There is no before to such actions, nothing anticipatory, as part of a logic of which the action is the inevitable consequence.*

Katherine and Alex rush towards each other and embrace in the midst of a religious festival whose crowd and hysteria had separated them. They realise the terror of their needs, find an awareness they cannot speak as they cling to one another.

Four

In 1912, Albert Kahn appointed Jean Brunhes director of the *Archives de la planète*. In the same year, Brunhes was elected to the Chair in Geography at the Collège de France that Kahn had endowed. The appointments were complementary. Kahn ensured that academic honour was given to Brunhes at the Collège and the honour given was conferred back through Brunhes on the *Archives*. A collection of miscellaneous photographs was given special value thereby. They became scientific, geographical.

The *Archives* classified the *autochromes* collected for them. Brunhes's geography provided the system of classification. Though there are no written records in the *Archives* – only wooden boxes of *autochromes* catalogued by country – Brunhes specifically instructed the *Archives' opérateurs* what to photograph.

His geographical categories were organised to collect the material that filled them. The *autochromes* exemplified the rightness of the categories and the categories determined the *autochromes* that would authorise them.

Container and contents were perfectly matched.

Géographie humaine, because it claimed to be a science, sought to be objective. The *autochromes* had the status, for Brunhes, of objective facts (reality), objectively obtained by categories devised to be true (they reflected reality). It was reality that was collected and, since it was reality, it was truth. The system was its own self-validation. It refuted all negation, all denial of its truths, covered all gaps. The material, the methods, the explanations cohere with each other blanketing doubt, suppressing secret or mystery. The quality of the *Archives* is self-evident and in full light. It is not, however, like an illumination. It is a truth known in advance, carefully prepared as one might prepare a stage set or draft a script for a film.

A photograph is an image of what has been. An archive is a classification of what has been in the form of objects or images, as in a museum. Brunhes saw no significant difference for the purposes of geographical study between a photograph and the reality it reproduced. The images collected were miniaturised images of reality, a direct transfer, not an interpretation. Image and reality were fused, not mirrored.

All that differed was scale, but it was a scale of exactitude.

Reflections, by doubling reality, throw doubt upon it – *Is that really me in the mirror?* But these were not reflections, nor was there doubt that the system for gathering images was not objective.

The archive and the museum document time as a time cut off from the flow of time by being completely *in* the past, not part of a becoming, or a process, but of a having-once-been. The emphasis is on proof, not movement.

Movement spreads doubt, compromises surety, unfixes security with time.

Five

The passage of time, the time it takes for awareness to settle, the time in which the camera waits, the time that flows but without end or direction, is the time the couple move through in *Viaggio in Italia* which unhinges their certainties, reveals the fragility of their ideas, their identity, the emptiness, and the substance, of their relation. All these things, but nothing very definite. It is the vulnerability and immensity they find at the close of the film in their desperate embrace.

The suddenness is astonishing and provisional.

Six

An archive of photographs is doubly evidential, once as photograph, then as inventory. Just as the photograph finds reality and reality imprints itself as image, so too does the classification system seem to be dictated by the order of reality. Thus, it is 'houses' that determine the category 'habitation', 'rivers' the category 'waterways', and 'doorways' or 'roofs' the sub-categories 'doorways' and 'roofs' within the category 'habitation'. Each category is as if a category existing in reality. There is no distance between category and reality, nor between observation and explanation. What you see 'is' and what is, explains itself. To observe is already to explain.

Brunhes said that photography was *the* geographical method. Observation was self-sufficient, like reality. The *Archives de la planète* was his '*encyclopédie du réel*'.[2]

The categories do not exceed or interpret reality. They coalesce with it. It is a system of adherence.

History written at the turn of the 19th century authenticated the past by means of a particular narrative form. Historical narratives were organised by a causative, consequential logic of events that made it appear that events, not historians, wrote history. Historians recorded what history (reality) dictated, else history would be opinion, not objective truth. This was the fiction of historical writing.

History, like geography, stressed the importance of the document and the irrefutability of fact. The historical narrative was an ordering of these facts, an order in time, nevertheless spatial (chronology is time measured) rather than temporal. History converted time into space by locating events, seeing them in their place as having taken place. It was like Marey's chronophotographs. Each moment of time is measured and calibrated, in effect, quantified.

Though the *Archives* were not historical, but sought a structured categorical reality where time did not enter (time was nullified), historical thinking and the geographical thought that created the *Archives* were similarly spatial. The difference was that history ordered space in a horizontal line (chronology), the *Archives* ordered it vertically (structurally). Though the vertical structure of the *Archives* appears less naturally motivated than historical succession, more meditated and discursive and therefore more open, this openness was only apparent.

Just as with history, where it seemed that events spoke and not the historian, in the *Archives* it was as if geographical reality spoke, not the geographer. The erasure of speech was a guarantee of non-interference and thus of objectivity. Structure was thought of as a consequence of reality, what reality gave rise to and what mirrored it, but not belonging to the discourse that constructed it.

The discursive followed, tracked reality.

The social sciences defined the goal of science as objectivity based on observation. The description of what was observed served as explanation.

Description, though structural, was thought to be the description of fact, fact being that which could be and was observed. Structure was like an optical device, a lens or a camera, assumed to be duplicative not formative. The optical instrument of photography became the perfect tool of observational social sciences like geography and ethnography. These sciences were the main classification categories for films in the early cinema.

The social sciences gathered up facts that related to each other as being similar, of the same type. As in a tautology, similarities constituted the categories of the gathering of facts, and facts were gathered in conformity to the categories so constituted. Thus 'irrigation systems' were categories for gathering details of irrigation systems, and the details so gathered verified the categories as true and descriptively accurate. The system could be infinitely expanded. Each particularity not classifiable within an existing category became the basis for a new category.

Every generality spawned lesser generalities as sub-categories: 'desert irrigation systems' to 'irrigation systems of the upper Nile'.

Categories were typologies of facts thought of as patterns of regularities *in* reality, which in turn served as the rules *of* the science of that reality, geography, for example. Facts were not what the discipline established. They were what it collected as self-evident and thereby obdurate and irrefutable.

The system adhered to reality and it made reality cohere.

The event structure in the historical narrative gave to past events their full sense of pastness as a result of the successive structure of consequence and displacement in which they were situated. Each event, *located* in time, was located thus by being immobilised, as time is immobilised in a photograph, caught in an instant of its fleeting passage, therefore able to be framed and measured as Muybridge would do and Marey did, measuring each instant in a continuity.

Immobility bestowed solidity.

Marey sought to measure every conceivable movement in a continuous line of movement to the infinity of their spatial divisions. This measure of each instant of movement was of each instant in the entire universe of movement for all of its creatures, literally a universal encyclopedia or archive.

His chronophotographs measured the divisions of the passage of objects in time, while they retained, visually, the trace of the passage as a measurable line. The vision of the passage was a vision of traces, wisps of time, overlaid, superimposed, and ultimately indivisible. His chronophotographs were created out of a positivist past but with a relativist vision. The wisps and traces of time in his chronophotographs could not be reduced completely to a measure. They exceeded measure by their evanescence and also by their overlapping and layering.

The objectivity Marey sought required his presence, not exterior to the time of objects passing, but interior to them, passing with them. Tracing time, he traced his own observing movement within time.

This was his modernism.

Each event in the classical nineteenth-century historical narrative, in order to succeed and supplant each other with clarity and consequence, needed to be delimited, spatialised, not a flow of events where time moves and interpenetrates and no event is ever complete, but time frozen, the time that encloses events in space. A sequence of historical continuities was composed of distinct, discrete units in a linear, causal succession, a thin reductive line of consequence. To say, this event, *then*, that event, removed events from time and relocated them in space that they might succeed each other, as numbers do, and be compared.

Mareyian science was as interested in a historical progress of movement, as history was interested in charting, infinitesimally, a chronology of events.

It was crucial for its claims of scientific value that the documents of the *Archives* were constituted by discrete objects irrevocably of the past. Process in time is something not yet concluded, therefore not measurable, as is an entity in space. It lacks the finality of boundary and the reductiveness of a single line.

In time and in memory there are no boundaries, only continuities, no line, only heterogeneity.

Because the *autochrome* of the *Archives* was considered to be a fact of reality, it was the referent that ruled it. An image of a house in rural Ireland was simply 'house in rural Ireland', not 'nostalgia', 'beauty', the 'picturesque', or 'poverty', not a cause for social indignation or social enquiry or political action. When the photograph is more than its referent it becomes interpretation, discursive, the house no longer belonging only to 'house'. If it is linked to interpretation, it is linked to the present of its enunciation, not to the past of its reference. It is taken from the past of the archive (historical) and placed in the present of utterance (political).

Interpretation opens a gap in reality by bringing the event into time rather than leaving it behind in space. It introduces into time the subject who speaks and the spoken of discourse and thereby creates a subject and discursive instances as instances in passing, in formation, uncertain unstable, unpossessable.

This was a lesson Marey learned of necessity.

Brunhes's captions for the photographs in the entirely photographic third volume of his *La Géographie humaine* were rigorously descriptive. A house by a river in Vietnam was captioned 'House by a river in Vietnam'.

In the films of Rossellini, it is not events, the referents, that matter, but the effect of events as time internalised. The effect can be materialised but the activity of time is unrepresentable.

The present is in movement, *en marche*. If, in the present, the past is returned to, it is no longer in the past, but in the present, and, like it, *en marche*. We are implicated in the past and made part of it, made to belong to the past and share in it as part of our present. The past as present is memory.

To render something as if wholly in the past is to remove it from time and give it to space, which removes oneself from time and places one in a space exterior to it and exterior to the past. This rendering of the past in space is not memory that flows and overlaps and is temporal, but the absence of memory, a dis-place-ment. These spaces of the past and exteriority do not belong to time but to a space where the past is *before* the present and the present is what comes *after* the past.

Chronology is in space, in an exteriority to time.

The relation of past *and* present is a relation of locations, unlike the relation of the past *in* the present which is a relation in time. To place the past in space (where it does not exist) and remove it from time (where it does) removes us from time (where we exist) to place us in a relation of exteriority to objects so spatialised (where we are not). It makes it possible to compare them in space and gives us a place, not within things, but *above* them. It provides a secure viewing space and viewing position, a vantage point.

Space and perspective so conceived are fictive.

The operation is based on a perspectival illusion.

The *Archives* compared and grouped under 'roads', or 'bridges', or 'rivers', roads, bridges, and rivers in Vietnam, Cambodia, China, Japan, the Auvergne and Yugoslavia, assuming an exterior observer.

Brunhes's ideal geographical perspective was to be in a balloon, above things, and, like God, able to see them clearly.

> ... élevons-nous en ballon ou en aéroplane tout ce qui est exceptionnel a pour les études de géographie humaine, moins de valeur que tout ce qui se rapproche de la notion de 'type' et à quelques centaines de mètres au-dessus du sol; et, l'esprit débarassé de tout ce que nous savons des hommes, tentons de voir et de noter les faits essentiels de la géographie humaine avec les mêmes yeux et du même regard qui nous permettent de découvrir et de démêler les traits morphologiques, topographiques, hydrographiques de la surface terrestre. De cet observatoire supposé, qu'apercevons-nous? Ou mieux encore, quels sont les faits humains qu'une plaque photographique pourrait enregistrer tout aussi bien que la rétine de l'oeil?[3]

Seven

Barthes had a different view of the photograph. Historically, the photograph belongs to positivism not simply because it is evidence of the real, but because it is evidence of the classification of the real, not simply the trace of reality, but its definition. Barthes fixed on realistic details in the photograph, a button, a gaze, the position of an arm, as testamentary evidence of what had once been but which now touched him. That touch escaped category because it was personal. Barthes added in this way a discursive dimension to the photograph that was at odds with the photograph and its objective realism, because what interested Barthes was a reality that could not be classified, that touched him in part because it escaped generality and category. It was emotional, passionate. Through this tear or fissure in time he entered the photograph as subject. Entering it as a subject, he re-inscribed the photograph in time.

What interested photography historically was reality defined as only that which could be classified, for example, Atget's photographs of Paris which obey a classificatory system of the library catalogue that it fills with 'doors', 'windows', 'facades'. The category pre-exists the fact and determines it.

The 'reality effect' of a button, a ribbon, a bracelet, a look that gave to the portrait its substance, its evidence as being real, were the details that undid the coherence of reality for Barthes since he noticed them as out of place, caught in his memory, moving him. This movement is beyond categorisation.

Barthes's *La Chambre claire* is a remembrance of his mother, of her particularity and his. No photograph of her appears in the book.

The book can only be felt.

It was Lacan who said that what we write is always written to show to our mothers.

When Karin and Alex embrace in *Viaggio in Italia*, they realise aspects of their interiority. More important, we realise our interiority, the passage of time of what we have seen and what is working within us, hence our astonishment, our displacement, and with it a sense of uncertainty as the Rossellinian precondition for understanding: an awareness of the fragility and provisionality of understanding.

In the classical cinema, time was converted into narrative space. In Rossellini's films, characters are in locations, but locations that have been narratively diminished. They are without consequence or line. These locations are temporal, not spatial – there is no accumulation of causes and their effects.

Rossellini was impatient with narrative connectives. His films are made of episodes, of fragments, with the connections left out. Connections are purely internal. They result in a view where you see objectively what the character sees without seeing the consequences of their sight, the understanding. You only see a disturbance. There is no external view to guide you to an understanding, only an objective one whose objectivity is so rigorous as to refuse any facile sense.

Rossellini's camera has no opinions.

For the most part, certainly in his early films, his main characters neither search for, nor are blessed with, understanding. They act and they are dissatisfied. Understanding finds them without warning or preamble as it does Karin, for example, in *Stromboli*.

It confronts them.

Rossellini converted space into time, but objectively, which is the shock of his films. In his interviews, he spoke of waiting, patience, being in attendance, of rhythms and moments. He did not exactly improvise on the set nor work without a script. Nevertheless, there was nothing very detailed.

His films, in their method, are open.

The externality of observer and observed in Brunhes's work was in a homogeneous space where likenesses and analogies could be formed and compared and rules and regularities defined. Homogeneous space is the space of morphologies, classifications, the archive, of classical film narratives. It excludes time, which is heterogeneous and multiple and not amenable to classification. Bergson shattered this space.

Modern perspectives overlap and superimpose. They are never singular, never single-sided.

Time is quality and space quantity, Bergson insisted.

You cannot make quality into quantity.

How much do you love me?

Such questions belong to the time of our childhood, a time we cordon off into space, unable to enter it or exit from it. One of Rossellini's most insistent metaphors is the prison. In the prison there is no inside or outside as fixity. You look out to look in and others look in and you watch them and they seem confined.

This is the lesson of *Europa 51*.

Eight

The *Archives* documented a pre-industrial world at the moment before it changed. Brunhes named the societies of this world before the modern, '*îlots*', 'islands of time past', as if they were caught at the threshold before the modern entered and they were engulfed. It was as a space rescued before the advent of time that gave the islands their scientific/geographical value to him. Industrial society was progress, modernity, change, the erasure of history and document, the flattening of perspective, the cancellation of line. The islands told us where we once had been, but were no longer, like a fossil record. They restored to us lost perspectives.

These islands of time, consigned to space, entered erudition as bulk and quantity, certainties added to knowledge at the instant before they would become part of time and no longer themselves, like objects in a cubist painting.

Nine

Claude Lévi-Strauss's *Tristes tropiques* recalls his ethnographic experience in Brazil during the late 1930s. He worked principally among the Nambikwara and Bororo indians. Both peoples, numbering more than 20,000 in 1905, have now disappeared, wiped out by disease. Already in the 1930s they were only the remnants of themselves.

Lévi-Strauss's ethnographic studies were based on these American peoples and the period he spent with them. He was interested in their social structures (for example, kinship) in relation to their structures of thought. He did significant work on Bororo and Nambikwara mythology. Lévi-Strauss revealed a universe of overlapping and connected structures of kinship, ritual, narrative, village organisation, tools, work and cuisine.

His intellectual models were Freud, who revealed that the most 'irrational' and incidental gesture or word was significant and meaningful; Marx, who revealed that society consisted of a series of overlapping connected structures, the most manifest of which were not necessarily the most important; and geology, a science of intersecting layers of time and its traces.

In these intellectual models the 'real' is not perceived and possessed by direct lived experience (living, in any case, is never direct), still less by its reproduction, but by an act of intellection, something synthetic as a way to understand. For Lévi-Strauss, only reality reconstructed in this manner had reality.

It was reality plus its comprehension/structure.

This was not simply a method. It was an insight into the workings of culture. The real for the Nambikwara was what they structured to be real, and it was in that cultural and structural impulse that they exhibited their humanity and thereby their equality with the ethnographer. Myths and other structures were ways of bestowing meaning. Meaning was not simply the understanding of reality, but its fabrication as the instrument for understanding. To fabricate is the way to understand.

There is neither nostalgia, sentimentality nor regret in Lévi-Strauss's book at the passing of the Nambikwara. Nor is there any attempt to regard them as pre-modern, pre-industrial relics to be recorded before they disappeared.

The Nambikwara are studied for a particularity that Lévi-Strauss does not dissolve into categories and typologies. He sees instead processes and structures of thought, analogous to our own and which form the basis for his understanding of the Nambikwara as related to ourselves. Lévi-Strauss's tools are not simply accumulated ethnographic knowledge (the discipline) but a method of sensitivity, awareness, care, and wit in search of a similar inventiveness in his ethnographic encounters.

For Bruhnes, categories form the basis for the gathering of facts; for Lévi-Strauss, it is the interplay of differences that forms the commonality and connections of culture. It is a way to ask questions and to make connections, not a method to take possession. On the contrary, it opens a dialogue, an exchange among equals. Lévi-Strauss is one of the least colonial of ethnographers. Brunhes was one of the most colonial of geographers.

Kinship rules, cuisine, the fashioning of tools, are not only these practices, or are never simply these practices, but ways to think, to make sense, to signify with nature and the 'real', as language creates sense through ordering the continuum of natural sound.

Culture is a natural impulse, like philosophy. All that is human is part of culture. Brunhes took cultural processes and found a way to naturalise them as 'facts' almost as if they were physical biological objects, literally data. His *géographie humaine* was a human geography that converted nature into culture, then reclaimed culture for nature as physical evidence to classify.

His model was biology.

Differences are important to Lévi-Strauss, but not 'otherness'. His studies are a colloquy between cultures. He tries to touch a perspective different from his own yet to which he and we are related. As the Nambikwara seek to make sense of the world and the sense so created indicates the impulses of their culture and inventiveness, so too Lévi-Strauss, in seeking to make sense of the Nambikwara, finds a way to signify himself and his own culture. It is the creativity of his ethnography.

Like Marx and Freud, Lévi-Strauss is that rare being among social scientists, an auteur.

His work is not simply science, nor simply specialised knowledge. It is something stronger. It is the creation of a system of thought.

The culture of the Nambikwara is a way to be human.

Dans la savane obscure, les feux de campement brillent. Autour du foyer, seule protection contre le froid qui descend, derrière le frêle paravent de palmes et de branchages hâtivement planté dans le sol du côté d'où on redoute le vent ou la pluie; auprès des hottes emplies des pauvres objets qui constituent toute une richesse terrestre; couchés à même la terre qui s'étend alentour, hantée par d'autres bandes également hostiles et craintives, les époux, étroitement enlacés, se perçoivent comme étant l'un pour l'autre le soutien, le réconfort, l'unique secours contre les difficultés quotidiennes et la mélancolie rêveuse qui, de temps à autre, envahit l'âme nambikwara. Le visiteur qui, pour la première fois, campe dans la brousse avec les Indiens, se sent pris d'angoisse et de pitié devant le spectacle de cette humanité si totalement démunie; écrasée, semble-t-il, contre le sol d'une terre hostile par quelque implacable cataclysme; nue, grelottante auprès des feux vacillants. Il circule à tâtons parmi les broussailles, évitant de heurter une main, un bras, un torse, dont on devine les chauds reflets à la lueur des feux. Mais cette misère est animée de chuchotements et de rires. Les couples s'étreignent comme dans la nostalgie d'une unité perdue; les caresses ne s'interrompent pas au passage de l'étranger. On devine chez tous une immense gentillesse, une profonde insouciance, une naïve et charmante satisfaction animale, et rassemblant ces sentiments divers, quelque chose comme l'expression la plus émouvante et la plus véridique de la tendresse humaine.[4]

Ten

Brunhes and Kahn reiterated the virtue of collecting what had disappeared at the instant it was being collected. The document was the record of what had been snatched from time before it had been passed by the present, arrested at the moment of its pastness, resurrected into an image that was timeless and ideal.

'... de facer une fois pour toutes ... des modes de l'activité humaine dont la disparition fatale n'est plus qu'une question de temps'.[5]

'Le but des *Archives de la planète* est d'établir, comme un dossier de l'humanité prise en pleine vie, à l'heure de l'une des "mues" économiques, géographiques et historiques les plus complètes qu'on ait jamais pu constituer.'[6]

The value of a document can be said to rest not with its veracity as having been, but with its freshness as still being. It is not a matter of whether the document comes from the past or not (the most antique record can speak to us) but, instead, of its belonging to a process still alive.

Discourse breathes life into fact as present enunciation.

Brunhes's geographical discourse depended on creating and defining a document whose veracity as document depended on the elimination of discursive marks. His goal was to establish facts. The photograph was facts taken from time, the *Archives*, their classification.

By removing the photograph from the present and from everything alive within it, Brunhes could exchange the photograph, as one might exchange currency with fixed values. It was more important for him that the archival be verified as true than activated as useful.

In a fixed past it retained a fixed denomination.

The *autochromes* were denominated into sums: 'habitation', 'roads', 'monuments'. These were imprinted and their likenesses compared, like currency notes, object quantities in abstract homogeneous space.

It was perhaps fitting that the *Archives* were founded by a banker.

Looking at the images each day at the Musée Albert Kahn, presided over by the portrait of Kahn who the curator referred to in privileged intimacy as 'Abraham', his name before he changed it in order to appear less Jewish (or more French), and surrounded by boxes of *autochrome* glass plates, a devotional silence, I imagined I was the reporter Thompson, in Welles's *Citizen Kane*, locked up in Thatcher's vault, reading his diary, in search of 'Rosebud' to conclude 'News on the March'.

Would I find the key to Abraham (Albert) Kahn?

Eleven

There are no longer pre-modern societies in the modern world. The rich field of cultures to which they belonged is gone for ever. On the other hand, our tools for understanding are finer now even if the field and world on which they can be turned is less rich. The richness Tahiti offered to Bougainville in the 18th century may be better understood now, although that Tahiti is gone.

The complexity of analysis and understanding we possess has been formed in part by contact with differences we have erased, which modern society helped to erase as it developed its tools of comprehension. When we travel now we discover only the remnants, the flotsam and jetsam that we have helped to create, that washes up on our shores like garbage.

The modern is not something outside primitive societies that the modern world encountered (and destroyed). Primitive societies are inside modernity itself, its creation. They help to define its characteristics.

The ruin of the primitive and the decadence of the exotic are crucial to the identity and formation of modernity.

Pasolini spoke of the genocidal tendency of modern society.

Tristes Tropiques is sad because the world has become poorer. But the book is immensely rich, like Pasolini's poetry.

There are no relics in Lévi-Strauss.

Twelve

G. K. Chesterton (*The Club of Queer Trades*):

'It is. It's a matter of fact,' cried the other in an agony of reasonableness.

'Facts,' murmured Basil, like one mentioning some strange, far-off animals, 'how facts obscure the truth. I may be silly – in fact, I'm off my head – but I never could believe in that man – what's his name, in those capital stories? – Sherlock Holmes. Every detail points to something, certainly; but generally to the wrong thing. Facts point in all directions, it seems to me, like the thousands of twigs on a tree. It's only the life of the tree that has unity and goes up – only the green blood that springs, like a fountain, at the stars.'

'But what the deuce else can the letter be but criminal?'

'We have eternity to stretch our legs in,' replied the mystic. 'It can be an infinity of things. I haven't seen any of them – I've only seen the letter. I look at that, and say it's not criminal.'

'Then what's the origin of it?'

'I haven't the vaguest idea.'

'Then why don't you accept the ordinary explanation?'

Basil continued for a while to glare at the coals, and seemed collecting his thoughts in a humble and even painful way. Then he said:

'Suppose you went out into the moonlight. Suppose you passed through silent, silvery streets and squares until you came into an open and deserted space, set with a few monuments, and you beheld one dressed as a ballet girl dancing in the argent glimmer. And suppose you looked, and saw it was a man disguised. And suppose you looked again, and saw it was Lord Kitchener. What would you think?'

He paused a moment, and went on:

'You could not adopt the ordinary explanation. The ordinary explanation of putting on singular clothes is that you look nice in them; you would not think that Lord Kitchener dressed up like a ballet girl out of ordinary personal vanity. You would think it much more likely that he inherited a dancing madness from a great grandmother; or had been hypnotized at a séance; or threatened by a secret society with death if he refused the ordeal. With Baden-Powell, say, it might be a bet – but not with Kitchener. I should know all that, because in my public days I knew him quite well. It's not a criminal's letter. It's all atmospheres.'

Thirteen

Borges said that we are not made of flesh and blood but of time, of evanescence. His *Atlas* is not an atlas of place, but an atlas of time. It passes through space in memory which circulates. Each moment as it flows in the *Atlas* is a glimmer of astonishment. In time, there is passing, retracing and intersection. A temporal moment calls to another and to things within it and these in turn traverse, coalesce.

The presence of a live tiger, who licked Borges, whose paw lingered on his head, who he could smell, whose weight he felt, was no more real to him than other tigers he knew in dreams and books. The tiger he directly perceived, with scent and feel, he described in his *Atlas* in an image.

The entries in the *Atlas* are brief, some no more than a few lines, a reflection whose traces only are visible. Yet, it is as if the universe was contained in this brevity and fleetingness. Because in the *Atlas* there is nothing solid or still, there is a perpetual calling between all things.

In the *Atlas* there is a photograph of Borges being licked by the tiger.

The train station for the blind man, I like to believe, was not the particular station I accompanied him to, but images of stations and their memories. The station was not external, but internal.

He did not observe it.

Each movement in space belonged to time.

Borges might have said that it belonged to the archetype of stations. The archetype is not like Brunhes's typologies. The archetype is part of memory and is alive, whereas the typology is a list.

There is a photograph of a brioche as an archetype brioche in Borges's *Atlas*. The archetype is neither perfect nor ideal.

Archetypes call to a range of images in Borges's memory, in books Borges had read. They evoke other archetypes or connect to them. These may begin as 'Geneva' , or 'Calvin', or the bakery at an intersection in Paris.

Intersections themselves can each be an archetype. In this way Borges can approach the infinite without endless nominations.

The archetype is not a category.

Borges recalled a meal in a Japanese restaurant in Buenos Aires with friends before he left for Europe. In this corner of Buenos Aires he perceived the flavours of the Orient. This journey pre-existed his departure.

M asked me, 'But don't you miss R? Did she give you what I can't? Is that what you miss in me?'

I said, 'but I am not the same person now.'

She tried to believe me. We both made believe.

I remembered with R, I felt the nostalgia that I would feel at this moment, including feigning that it would not be so. I was feeling it now with M.

Fourteen

The modernity of Proust's reaction to Vermeer is in its passion, almost a hysteria, a lack of measure, added to the object. This passion characterised the contemporary revolution in painting evident in Delacroix, dramatically in Impressionism.

The passion is physical and tactile. Tactility is the constituent of the visible without sight.

Borges's tiger is a sensation seen.

This is the nature of modern painting, not the visible, but the sensational. The eye, like a finger, caresses.

Borges's tiger is thoroughly modern.

Fifteen

The morphology of *géographie humaine* determined, *in advance* of observation, what would be seen and classified. The classification system made it appear that what was observed (and classified) were realities exterior to the classification system that catalogued them. In fact, the system had created its realities along with the illusion that it had not done so. The realities belonged to the system that framed and denominated them. Brunhes believed that he could observe by means of his system what was independent of it. The system presumed to efface itself before the objects it perceived, and that effacement, he believed, *enabled* reality to appear.

The system was coloured by nostalgia. It was a geography of lost things that it hoped it could fix forever.

In a photograph the referent of the image can cause the quality of the image to be neglected. The photograph becomes *no more* than its subject. In Brunhes's morphology, the reality depicted caused the system of classification to fade before it. The same is true in certain films whose logic works to efface the evidence of the logic and make it seem that events have not been ordained by a thought but by nature, naturalising logic as if the world were reasonable (which it is not), rather than astonishing (which it is). In the case of films, the seeming-to-be-true knows it is not true.

Brunhes's scientific system was more illusory.

Chesterton speaking of ethnographers: 'Suppose it is we who are the idiots because we are not afraid of devils in the dark?'

While it may have seemed to Brunhes that the real had imposed itself on his system, in fact the real was its effect.

Reality was that which was defined as real.

Though Brunhes laid stress on observation, his geography was not designed to see, but to catalogue. He saw what the catalogue made it pertinent to be seen.

The classifiable was that which belonged to a generality and could be typed. Particularity lost its unique qualities in order to fit within a typology, or else the particular could not be classified. Only what could be classified was given the status of fact, that is, significance. The classification system, though reductive, could be filled with infinite examples. Each category was a generality based on analogies. An object that did not conform to a type, or could not be typed because irreducibly particular, was as if non-existent. Brunhes's real, in order to maintain itself as real, had to be stripped of most of its qualities. These were impertinences, excesses, that scandalised the system. Impertinences were banished to a beyond called chaos or simply ignored.

The Borghesian archetype banishes nothing.

Barthes's *punctum*, what pricks, is an impertinence.

Brunhes's system did not classify reality. It classified significance and called significance reality. What was not significant was not worth considering. Yet it was exactly this addition of significance, of turning reality into signs, that Brunhes surreptitiously denied by proclaiming that his discursive system was determined by reality, not by the logic of the system that, for him, had no more systematicity than a lens.

Reality was known in advance, shaped for the archive already in place.

Brunhes had harsh words for the contingent, time and the subject. These were disruptions of system.

Borges's archetypes are not systematic but poetic, unclassifiable and unspeakable.

The same is true for Barthes. Attempts in textbooks on photography to summarise Barthes's ideas and theoretical propositions in his *La Chambre claire* are unconvincing.

Borghesian archetypes exist in time and memory. Brunhes's classification system only classified what was *there*, what you can see and was deemed irrefutably present, a system of verification. It abolished time and memory (which causes reality to quiver). Where Brunhes strove for exactness, Borges strove for approximation (more difficult). Borges's words are exact while the images they evoke whirl and pass. Brunhes's words are abstract while his images of objects are solid, cementing reality to them.

Had Brunhes read Borges's remarks on evanescence, he would have thought them poppycock.

Borges's *Atlas* and his *Labyrinths* are purely temporal, as is his *The Book of Imaginary Beings* whose order is alphabetical (arbitrary). The alphabet cannot contain the migratory nature of imaginary beings, only approach their reality, skim it. Borges's order recalls Calvino's *Le città invisibili*, whose dreams create cities, and Primo Levi's *Il sistema periodico*, whose chemical elements evoke memories and astonishing tales.

The *Archives* authenticated reality in collecting it. It was a museum of erudition, a bourgeois exhibition of wealth, piled up, added to, stored, as in a safety deposit box in a bank.

It earned no interest.

Its documents are musty, perfectly assimilated illustrations of a world already known and which the documents attempt to shore up (hopelessly).

It is not reality one encounters in the *Archives*, but hope (despair).

Sixteen

From the 17th century, artists, and later photographers, accompanied scientific missions, journeys of exploration, military campaigns, and voyages of discovery: Bougainville, Cook, Darwin, Livingstone, Napoléon.

Artists recorded what they observed. Emphasis was on accuracy and immediacy. Scientific needs transformed artistic techniques. The pencil drawing, watercolour, sketch, wash and charcoal displaced the finished canvas. The instant was important. It provided a direct view, not a synthetic, idealised summary of instants as in the painted canvas. It was both more and less objective than idealised views. It was more objective because it was not idealised, but less objective because instantaneity interposed the presence of the subject and thereby of heterogeneous views.

Towards the end of the 19th century, these techniques of the instant were displaced by the photograph, more instantaneous still and closest to natural sight and closest also to the personal.

Travel diaries are coincident with the techniques of instantaneous renderings.

The instant was excessive. It multiplied perspectives, making all points of view provisional and equal. Instantaneity abolished fixed vantage points and ideal orders. This shift was more apparent in late nineteenth-century paintings than in the photograph: the unnatural perspectives of Degas, for example, or the flattened frontality of Manet that swept away depth like a Godard travelling shot.

The Impressionists were not realists. They used empirical insights to go beyond classical measure.

Time, passion, desire, the moment, exploded the confines of painting. When Bougainville came to Tahiti he believed he had arrived in Paradise. Diderot's *Supplément* to Bougainville's account of the voyage was a fictitious dialogue made to seem true, as if Diderot had come upon the *Supplément*, rather than having written it. The *Supplément* 'demonstrated', as in a scientific demonstration, that what had been met with in Tahiti was natural man and woman, a culture of nature, not convention, and this nature was more civilised because natural while civilised convention was civilised because it was unnatural. The real was not only true, but good.

Nature was seen to conform to the way human beings were. Convention was seen to be an artificial constraint upon nature.

No good could come of such artifice.

Diderot concocted fictions as true documents: *La Religieuse*, for example (made into a film of the same title by Rivette). For someone keen to praise the natural order, he was equally keen on presenting a deceitful truth to demonstrate the deceits of civility while fervently practising these.

La Religieuse is a story made to seem a true document in the form of letters from a nun, cloistered against her will, to a nobleman. The origin of the novel was a set of letters that Diderot addressed to an aristocrat *as if* written by a nun and which Diderot did in fact send to a French aristocrat who had no reason to believe that they were not truly the letters of a cloistered nun.

That nun was Diderot.

In Rivette's film, every move by the nun to free herself from the convent life she has been forced into results in her being more bound by that life. When she escapes, other constraints pursue her until only the complete annihilation of suicide offers her a way out. The plot, diabolical and sadistic, tightens around her, like a noose.

There is no escape from the fiction.

The nun is played by Anna Karina. Her role in Godard's *Vivre sa vie* is an improvisation/impromptu of the American gangster film plotted with the sadistic play of the Rivette film.

Rivette has made films where his actors are given relative freedom to compose the play they are in and the lines they speak. The actors in this situation always come up against a natural limitation, inherent in their freedom, whose logic limits them more and more and into smaller and more restricted spaces. Left to themselves, it is they who restrain themselves and become devilish.

So much for natural man.

The erotic adventures of Bougainville and his crew in Tahiti were crucial for Diderot's arguments. He criticised the moral/social constraints of civilised society by measuring it against the freedom and happiness of primitive natural society.

Diderot's *Supplément*, Bougainville's *Voyage autour du monde*, and the diaries and log of Captain Cook are, among other things, ethnographic and geographical works, works of empirical science, based on direct observation.

If Diderot and Bougainville erred in displacing culture with nature in Tahiti, they nevertheless understood that culture was not natural and social rules not God-given. It was the conventional nature of civilised society that was exposed by the natural culture of primitive society. The argument was false (because the Tahitians did not live in a natural state) and their observations less than accurate, but the argument was also true (because the French lived in a cultural state).

Bougainville's *Voyage* is a lesson on the unreliability of images for the stories we tell with them.

Cultural arrangements could be socially altered and other rules substituted for existing ones. The merely contrived could be displaced by the truly natural.

The primitive example, though idealised, had radical consequences.

The Western encounter with the primitive altered the West as thoroughly as it did the primitive.

Seventeen

Rohmer observed that literary adaptation for the screen is a problem because most literary dialogue contains visual clues. To translate literary dialogue to the screen results in redundancies that make the transcription seem artificial, in effect, literary.

A scene of dialogue in a film does not require visual pointers. Literary indirect speech is more easily translated for the screen because visual qualities are seldom *in* the dialogue. They surround it.

Contrary to expectations, indirect speech is more cinematic than direct speech because it is less visual.

Rohmer called dialogue scenes in the cinema *hyper-direct* because you hear and see the dialogue. In literature there is only the *direct* and *indirect*.

Rohmer's *Le Beau mariage* opens with Sabine and her lover embracing. Their love-making is interrupted by a telephone call from his ex-wife. Sabine gets out of bed, dresses, and announces that she is to be married and leaves. Who she will marry is not clear.

In fact, there is no one.

By chance, she encounters Edmond, a lawyer, and resolves, without cause or encouragement, that he will be her husband. She assumes, on no evidence, that he is fascinated by her. In fact, he has no interest in her. Everything he does to express his disinterest, she takes as signs of the contrary. Her pursuit is based on nothing except her desire to be desired and to be the heroine of a story rather than a minor character interrupted by a wife's phone call.

What she sees, she misreads. Because she sees it, she believes her misreadings to be true. It is like the effect of the *hyper-direct* but on a character, not on the audience. To see and hear something might make it more believable, but not that it is not thereby true. In fact, it is only an image (*juste une image*) and doubly so: an image for a character, the image for which is an image for the audience.

Rohmer presents to his characters and to his audience images that are plain, realistic, casual. They are like documents of reality. His characters spend their time discussing what they see, trying to fit what they see into what they imagine, unable to distinguish their imaginary from fact.

The characters are narrators or behave like narrators telling (false) stories they believe to be true on the basis of images into which they have projected their desires. Their understanding is blind, often fatuous, a projection, and cannot be trusted. Nothing seen nor said can be trusted. The stories the characters narrate are stories of themselves as heros and heroines of their fictions that they are convinced are not fictions. The truth is what they concoct it to be.

The films reveal the gap between what is seen and what is said, between images and the narration of them. It is the play and pleasure of Rohmer's cinema raised to the level of a play and pleasure with the cinema.

The directors of the French *nouvelle vague*, such as Rohmer, Rivette, Godard, never ceased to make cinema with every film they made, dissolving the difference between critical awareness and artistic practice.

It is by making deception the subject of his films, as Hitchcock does and perhaps all the best films do, that Rohmer turns his films to the cinema and its effects as openly as does Godard.

How else could you otherwise enter fictions except by a deceit?

Deception is an opportunity not to reveal the truth but to play with it, to perform, to exhibit mechanisms, to open up. Deception is an instrument for revelation.

Images are as blank as reality. Rohmer corrodes certainty, not by proposing the fantastic but in maintaining the matter of fact and the everyday. Vision is not a guarantee of reality, but its risk. All images are traps and lures. Rohmer's plain speaking seduces you into a labyrinth.

Reality duplicated is not real: it is meaningless. Reality is what has been transformed by meaning. It belongs to discourse, not true, but meaningful.

Stories are a means of knowing and entering fictions a means to approach reality.

The hero, Frédéric, in Rohmer's *L'Amour l'après-midi*, carries Bougainville's *Voyage autour du monde* with him on the suburban train to work. He imagines sexual adventures with the women on the train, in the street, during his lunches in the afternoon. He never confronts what he imagines with the reality of a meeting. He meets these women in his reveries. They are images all the more tempting because they are there in reality yet a reality constructed of images narrativised. Like Rohmer, Frédéric tells stories with images. Frédéric is unlike Rohmer, because Rohmer's stories are the stories of the making-believe, the story of telling stories in images.

Rohmer presents you with the real and the image of that real. Together they affirm and deny each other in a web and layering of projections.

The avowal/negation is the pleasure of his films.

Frédéric, like Sabine, is a character of his own fiction, an effect of his imaginings. He is what he narrates himself to be. By investing reality with images narrativised, he transforms himself into an image in the image world in which he lives, that is, in fiction. He sees something (*une image juste*) where there is nothing (*juste une image*), as Sabine spies a husband where there is none.

Chloé, an old friend of Frédéric's, turns up one day at his office. As their friendship renews itself, she offers herself to him one afternoon. She is lying naked in bed in the pose of Manet's nude in *Olympia* or Ingres's *La Grande Odalisque*, the real mixed in her own self-presentation with an image, a play with the real. Frédéric's erotic imagination can now be realised in fact, unlike with the women he erotically imagines in his dreams each day but can never approach. Now he flees from the reality of Chloé, the image made object.

To consummate an image in reality is to lose it in fantasy, often the case when you miss someone until they appear and longing dissolves. Imagining Chloé is one thing, having her is quite another. An image actualised can be disappointing. It effaces the openness of an image, hence the possibilities for fantasy and narrative investment.

To think of your love, to fabulate and to masturbate, can often be more satisfying than the presence of the love.

Rohmer's characters play, flirt, dream, imagine, spy, pursue, and narrate, but seldom act, even less seldom embrace.

Frédéric, in his narration of himself, forgets that others have their stories, not only Chloé, who interrupts his imaginings with her reality, but his calm, devoted, well-organised wife of whom he is certain, whom he knows, takes for granted and never notices.

Chloé remarks to him, as she beckons him to bed, that she had seen his wife the other day at the Gare St Lazare, with someone.

Two realities in a single day are too much for poor Frédéric.

In the early 1950s Rohmer interviewed Rossellini for *Cahiers du cinéma*. He interviewed him a number of times. Rohmer admired Rossellini, as did most of the film-maker/critics of the *nouvelle vague*. Just as the cinema of Hitchcock is related to the films of Rohmer, so are in equal measure the films of Rossellini, especially *Viaggio in Italia*.

It is too much to say that the discovery of the characters at the end of *Viaggio in Italia* could be a Rohmerian ending; nevertheless, the sense of a revelation of realities, a knowledge of reality the characters suddenly encounter, including encountering the reality of themselves, is as central to Rohmer as it is to Rossellini, and to Hitchcock.

The themes of revelation/error/misapprehension/projection/ambiguity/ false identity/false pursuits, and, related to these, the uncertainty of vision and of reality and the consequent gap between images and their narration, a gap within which the films of these directors play, are not themes, but methods. And they are also the subject of the films.

Notes

1 'Phenomena, which for others are deviations, for me are the givens which determine my route – My calculations are based on time differentials, which for others, disturb the 'main lines' of research.'

2 'encyclopedia of the real'.

3 '... from a balloon or an airplane, at some hundreds of metres above ground, the exceptional has less value for human geography than the "typical"; and the mind, liberated from what we know of human beings, let us try to observe and make note of the essential facts of human geography with the same perspective and regard which allow us to discover and map the morphological, topographical and hydrographic details on the earth's surface. From this supposed vantage point, what can we see? Or better, what facts can a photographic plate register as accurately as the retina of the eye?'

4 'The fires of the camp glowed in the darkness of the bush. Around the huts, the only protection against the coming cold, and behind the fragile screen of palms and boughs hastily erected against the wind and rain and close to the sacks filled with the mean objects that were the sum of their earthly possessions and sleeping on the ground, haunted by other bands who were

equally hostile and fearful, the couple, tightly intertwined, thought of themselves as the support for each other, the comfort, the only solace against everyday difficulties and the dreamlike melancholy which, every now and then, enters the soul of the Nambikwara. The visitor who, for the first time, camps in the bush with the Indians, is overcome by anguish and compassion at the spectacle of this humanity so totally bereft, crushed against the ground, it seems to him, by some terrible cataclysm, in a hostile world, naked, shivering close to the flickering fires. He feels his way in the undergrowth, trying to avoid a hand, an arm, a body whose warm sheen one senses in the light of the fire. But this miserableness is alive with murmurings and laughter. The couples embrace one another as if nostalgic for a lost wholeness; they don't stop their caresses at the passage of a stranger. One senses among them an immense kindness, a profound carefreeness, an innocent and delightful animal happiness, which, taken together, is the expression of what is most moving and most genuine in human tenderness.'

5   '... to observe once and for all ... the modes of human activity whose fatal disappearance is only a question of time'.

6   'The goal of the *Archives de la planète* is to establish a dossier of humanity at the moment of its fullness, when we are undergoing one of the most complete economic, geographical and historical transformations that have ever occurred.'

7   'Moreover, the cinema is a language.'

Chapter Four
Naples/Calabria/Jerusalem

'D'autre part le cinéma est un langage.'

'Le cinéaste est non plus seulement le concurrent du peintre et du dramaturge, mais enfin l'égal du romancier.'[1]

One

Photography was supposed to have overcome the deficiencies of language by direct visual representation including the objectification and measurement of movement in time as is the work of Marey.

The cinema at its inception would reinstate narration to the image and offer to images another dimension of reality. Film narration made use of the objectivity of images to create stories that seemed true, not an analysis or measurement of images in time as in Mareyian science, but the reinscription of time to the image for fictional ends and for the creation of dreams.

Even the most minimal Lumière image provokes a story.

Marey's contributions stimulated the Italian Futurists, the fantasies of the Dadaists, and the imagination of Duchamp.

The Soviet film-makers realised the openness of film images. This was the lesson of the Kuleshov effect and of Eisenstein's practices, lessons learned from Griffith.

Griffith understood that images were without a specific sense but filled with the possibility of sense, a possibility he could direct towards a given end by the juxtaposition of images. He knew that an image is never more than *juste une image* and for that reason can be turned into *une image juste* by a narrative to satisfy desires. ' … il substitue à notre regard un monde qui s'accorde à nos désirs.'[2] The phrase is Bazin's recirculated by Godard in *Le Mépris.*

Juste une image contains the real, the grain of it, from which fictions can grow.

Two

Howard Hawks's films are filled with rapid-fire dialogue, sometimes punishing. Words are actions in his films: the wisecrack, the taunt, the tease, abuse, a challenge, prodding. They test values.

The delivery is sharp. A response anticipates a provocation and is in turn a provocation, defensive and aggressive. Dialogue functions to try character, character in the sense of having character, to find out if characters are worthy, deserving, up to it.

Hawks's characters submit to two tests, a test of action and a test of words. The films alternate scenes of one with the scenes of the other as if verifications. This testing is the beauty of *Red River.* Do the words match the deeds and does what we hear measure up to what we see?

Hawks is another cinema model for Rohmer. Hawksian men and women have to prove themselves in action as professionals (driving cattle, racing motor cars, flying planes, capturing wild game, capturing each other), and through words. Action and words produce the moral dimensions of character. Characters need to demonstrate their reliability, intelligence, courage and truthfulness by what they do in relation to what they say.

Hawks's heroes, though they emphasise self-reliance, are never self-sufficient. They require others. It is a hard lesson sometimes for them to learn. It teaches them their vulnerability. The lesson is learned in couples: male/female, male/male, female/female fighting it out to be loyal to each other, loyal to themselves, and to accept equality, and thereby vulnerability and to be compassionate. Love is the struggle for these.

Hawksian heroism is based on friendship, co-operation and loyalty.

Love in his films has these qualities more than that of passion whose expression is awkward, gruff, self-protective, unaccustomed. Dialogue seeks out values as the foundation of relationships and as the limits and constituents of the individual and of heroism. Hawks's films are as choral as the films of Renoir. The chorality is not assumed as being there at the outset, but is achieved, arrived at in the end, by actions that are understandings. Understanding is a demonstration, as exact and precise as a theorem.

Rio Bravo is the logical refutation of *High Noon*. In *High Noon*, the hero stands alone, deserted by the brave who are only their words. In *Rio Bravo*, the hero stands with his friends, the drunk, the limping old man, the young kid, who are their actions. It is not appearances that matter, but what one does, ethics performed.

Maréchal and Rosenthal battling each other after their escape from military prison in Renoir's *La Grande illusion* reminded me of Tom and Matthew in *Red River*, Walter and Hildy in *His Girl Friday*, Dorothy and Lorelei in *Gentlemen Prefer Blondes*.

The dialogue scenes in Hawks's films attempt to give sense to the action that succeeds them, and thereby to the world that surrounds them, a Hawksian world that is senseless and absurd, hence the need to establish values for oneself and with others, not abstract values, but real ones, those between friends and professionals in which the stake is survival.

For Rohmer, the game is a play with the audience between the openness of images and the will to narration. For Hawks, the game is bitter and serious. It involves the openness of images to be filled with meaning and the meaninglessness of the world and its implacability. In a Hawks film you are at risk.

Three

Pasolini identified two languages in the cinema: one, a narrative language, an artificial sign system, socialised and conventional, that imposed sense; the other, photographic and duplicative that imitated reality and was analogous to it. The photographic in the cinema, said Pasolini, spoke *with* reality, without a definite sense, as if unsignified. Meaning appeared when images were organised and grouped in structures that were perceptual and interpretative.

This distinction was similar to Bazin's between those who put their faith in reality and those who put their faith in the image.

One sphere related to chemistry, science, optics, the imprint, direct reproduction; the other to perception, the subject, manipulation.

These two poles have defined the central debates about the cinema. Godard restates these in the opposition *juste une image/une image juste*.

The modernity of the cinema rests within this dichotomy. Griffith and an American tradition were not realistic in a duplicative, photographic sense, but understood and exploited the perceptual/perspective qualities of the cinema that they grounded in a psychology and a verisimilitude, anchoring images away from their inherent ambiguity and away from a blank, stark reality. Reality unmediated threatened to disrupt fictional truth-seeming, the illusion of reality, seemingly more real and powerful than 'nos désirs' and more convincing and comforting than the duplication of it.

A way of undermining verisimilitude was to multiply perspectives: for example, by creating more than a single fiction and having levels of reality that do not join, as in a collage effect, radically used by Godard.

Another way, the way of Rossellini, and the direction of Bazin's thought, was to reintroduce duplication, photographic reality as a means to disrupt verisimilitude, in part a return to origins. Bazin was interested in nature, exploration and medical films. Rossellini was inclined towards science and history. Godard had an abiding fascination with documentary and ethnography. Jean Rouch *and* Bazin were his models.

Godard broke up verisimilitude by playing within the gap of fiction and documentary. Perhaps these two paths are evident as well in Rossellini. Reality for Rossellini was an unresolved multiplicity, perspectives that intersected but could not be reconciled, as in *Viaggio in Italia* within Catherine and in relation to Alex and in *Germania, anno zero* interior to Edmund and most starkly in *Europa 51*.

Godard's cinema is open.

Four

Kim Novak in *Vertigo* has multiple identities. She is Judy Barton making believe she is Madeleine Elster to mislead the detective, 'Scottie' Ferguson (James Stewart). Scottie is doubly misled. He follows a false trail and a false person *and* falls in love with a false identity, with Madeline Elster who is not Madeleine Elster.

And Judy Barton/Madeleine Elster is never not Kim Novak, as Scottie is never not James Stewart. And Novak and Stewart are stars, that is, masquerading, in play, not themselves, not even, not even especially, as Novak and Stewart.

Madeleine Elster is doubly not herself. Judy Barton pretends that the Madeleine Elster whom she falsely plays thinks herself possessed by her dead grandmother, Carlotta Valdéz, whose death threatens to be Madeleine Elster's destiny. A false character has been constructed with a false history which doubles her in distorted mirror images.

Scottie falls in love with an image ... from the beginning, and so do we. These images are never singular even when they appear to be.

Scottie is employed by Madeleine Elster's husband to protect her from herself. But the husband has created Judy Barton to be the image of his wife. The characters played and impersonated by Novak produce other similar characters who resemble each other. No one is who they appear to be. Scottie, straight as he is, is not himself, having been traumatised by an accident that gives him vertigo, preventing him from being himself. Vertigo is a state of unbalance. The false drama Scottie is enmeshed in and the true passion it evokes in him depend on an internal split and an unresolved trauma.

At the end, the film restores Scottie to himself and the truth. The price of truth is dreadful: he loses Madeleine, and twice over, as Madeleine who fictively died, then as Judy who really does die, taking with her his illusions and his happiness.

Five

When you are being betrayed you are not unhappy. You are unhappy when you find out you were betrayed. The unhappiness you feel at that moment, the

moment when you know the things you did not know at the time you were
happy, you project back to the time that now seems to have been a time of false
happiness. But that is what you understand now. Then, your happiness was not
false.

You were happy then, as you are truly unhappy now.
The unhappinesses provoked by deceits or infidelities are tricks of time.

Six

When Judy Barton returns to herself, no longer Madeleine Elster, she plays being herself. Judy Barton, however, was she who had assumed the false identity of Madeleine Elster. The true Judy Barton is a fraud, impossible to redeem or to be reconstituted either as herself or as another. Her true identity is for ever lost. To appear true she needs to deny her fraudulence, which is only possible if she maintains her falsifications.

She becomes herself, with her most crucial aspect left out, her masquerades of not being herself. Judy can never return to herself except as an act, a falsity.

Scottie, in love with Madeleine (who he thinks he loses in a suicide which in fact does not occur but is the murder of the *real* Madeleine Elster), meets Judy one day by chance in the street who resembles the lost Madeleine. He tries to make Judy over to be exactly what he remembers her to be (as the husband had done), an illusion that deceived him and still deceives him. Judy, when she was Madeleine, fell in love with Scottie as he did with her, an impossible love because she was not herself, nor was he himself.

Judy as Judy seeks to efface her falseness to Scottie by remaining for ever false, never admitting to him her masquerade.

When she is herself she is always false.

It is difficult to always distinguish original from translation. Scottie takes the copy for the original, then tries to translate the original to the true of its copy. Perhaps, as Borges suggests, every original is already a copy and already a translation.

To sustain a love, perhaps to sustain all love, one can never be wholly genuine or completely oneself.

No image of Judy, no representation of her, no words that she speaks, can be true. Even to say 'I love you' would be false. The 'I' who speaks has no identity except as this double, this masquerade of representation.

Scottie pursues a Madeleine who is not Madeleine and a Judy who is not Judy, who he seeks to return to being Madeleine.

In the end, recovering the truth, he recovers himself and is reunited with himself.

That is his loss.

Seven
Pascal Bonitzer quotes this story by Béla Balàzs:

Un jour, Asta Nielsen a joué le rôle d'une femme qui a été soudoyée pour séduire un jeune homme riche. L'homme qui l'y a contrainte l'observe dissimulé derrière un rideau, attendant le résultat. Consciente d'être épiée, Asyta Nielson simile des sentiments amoureux. Elle le fait de façon convaincante, son visage reflète toute la gamme de la mimique amoureuse. Nous voyons que c'est joué, que c'est faux – ce n'est qu'un masque. Au cours de la scène, Asta Nielsen tombe réellement amoureuse du jeune homme. Ses traits changent de façon imperceptible, puisque aussi bien elle avait jusqu'alors montré de l'amour – et ce la, à la perfection! Maintenant qu'elle aime réellement, que pourrait-elle montrer de plus? C'est seulement une lueur différente, à peine perceptible, immédiatement reconnaissable, qui fait que l'expression de ce qui auparavant était simulé devient celle d'un sentiment profond, authentique. Mais Asta Nielsen a soudain conscience d'être observée. L'homme caché derrière le rideau ne doit pas lire sur ses traits que ce n'est plus un jeu. Elle fait donc de nouveau comme si elle mentait. Une nouvelle variation, désormais à trois voix, apparaît sur son visage. Car son jeu d'abord simulait l'amour, puis le montrait sincèrement. Mais elle n'a pas droit à ce dernier. Son visage montre donc de nouveau un amour faux, simulé. A présent sa simulation est devenue mensonge. Elle nous fait croire qu'elle ment.[3]

Eight

Ferdinand de Saussure's semiotics was contemporary with the establishment of the collection of the *Archives de la planète* and with the philosophy of Bergson.

Semiotics generalised the notion of language as a system of signs to include more than ordinary language. Its insight was that all of language was a system of signs and all systems of signs like language. Semiotics embraces different forms of communication and expression, verbal, visual, ordinary language, artistic languages, photography, the cinema, painting, theatre, music, literature. It insinuates a system of signs and signification, with their relativity and uncertainty, into the sureties and assumed objectivity of positive notions of reality.

If reality is reality only as signified then it belongs to discourse, not nature or fact, and therefore is subject to argument, refutation and desire.

Semiotics is not paranoid.

Every fact is an enunciated fact, every referent a construction.

The realities of positivism were established by conventions of non-enunciation. Things were objective and true because there was no speaker who spoke them. Reality had spoken them.

Semiotics compromised a simplified relation of an observer exterior to that which was observed, challenging the idea of the facticity of reality that issued from such a relation. Between the observer and observed, semiotics introduced the mediation of the sign and the attendant complexity of reality in representation (reality is always represented) that the notion of the sign suggests.

Reality can only be recognised in what it is not.

Practices such as Brunhes's *géographie humaine* sought to expel language from reality in the name of science. Brunhes's ideal writing was a writing without a subject, a referent unenunciated.

He believed photography was that ideal writing.

A geographical archive of photographs was a Utopia.

Nine

Pasolini went to Palestine (modern Israel) in search of locations for his

Gospel film, *Il Vangelo secondo Matteo*. The journey of that search he made into a film, *Sopralluoghi in Palestina*.

Pasolini was unable to find the likenesses of what he imagined was the Palestine of the Gospels. He found the likenesses he sought instead in the backward regions of the Italian South: Sicily, Puglia, Basilicata, Calabria. These regions seemed to him like ancient Palestine and their people like the figures of the Bible. The analogies were second-order representations of an imagined hypothetical reality, nevertheless actual, whose fictional likeness to a presumed reality is open and acknowledged.

The world of antiquity no longer existed in Palestine, but seemed still alive in southern Italy, though in tatters.

In *Il Vangelo* the villages of Calabria appear as if they are the towns of ancient Bethlehem and Jerusalem. This is not an illusion. It is a citation. The villages do not lose their identity as Calabrian villages. This true identity is necessary in order to posit a likeness with ancient Palestine and thereby the difference and the gap without which likeness could not be composed.

The reality of Calabrian villages is transposed into a linguistic, metaphoric relation by which the reality of Palestine can be born, but as a linguistic effect. Reality comes out of language, to Pasolini, out of poetry.

If Calabria were represented not as if it were ancient Palestine, but as the illusion of Palestine, as really seeming that, then the reality of Calabria would be lost and with it the possibility of forming the analogy with ancient Palestine. The loss of reality would occasion the loss of language. It is only through metaphor, analogy, citation, that reality can be sustained. Language is based on difference. The marking of difference in metaphor is the mark of poetic language, hence poetry's guarantee of reality.

Pasolini compares an existing reality to one that had once been and is now only imagined. He overlaps memory and time in metaphors that condense two phases of time and two levels of reality. He makes them indivisible and paradoxical, Calabria being and not being Palestine and being and not being itself, each term at once different and like. Calabria, made to serve as the citation of Palestine, enables Palestine to serve as the citation of Calabria. As the one (Palestine) disappeared to necessitate the other (Calabria) to mark that disappearance, the other, in turn, will disappear.

Pasolini does not speak about Calabria or about Palestine. He speaks with them as if they are linguistic or poetic units. Each term is necessary as terms of difference to produce likeness. Instead of creating a make-believe reality, he uses reality as a form of speech, to speak with it in order to speak of it. Reality can never be touched directly, but nor can it be touched through the illusion that it is being touched. Only metaphor, which admits and acknowledges the gap and points to the citation, can retain the reality that can never be reached.

Representation, which is an illusion of reality, is not good enough. What is required is a second order of representation, to reveal, or rather block the illuson.

In Pasolini's films, you watch a linguistic transformation taking place, a metaphor enacted, language performed. You see the play of sign and reality which is the subject of the film whose continuous labour is to sustain and renew differences in language by means of reality. This for Pasolini is poetry.

The fact that Calabria was used as a real setting analogous to the sacred and belonging to the Gospels emphasised how precious difference was and how terrible the threat to it. Palestine had been effaced in modern Israel, Calabria was being effaced in modern Italy. They were like, not only for what the one was, but for what the other was becoming. With their disappearance would disappear the ability to form the metaphor by means of them.

To Pasolini, modernisation homogenised difference, turning reality into the same. Sameness threatened the metaphor, hence poetry, which was the defence of difference and thereby the defence of reality.

Il Vangelo is not a re-enactment of the passion of Christ, which would have been false, but the citation of the Gospel, which is true. The Gospel is not thereby lost, but rescued by being returned to its specificity, its pure difference. Pasolini literalises the Gospel. As you watch this enactment and literalisation they appear astonishing, something never seen before.

Re-enactment as verisimilitude falsifies the real because difference is missing and analogy nullified. Re-enactment compromises reality, thereby debasing language. It makes believe we are in Palestine (where we are not) and not in Calabria (where we are).

To understand where one is it is necessary to understand where one is not and why one is not there.

Illusion fuses language with reality.

Pasolini doubles reality, causing it to vacillate.

Ten

Pasolini openly declares the analogy of Calabria/Palestine. The openness of the mechanism is evident in all his films. It operates by a double reversal. Calabria is original *and* translation and Palestine is translation *and* original. Calabria is *like* Palestine and Palestine *like* Calabria, both necessarily different else without the difference there could be no analogy, no translation as the play of difference.

A similar play is present in Pasolini's dialect poetry where the original in dialect is translated at the foot of the page as its Italian copy.

In fact the original in dialect is not the poem in dialect but the poem in Italian translated into dialect presented to the reader as the (false) original. This is not a double falsification but a double movement. Each poem is as if a poem about to become another poem as every Pasolini film and every location in the film was also another film and another location which the film and the location sought to be, but was not yet and was and might become. The film was nothing in particular but these possibilities taken together, co-present, overlapping and contradictory.

Many of Pasolini's films were explicitly titled and organised as films to become other films. They contained their otherness within them as part of themselves, their not-being and erasure.

They were their own incompleteness, disappearance and negation.

Otherness was the feature of their structure. It denied structure, centre or fixity. It pointed to what it was not. Negation was evident no matter what vantage point you had to view it and no matter what positive you assumed.

No matter where you looked what you saw was elsewhere than where it was or would be or was passing to an elsewhere of its own denial.

Pasolini's theoretical writing is paradoxical and metaphoric. It is poetic writing masquerading as theory. If you like, it is poetry seeking to be theory and theory seeking to be poetry, neither quite one or the other. Translations are almost impossible of this kind of writing because they seek one or the other side of the reversal, turning poetry into bad theory or theory into bad poetry. The translations of Pasolini's theoretical writings are usually unsuccessful.

Metaphors are difficult to elucidate. Pasolini used them as instruments for explanation: film is like language, language is like reality, writing is like reality, the written language of reality, and so on.

Such theory is not explicative. It is expressed in extended metaphors, the paradox, riddles of language. It calls out to be comprehended and blocks comprehension save by recourse to a further analogy. It is theory which spins beyond itself.

Eleven

For Brunhes, the relation of image to reality was not contradictory, but cohesive, not an analogy, but a connection of similarities, the conjunction of difference as the same thing. The photograph, to him, was not a likeness to the object it reproduced, not an analogy, but sameness, which erased difference.

Baudelaire's comment on painting as creation (art) and photography as duplication (science) was a comment on a threat to difference by a poet.

Bruhnes's ideal language was plain speaking, like the photograph. He was not troubled by a loss of reality in the image nor motivated to deal with it as a problem. On the contrary, the image contained and preserved reality as duplication. Reality and the image were collapsed into one. Brunhes's interests were with the real in so far as it could be typified and classified. To collect and sort photographs of reality was like sorting reality.

What was geographical reality for Jean Brunhes?

It was visible surface marks: 'lignes', 'points', 'tâches', 'vides'. 'Placer sous les yeux ...' '... voir ... voir ...' '... ouvrir les yeux et voir...', '... fera voir ...'.

And in that seeing you would be absent: '... Ne voit pas qui veut.'[4]

Géographie humaine had delivered nature to culture, but was unable to understand culture except in its physical manifestations. The human, geographically speaking, was defined as an evidential trace, the mark left by human activity, a mark, therefore, with the full presence of the physical.

The *humaine*, after entering geography, was evacuated from it, leaving only its stain, a melancholy *tâche*.

The reality of physical marks of a cultural kind (canals, tunnels, towns, roads, and so on) were for him imprinted (*imprimés*) on the surface of the earth, his *tâches, lignes, points*. Geographical reality was this printing, an etching, which the earth, like a photographic negative or lithograph, registered and which the geographer (like the photographer) or artist developed into a positive image.

'... l'empreinte (materielle, concrète, tangible) ...'. 'Les actes essentiels du travail humain s'impriment en caractères materiels et visibles sur la surface de la terre ... les territoires habités comme des traits physionomiques qui reflète la manière dont l'homme se comporte vis-à-vis de la terre.' '... les traces et les traits superposés par lesquels s'inscrit depuis un siècle sur l'épiderme de notre planète, l'ingéniosité active de notre espèce.'[5]

The *autochrome* of the geographical vestiges of human activity was a photograph of a photograph, the imprinted surface of the earth. Human geographical reality was an inscription and the *autochrome* a reinscription, doubly evidential and sure. Man had passed, made his mark, recorded himself, and the *autochrome* recorded the passing in an imprint which superimposed itself on reality, reinforcing it.

Upon the inscribed has-been of human action was the has-been of the photograph of the action.

La géographie humaine was emphatic, a tautology that authenticated.

Twelve

Do you remember, one summer, in Naples, we retraced the steps of Ingrid Bergman in Rossellini's Viaggio in Italia? *We took photographs in Il Bersagliere, posed in front of the Excelsior, walked along the embankment opposite where George Sanders had picked up a whore who he took for a melancholy ride to nowhere. His reality and its sadness were exposed without a word, like ours. Do you remember? And the time at Pompeii, when they discovered the clay mould of a couple embracing at death, and their own desperation? And the ferry ride of anguish and silences and hurt in the Bay of Naples?*

I wonder what we reproduced. Why did we choose to do so? It certified something disquieting. Then, I only wanted to translate what had happened in the film, just for fun, I thought, like a game, like children. But now, I know other reasons. If you know the result beforehand, Rossellini said, there is little point in filming it. To film, like 'to write', is to reveal something, not to record what has already been revealed and that you already know. When Sanders and Bergman find each other during the hysteria of the religious festival, after having been lost to each other, it is like a miracle. I am certain Rossellini came upon the ending as they came upon each other.

The experiment has to be done with care to avoid coming to a conclusion and thereby cheapening the journey. Viaggio in Italia *is never cheap. Film narratives, most of them, impose sense. Rossellini had to decompose sense, to allow sense to flourish, giving birth to significance by making it uncertain.*

If I had said anything like that to you, you might have looked bored.

The game I played and the one you played were different even if it seemed that we were playing together.

Thirteen

Brunhes's major theoretical work was *La Géographie humaine: essai de classification positive,* published in 1910. It formed the classification structure of the *Archives de la planète*.

There are three essential categories to it. Each consists of two subordinate categories, in turn further divisible. Potentially, all of geographical reality could be absorbed and classified in the system. There was no end to it being cut into fragments, more and more finely described and exhaustively detailed.

The system read:

A. Facts of occupation (unproductive)
  1. houses (*points*)
  2. roads (*lignes*)
B. Facts of animal and vegetable conquest (productive)
  3. agriculture (*tâches*)
  4. domestication of animals (*tâches*)
C. Destructive economic pursuits
  5. mining (*tâches*)
  6. vegetable and animal destruction (*tâches*)

Roads could be extended to include patterns of settlement, trade routes, economic activity. The domestication of animals could be extended to include nomadism, the construction of villages, population densities. Mining could be extended to include the formation of towns, cities, ports, railways. One could then return to patterns of transport, houses, cultivation, or whatever, caught in the infinitude of these microscopic divisions that were reality's order.

Brunhes stressed connections that bound, continuities that reinforced, a world that cohered.

It was an ideology of cohesion, a regionalist conservatism.

He wrote on the eve of the First World War.

Notes

1 'The film-maker is no longer a rival to the painter and the playwright, but, at last, the equal of the novelist.'

2 '… it substitutes for what we see a world in accord with our desires.'

3 'One day, Asta Nielsen played the role of a woman who is bribed to seduce a young man. The one who hired her watches her, hidden from behind a curtain, awaiting the outcome. Conscious of being spied upon, Asta Nielsen fakes being in love. She does it convincingly, her face mirroring the whole

gamut of love's expressions. We see that she is making believe, that she is false – that it is only a mask. In the course of doing so, Asta Nielsen really does fall in love with the young man. Her features imperceptibly alter, since she had so well up to then showed herself to be in love – and to perfection! Now that she is truly in love, what more can she do? It is only a slightly different glow, hardly perceptible, immediately recognisable, which makes the expression that she had previously simulated become genuine, authentic. But Asta Nielsen is suddenly aware of being observed. The man hidden behind the curtain must not be able to read from her expression that it is no longer a game. She thus pretends to be faking again. A new variant, henceforth in three voices, appears on her face. Because her earlier play of simulated love now shows itself to be sincere. But she has no right to this attitude. Her face shows once more a false love, simulated love. Now her simulation has become a lie. She makes us believe that she is lying.'

4   'lines', 'points', 'stains', 'blanks'. 'Use your eyes ...', '... observe ... observe ...', '... open your eyes and see ...', '... you must look ...'. 'Whoever sees what he wants does not see.'

5   '... the imprint (material, concrete, tangible) ...'. 'The essential actions of human endeavour are imprinted materially and visibly on the surface of the earth ... inhabited places are like physiological traits which reflect the way man acts in his relation to the earth.' '... the superimposed traces and traits through which the active genius of our species has been inscribed for a century on the epidermis of our planet.'

Chapter Five
Cracow/Pesaro/Xanadu

Once a thing is known it can never be unknown. It can only be forgotten. And, in a way that bends time, so long as it is remembered, it will indicate the future.

Anita Brookner, Look at Me

One

I met a man called Josef who told me his story. This chapter retells Josef's story and the effect it had upon me.

I always knew I would retell the story of Josef. It may be that, had Josef not told me his story, I would not have written this book.

Two

In Orson Welles's films, in films such as *Othello*, *The Trial*, *Citizen Kane*, the films seem realistic because the worlds created are dreamlike. The realistic space Bazin noticed in Welles's films constructed by depth of field is a space of dream, enclosed and hermetically sealed. The world as dream is the terrifying world inhabited by Joseph K in *The Trial*, who reacts to the horrors, illogic, persecution and astonishment he encounters as if these were normal. The strangeness of reality is never acknowledged. No one is surprised. That is the terror, this acceptance.

Welles's films are claustrophobic. They press upon you and there is no way out.

Everything seems alien, especially the scale, the monstrous depth, like

the lips of Kane when he utters his last word, 'Rosebud', the hollow resonance of the sound, the camera that transports you through dizzying spaces
in *Othello*. I, like Joseph K, am asked to take astonishing things as ordinary. This is the reverse of a dream where the banal seems fantastic. In my
dreams, the dream is more real than reality because it has none of reality's
dreamlike qualities.

Like fiction, the dream seems familiar.

The terror of Welles's films is that you are provoked to ask, 'But, what
if this is true?'

In Pasolini's *Edipo re*, Oedipus in a modern present dreams the Oedipus
myth of the ancient past. The dreaming and the myth dreamt is the film
you see. It can be thought, however, that the present is dreamt by Oedipus
from the past. The dream is a projection from a mythological time. The
possibility did not occur to Pasolini. When Jean Narboni suggested it,
Pasolini agreed, laughing.

Jean Rouch, shooting the possession rituals of the Songhai and following
the lion-hunt rituals of the Dogon, entered into these activities, as if he
were possessed by them. The camera is inside the action, not an observer
exactly, but inside and outside at once, like the participants, perhaps.

This position is difficult to define (and achieve). It depends on delicacy,
tact and responsiveness.

The rituals were real enough, though possession is a matter of mind.
They make sense only internally. By entering the worlds of Songhai and
Dogon myth, Rouch entered their reality. Reality was a perspective, nothing
very solid. To film and document it, Rouch needed to document the fictional world of these peoples, what they felt and imagined, how they shaped
things. Reality was their dream of reality, which possessed them.

Could that be what Rossellini meant when he spoke of his love of reality?

In Jean Renoir's *La Carosse d'or*, Camille (Anna Magnani), an actress, finds
that off-stage she is in a world of spectacle, masquerade, make-believe, falsity. Renoir organises the off-stage space in his films as a theatre space: the

courtyard in *Le Crime de monsieur Lange*, the chateau in *La Règle du jeu*. Here too, as in Welles, the effect of depth of field is not realistic, as Bazin maintained. It is a play of artifice whereby reality is not falsified but theatricalised without thereby losing its realism; in fact, on the contrary, realism is gained in the openness of the theatrical.

It is on-stage, in the theatre, in *La Carosse d'or*, that Camille feels most herself, most true to herself. At the close of the film the curtain comes down on the off-stage reality in which Camille has lived, and as this curtain closes the space of the off-stage, Camille re-enters the world of theatre, with its mountebanks, tumblers, clowns, Pierrots and singers. Asked by the master of ceremonies if she will miss reality and her loves, her new wealth, her high social place, she sighs, 'Just a little.'

The golden coach, given to her by the viceroy, is a compressed sign of all the realities in the world that she will lose in returning to the theatre. It is the most fantastic, most fabulous *coup de théâtre*: absolute reality and the purest artifice.

Three

I can just glimpse Josef's diminutive figure, his gentility, softness, the intensity and determination in his eyes. If you asked me to recall Josef to you in detail, even his story, I could not do so. I feared at the time he told me his story that I might forget it. So, when I heard it, I wrote it down so that I would not forget. Returning to it now, I can't help reworking it.

You remember things because something current causes you to return to the past. Memory is immediate and detached. Immediate, because you require it now, detached, because it is in the past. When you reach it, you find the absence. Memory is unstable, like the present to which memory returns; both pass.

My daughter, when still young, lived with me in Melbourne. She returned to her mother in London. There were bad feelings between myself and her mother. I realised she would not be coming back. I missed her even before she left. What I missed were the things I remembered even as I could still feel, smell, touch, listen, and watch them. She had not yet gone.

Memories are images. In time they fade until what is missed is the memory of them. At that moment she was gone.

When I met Josef, I could not know where I would be in the future and whether in the future I would remember. I knew that I wanted to remember later. Now the memory is less intense than I thought it might be then.

Hearing his story caused me to return to my past. That instant too is now gone. The story, and what I recalled as a result of it, are connected. Borges retained things in the flow of time, like the smell of the tiger in his *Atlas* and the weight of its paw. What he remembers enters time, and he enters time along with it.

I seem to lose things.

I lose them because I try hard to hold on to them. Borges lets them go, gives them life.

I tried to hold on to Josef's story so that it would not fade or disappear. Fading and recall have been methods in this book.

Four

I met Josef at a hotel reception desk in Italy, in Pesaro in June last year (1998). I was in Pesaro for the film festival. Josef was in Pesaro for a holiday.

He spoke German to the hotelier and Swedish to his wife by his side, a shade behind him. I felt her to be withdrawn. We exchanged banalities about the weather. I assumed, wrongly, that he was with the festival.

He was a hydraulic engineer. We spoke to each other in English. We went out to a shaded table by the side of the pool. He had apricot fruit juice. I had a Prosecco. We shared pistachio nuts and crisps.

Going outside, sitting down, talking was natural, as if it had been organised that we would meet, sit at a table by the pool, order drinks, chat, that we had been waiting for the encounter.

Five

Josef is from Cracow. His mother died when he was seven. Soon after her death, the Germans invaded Poland (1939). His father enlisted in the Polish army. With the surrender of Poland, his father went to Syria to join the Free Polish army. He was killed by the Italians in North Africa.

When Josef's father left for the army, Josef was put into the care of the nanny/domestic of the household. Josef's family was comfortable, middling bourgeois, and Jewish. He was in Poland occupied by the Nazis. The domestic, like many Poles, was anti-Semitic. However, she loved Josef.

Josef, orphaned and defenceless, found a mother. The domestic, unmarried, without children, found a child to love, though a Jewish one.

After the Nazi conquest of Poland, the Jews were made to live in a ghetto. It was a return to the middle ages. Jews who lived in the countryside were relatively untouched at first.

Josef had relatives near Cracow. He went there, thus managing to avoid the ghetto. Later, the Jews in the countryside were rounded up by the Germans, classified, numbered, and sent to concentration camps. Most were murdered.

By then the Jews of Poland knew their fate.

Josef was hidden for the remainder of the war. His sister, less fortunate, was discovered and sent to Auschwitz. She survived. She is seven years older than Josef and still alive.

Josef has cancer. When I met him, he only had a few weeks, perhaps a few months, perhaps only a few days, left to live. He was in pain most of the time. Every day there was more misery in store for him. Neverthless, he had a light in his eye, more than a light, it was bright and it glowed. The light was soft and could laugh and be joyful. The pain was difficult but he was not afraid to die. His arm was bruised from needles and drips. He was very thin.

Josef regretted that when he died, more precisely when he will be dead, he will miss one of his grandchildren. The missing was now, already. There is no missing once you are dead. The grandchild will also miss him.

Joseph regretted these missings in advance of them.

He has four grandchildren, all boys. The one he was concerned about and who he most loved was seven years old, the same age Josef was when

the war broke out and Josef's mother died and left him, and then his father
was killed and left him.

When the little boy, the grandchild, was born, his mother, Josef's daugh-
ter-in-law, became depressed. It was not possible for the boy to live at home
in that atmosphere of rejection and gloom. He went to live with Josef and
his wife. Josef and his wife stood in the place of the boy's father and
mother. To die, for Josef, would be to desert the little boy who is, in imagination, himself.

   He would miss the boy who had become part of himself. Thus Josef
could relive the death of his own parents and its anguish. The little boy that
Josef would soon leave allowed Josef to return to a pain of leaving he did
not want the little boy to feel. Josef already imagined the little boy feeling
it. He had been that little boy and still was.

Josef's wife was troubled that Josef would soon die and leave her. She
already seemed shattered. He regretted leaving her too. For her, being left
was a feeling. For him, leaving her was only an idea. The pain of his grandchild was imagined and felt by Josef because he had been left in that way.
It distressed him that he was the cause of it. When he spoke of the boy, he
shined. When he spoke of his wife he was dull.

   Love is not something you understand.

   Josef's love was not understanding.

   Its power depended on not understanding.

Was his wife only mourning that she was an idea?

   To miss something when you are dead, when you will no longer miss anything, anticipates an impossible sentiment that you will not have when you
reach the state you imagine. Missing is now. It is like regretting the end of
a love affair while you are in love, that you will not regret when it is over
because then you will no longer be in love. Perhaps, to regret this end is
already to begin to approach it, the first sign of its ending.

Josef, the Jewish boy, was loved by the anti-Semitic nanny. She saved his life by keeping him fed and hidden and saved his soul by loving him. She loved him beyond her principles and her culture. With her help he learned to live his life with intensity and energy. It was not a debt he owed to her, but a gift he reciprocated. Joseph was happy. I think it was because of the way he was loved by his fictitious mother.

She did not annul his being Jewish or anything of him.

He was proud of being a Jew. For him it was a mark of determination and the key to his survival. To be a Jew was not to be a victim, but to survive, to succeed.

Josef was, in fact, orphaned. His grandson was only as if orphaned. Josef may have identified with his grandson, but he also thought of himself as the boy's fictitious father, as his nanny had been his fictitious mother.

Josef was to his grandchild what his father had been to him who deserted him. Desertion, understandable to an adult, is not understandable to a child. The child remains in us, uncomprehending, even when we become adults and can understand. The desertion continues because it is a wound that never heals, not a memory. It never fades nor passes.

How awful it would be to leave this little boy as Josef had been left, despite the warmth of a fictional mother.

Josef was adored because he was Josef. He was despised because he was a Jew. He said to me that Jews could always succeed in whatever they wanted. It was true for him. He was loved, he said, more than any mother could or would love a child, by his adoring, anti-Semitic fictional mother. If she loved him as he felt she did, she would have had to do so not despite Josef being a Jew, but in his being a Jew, which was his success.

I wondered, though, did he make all this up while talking to me as a need just before dying, a memory that he impossibly wanted to die with but which was not remembering, but something wished for, the fictitious loving mother, loving you despite everything, unconditionally?

All his life Josef held on to his Jewishness. He was loved for what he was. It allowed him to be himself and still be loved. Often we complain that our parents love us for what we are not and can never become.

It is a formidable accomplishment to shape and to hold on to your identity against all that. I felt that Josef was seldom lonely, or at least he seldom felt the loneliness of non-recognition, which is a terrible abandonment.

When the Germans established themselves in Poland, and before the deportations to the death camps that would make all Nazi decrees of exclusion superfluous, Josef, like all Jewish children in Poland under the Nazis, could not go to school.

Every day, in hiding, his nanny brought him books and paper and ink. She was determined that he, her impossible Jewish son, concealed from the Germans, would be educated. Little Josef read the books.

He cried for a perfect mother who was not a true one. I cried for not having the experience of that love, nor the experience of imagining it until that moment. I longed for it but not knowing it, it seemed inconceivable to me, even as I imagined it, by the pool, sitting with Josef.

Josef learned at an early age what most of us never learn, not the meaning, but the value of life, how precious it is simply to be alive and to accept that as something to be enjoyed, a gift. Love can make us responsible in the best possible way, and the lack of it can make us irresponsible in the worst possible way. Not responsibility as duty or ethics, simply a respect.

Despite the horror of the events in his childhood, it was a childhood I envied. It gave him happiness. It shaped a character of fineness that his nanny had helped to sculpt. She was simple, uneducated. Josef was not her object or her creation. He was her companion and apprentice.

Together they made Josef.

When the war ended and the few remaining Jews left in Poland came out of their hiding places from under beds, in haylofts, up from cellars, down from the attics, Josef went back to school. There were only 10,000 Jews still alive in Poland.

The Polish authorities wanted to place Josef in the class he had been in when he was no longer permitted to be at school rather than in the class he would have been in had he been permitted to be at school. His nanny fought against the ruling of the school authorities. She wanted Josef to be in his rightful place as if he had been at school for the past six years. It was a practical lesson for Joseph. Do not accept a disadvantage. Imagine something better. Insist on what you imagine.

Defend the as if, the fiction, the possibility, and realise it.

Josef went to Sweden when he was seventeen years old. He had relatives there. In Sweden, at school, Josef was given two choices. One choice was to study business. The other was to study to be an engineer. He said it was no choice. He had learned that to be a Jew was to be in business, and to be in business for a Jew was to be Jewish. So he chose engineering, which had no interest for him, rather than business in which he had, like it or not, an interest. It was not not to be a Jew that Josef chose engineering, but not to accept a disadvantage.

Josef met his wife in Sweden. She is Polish and not Jewish. Though the language and culture they share is Polish, they speak to each other in Swedish. They had two sons who are more Swedish than Polish. In this last year of his life, he wrote a story of his life to give to his children so that they would know his story and thereby know part of their own.

They cannot recognise themselves in Josef's story. He gave them his story that they might, in understanding him, recognise themselves, to ease his dying.

This strengthened his attachment to his grandson.

Josef's two sons married Swedish women. Each son has had two children, both boys. One day, Josef's son came to him and asked him to attend the baptism of his son. Josef refused. Of course, he said to his son, he should do as he wished with his children, but he would not attend the baptism and he disapproved of it. There are fictions to help find the truth and cause us to remember, and there are lies that make us forget and lose the truth which for Josef could only be sustained by insisting on his difference, not his sameness, that difference that gave him his determination to be different.

He said to his son that there was no substance in the baptism, no truth to it. Why not let the child first grow up, then choose himself? The baptism offended him deeply. I wondered if that was what he cared about. I suspect it had more to do with distancing him from his grandson, making the identifications he had made in the course of his narrative to me no longer possible.

Six

I had an uncle I loved and a father who seemed hardly to exist. It is impossible to say whether I loved my father or not. My father lived a life of being a shadow of himself. You were aware of him without his ever being fully present.

When he was absent it seemed a superfluity.

He neither appeared nor disappeared. When he came home, there was no sense that he had ever been absent, and when he left home no sense that he had ever been present. My father's extraordinariness was in his nonexistence. He did not even impress that sense upon you that he did not exist.

He was the negation of himself.

Once he came to see me on his own when I was at university. My father had always been, when he had been at all, accompanied by my mother, who blotted him out. She effaced him even as she shook him to try to make him come alive. The more she shook, the more limp he became.

It was a nagging.

His resistance was passive.

It was my mother who wrote me letters. When my father wrote, which was seldom, it was clear she made him write. He had no emotional initiative. His letters were letters of reprimand, written in his hand but without heart. He was making believe he was a father, doing fatherly things as he imagined them, scolding. It is hard to say whether he had his heart in anything.

The thing I remember most was him saying to me, and that in a mumble, 'Don't tell your mother.' I was tempted to tell my mother whatever it was I shouldn't tell her, out of curiosity.

He came to see me at university because he had decided to leave my mother. It seemed as if leaving her enabled him to speak to me. He didn't leave her in the end. Aside from banalities, we never spoke again. I did not mention the visit to my mother.

My father died of cancer. I went to see him before he died. His dying was lengthy. His body had become smaller, thinner, weaker, disappearing. He had nothing to say to me. No memories. Nothing. It was as he had lived. He was as reluctant to die as he had been reluctant to live. I woke up in the middle of the night calling out his name. It was near three in the morning. I telephoned to his room in the hospital. We said a few words. I can't remember what. We rang off and he died.

My father's brother, my Uncle Joe, was like a father to me. There was no particular motive in the relation, no obligation nor responsibility, no bad faith, just love.

My father's father, my grandfather, had a bushy beard, an old Jew from albums of old Jews, and was a bad father. One of his sons he reviled, another he was indifferent to (my father) and for his daughter he felt contempt. She was too tall, he thought, too dark, too striking. He despised her for being a girl without being sufficiently girlish. It was Joe he truly loved. When the once-a-week roast was served at dinner the finest piece was reserved for Joe, who played the violin.

It was in America that he played the violin. I always imagined, however, that it was in Galicia.

Seven

The quest for the meaning of 'Rosebud' motivates the whole of *Citizen Kane*. The film is organised as a journalistic enquiry/voyage into the sense of the term. None of the narratives told by the various characters in Kane's life directly elucidate 'Rosebud'; indeed, none of the narratives even touch it.

The film has two orders of narration. One is objective and exterior, with which the film begins and ends and which reveals to the audience, if not the meaning of 'Rosebud', at least its referent, Kane's sled consumed in the flames. The other order is subjective, elicited by interviews, and is interior to the film. It is the narrative of characters, none of which are privileged, and all of which are partial and blind. The newsreel belongs to these interior narrations.

The exterior narrative, which takes us into the world of Kane, reveals the sled, and then exits, as if back within the space–time of the audience. It is silent. It has images, not words. The other narratives are directed by language. Stories are told, enunciated by a speaker that become images where dialogue is reported and indirect. The stories in words are stories in search of appropriate images or which give birth to images that function as illustrations of a story. This parallels the mystery of 'Rosebud', a word in search of an image.

But 'Rosebud' is more than that and less.

It is presented as the possible explanation of Kane's life and as that which requires explanation. It is the enigma or puzzle and the principal clue to its unravelling and solution, a solution that is withheld.

The narrations, and the film, are divided by the contrast between the public and the private. The purpose of the quest by the reporter is to find what is private and intimate in Kane's life, in contrast to what is known of him publicly. The private narrations, however, which are posed as private explanations and private views of a public figure, never seem to penetrate privacy satisfactorily.

Each of the stories become stories of Kane's remoteness and of a character larger than life and beyond explanation.

Citizen Kane is a film whose only events, strictly speaking, occur within the exterior narration, the death of Kane with which the film begins and the disposal of his possessions, including the sled, with which the film concludes. Otherwise one is not watching events, but stories of events. The film is not a film in which events take place, rather a film in which stories are told. Meaning, significance, conclusion, clarity, resolution, elements usually associated with the presentation of stories, are not forthcoming. Each of the stories is incomplete. None are explanatory. Rather than being stories that elucidate, they make things more obscure. They overlap each other, creating a narrative density that is opaque and impenetrable. Though the film seems to have a centre consisting of Kane and 'Rosebud' (as Kane's exemplification/explanation), the centre is empty. The film revolves around nothing at all. If the character of Kane is centre-stage, its centrality is defined as absent, blank, a void. Kane is absent (he is dead) and also absent in the sense of no story being able to reach him or possess him. It is the absence the film seeks to make present and tries to fill. Kane is what the stories aim at and also what they miss and what escapes them.

The film functions, in contrast to most films, as a kind of inside-out, topsy-turvy, upside-down film. In the place of events, there is the story of them; in the place of full stories, there are partial ones. None cohere or connect. In the place of character, there is character as that which needs to be explained, the shadow of character, the image of character, the emptiness of character, never its substance.

The usual elements of film and fiction are evoked in *Citizen Kane* yet absent from it. What constitutes a film or story in the usual sense is what *Citizen Kane* makes problematic. They are elements separated from themselves and from each other, as one is from one's image in a mirror.

If the meaning or significance of 'Rosebud' remains obscure, its function in the film is clear. It is the motive for the quest and the motive for the stories. It is, like Kane's character of which it is the sign, the emptiness around which the narratives of the film revolve and vainly try to fill. For a meaning you are given a device, for a significance you are given a form, for a referent you are given a sign.

On the one hand, words are in search of images but images that do not explicate the words. On the other hand, words do not explicate images even when they are brought together in the stories or matched to the image of 'Rosebud' as a sled. You are left with words and images, but never the right ones. Rightness is deferred, marked out as unattainable.

'Rosebud' is three things, independently of its function as a device for a narrative or narratives. First, it is the privacy of Kane and literally unspeakable; second, it is full significance and meaning, and unrealisable; third, it is a lure of fullness as meaning which is revealed as emptiness.

While 'Rosebud' is the goal of the film, the conclusion it seeks, it is the sign of inconclusiveness, what cannot be resolved or understood. The film is not a vehicle of meaning, but its play, necessarily therefore irresolute yet strong.

Welles made twelve films. In these, save one, *The Magnificent Ambersons*, Welles played the main character. These characters are all swines – vicious, dishonest, egotistical, destructive, immoral, selfish, vain, inconsiderate, sometimes murderers. They ruin lives and are loathsome.

Welles, as an actor, gives to these characters his energy, talent, and his love. He tries to do his best for them and in such a way that no matter how loathsome they are they seem super-real, larger than life, and though not sympathetic or lovable, one is drawn to them beyond judgement or morality.

They have 'character'.

Whatever Kane is, he is something more than loathsome. And, like all of Welles's main characters, Kane loses everything.

'Rosebud' is this humanity, this comprehension, this generosity and, as a result, it cannot be spoken or summarised, but only played, narrativised, made into story because stories and play, hence 'Rosebud', are valuable, not because they explain, but because they present what cannot be explained.

'Rosebud' is the story of Charles Foster Kane which, like the sled, vaporises into thin air.

Chapter Six
Roma/Stromboli

Il est tout à fait possible qu'en désavouant mon passé j'établisse une
continuité avec le passé d'un autre.[1]

Walter Benjamin

The Garden of Forking Paths is an incomplete, but not false, image of the
universe as Ts'ui Pên conceived it. In contrast to Newton and
Schopenhauer, your ancestor did not believe in a uniform, absolute time.
He believed in an infinite series of times, in a growing, dizzying net of
divergent, convergent and parallel times. This network of times which
approached one another, forked, broke off, or were unaware of one
another for centuries, embraces *all* possibilities of time. We do not exist in
the majority of these times; in some you exist, and not I; in others, I, and
not you; in others, both of us. In the present one, which a favourable fate
has granted me, you have arrived at my house; in another, while crossing
the garden, you found me dead; in still another, I utter these same words,
but I am a mistake, a ghost.

Jorge Luis Borges

One
*The facade of the Villa Medici in Rome is at the moment (July 1999) covered
with scaffolding and netting. Like most of the villas, parks and palaces of Rome
it is being readied for the Giubileo. The Villa Medici belongs to the Académie*

Française. It awards prizes each year for artists to come to Rome and work. They are housed in the villa, given a studio, and are supported. The villa is 16th century. It has beautiful, vast gardens, rarely open to public view or only so for a few hours one day a week during parts of the year.

The present exhibit at the villa, called Mémoires, principally involves the gardens. Some of the gardens have been specifically excavated for the exhibit and they are surrounded by construction gates; in some parts of the gardens, large holes have been dug and paths, casual and labyrinthine, which go nowhere, constructed. From out of some of these holes come voices, reading poetry, singing, proclaiming, incanting, enumerating names or places. Around the garden are various structures and rooms and these have been taken over to be exhibits as well; for example, there is a room of madness in which there is a vase of dried-out flowers.

There are voices as well within the villa which speak from out of its walls. Sometimes speech is mute, pointing to its absence. Inlaid, in some of the steps, are miniature TV screens, almost like windows, on which various performances are enacted, not narratives, but dance and acrobatics, also with voices. These screens and sounds pierce the steps.

The stones not only speak, they seem to move and be illuminated from within; there is no exterior or interior to these memories, no surface and no depth.

The effect of all this is startling. The villa literally comes alive from out of itself and this life is memory, at once recovering something and making you aware of its unrecoverability, that is, of loss. The recovery is a memory, a trace, fragments, a ruin – stones, broken columns, an empty garden, a room of madness with faded flowers, a couch on which hundreds of 'names' have sat, galleries of portraits.

What is alive is the labyrinth. There is no itinerary. The villa provides you with arrows but without a set course. You wander through shards, evidence, as in a mystery. You come upon things and what you come upon are memories without authorship, which are not pointed to nor centred, which belong to no one and to which you are provoked to add your memory and become part of a movement going nowhere, part of innumerability and passing identities in a void.

One untitled work consisted of a hole in the ground and a large mound of earth and stone beside it. This work had no divisions, no differentiations, no frame, nor the slightest hint that this was contrived or that it had been found, that an excavation was actually taking place or only made to seem that it was taking place, and that tomorrow all this would change and be effaced and become memory, yours if you had been there that day.

There was the name of the artist and no title for the work. This seemed preposterous, a mockery.

These events(?), locations(?), works(?) were mirrors without object or reflection, where sameness permitted a permeability that made you recognise difference without being able to specify or locate it. It was both concrete and non-representational and not realistic, because you could not tell if this was a construction or made to seem like one, nor could you decide, and not ever, because sameness and resemblances were ubiquitous.

Difference was invoked by analogies, present and absent. The line between these states existed, but faintly. Was the real the one that was absent? Or was it the similitude of it that was absent?

The lack of boundary was everywhere, as in memory, and that was the labyrinth. For me, everything became precious because of its passing, its momentariness and above all by the fact of undecidability.

Wherever I was, I was in a quandary.

There was no clear value or significance the exhibition could give.

You might have thought that a lack of differentiation would be a blur, but in fact, it was a condition of clarity, and a lure.

Two

In Fellini's La dolce vita, Anouk Aimée and Marcello Mastroianni, during a party at an immense villa just outside Rome, find themselves, each alone, in the maze of the villa's infinite rooms.

A whisper in one room can be heard in another at a great distance. Anouk whispers words of love to Marcello that excite him. He can't reach her, can't know where she is. Voice is disembodied, dislocated in a labyrinth of murmurs.

As Anouk sighs her love and passion, a young man embraces her. She cleaves to him to meet his lips.

Three

In the park of Villa Sciarra, Marina remembered her childhood (she had been to the villa in her pram). And she remembered a love affair with the help of the trees, all of which she could name and to which she gave a history. Some trees, she said, were one of a kind and then we spotted another one just like it.

Often you are alongside people who are not with you who seek to touch you with their memories.

Villa Sciarra was faded, its plaster facade discoloured rose-pinks, ochre, touches of yellow. Like the Villa Medici it was being repolished for the Giubileo. The Giubileo, the memory of an ancient birth, is causing Rome to erase the signs of its age, of time. In bringing Rome back to its presumed former splendours, for example the Villa Borghese, the Villa Farnese, something has been lost. The villas seem fake.

Except for a tree, here and there, Marina would have no future landmarks to remember with.

Four

My knowledge of my origins is sketchy. Emotionally, it is always the case. But for me the bare facts are obscure, not only my feelings for them. I am not sure of my feelings. I am unsure of the facts. I use feelings to approach facts, to invent them. I believe I have always done so.

Where did I live? With whom? And what happened? Did I remember it? Or did someone just tell me? Or did I invent it, with the excuse of a photo to make it seem real? A toy tank that spat fire on the beaches of Seagate near Atlantic City during the war? Only that as the compression of my childhood? And did it occur? My mother rather plump in a bathing costume saving me from drowning, or was it a small wave and my self-dramatisation?

One day, I felt, I would wake up and enter reality.

Where were my parents born? Was it in Georgia in the Caucasus, where

Stalin came from? Was it Latvia where the Jews mournfully played violins? Let us say Georgia. It is a better beginning. And then? Was I molested by my mother's uncle or did we only shoot at trees in the mountains beside waterfalls? Once I went riding in the moonlight in those hills, just outside Tucson. I was scared I would be eaten by a mountain lion. I saw hundreds of mountain lions that night.

Are those events and therefore myself only imagined? Stories I have been telling myself? Am I the consequence of my own fable?

Five

Sometimes, away from you, your outlines begin to fade and you are blurred. I try to refocus you, which is a way to refocus my feelings, by writing to you and imagining you again. It is often temporary. You shine at times close by. At times you are dim from far away.

At times you disappear entirely when I lose myself. I am unable to reach or touch you. Resolution or effort does no good. Touching you is not a matter of resolve. Perhaps, it is my occasional wish for you to disappear. My inability to write to you constitutes your absence and the awful presence of myself.

For the most part, I write because you are absent and writing brings you near and I can console myself in the solitude where I write and feel secure.

I smile at the thought of making you happy.

I have been thinking of our future and what I shall never say. I wonder at what you will never say and the promises we shall make to ourselves and to each other. I wonder at our hopes that mirror the anxieties of our disappointments.

This future which is not yet is our only past.

I can't remember anything before it.

Six

Avant d'écrire on ne sait rien de ce qu'on va écrire. Et en toute lucidité.

Si on savait quelque chose de ce qu'on va écrire, avant de le faire, avant d'écrire, on n'écrirait jamais. Ce ne serait pas la peine.

Écrire c'est tenter de savoir ce qu'on écrirait si on écrivait – on ne le sait qu'après – avant, c'est la question la plus dangereuse que l'on puisse se poser. Mais c'est la plus courante aussi.

L'écrit ça arrive comme le vent, c'est nu, c'est de l'encre, c'est l'écrit, et ça passe comme rien d'autre ne passe dans la vie, rien de plus, sauf elle, la vie.[2]

Seven

Travel is often a search to find a reality to confirm a prior image of it, that on a postcard, a tourist brochure or a travel guide, itineraries and sights set in advance. In theory, these images are unlimited. In fact, they are not. In practice, reality transformed into images becomes the limit of the reality we see.

I was invited to a house on Via Garibaldi in Trastevere in Rome. I was in that house before, forty years ago, when I first came to Italy.

A friend of Uncle Joe lived there. Joe gave me his address. They had met during the war. He was called Mischa. He had a fictitious Russian identity and a rich, powerful voice, like Orson Welles, and a Wellesian stature. He was an American. He had been part of the occupation administration in Italy after the war and had decided to stay on.

He spoke perfect Italian. He had been an opera singer. In Rome, he acted in films and dubbed films (into Italian).

He was homosexual.

Someone told me he was in love with a Roman whore. He had a maid who was silently present. When I came to his house, I came with an American called Diana, who had hair down to her waist. Mischa was delightfully attentive to her.

We brought food, veal, and made it for him. His flat was filled with objects from Roman antiquity and medieval Rome. The flat had its own sounds, water from wall fountains, murmurs I felt from the wall hangings. The flat was in dim light, yellow and dark, with a soft scent exuding from the carpets and furniture, and the mahogany boxes. It called up for me the light of Rembrandt, which reminded me of the synagogues of my childhood.

It was a world closed off to the outside, erasing it. Its sounds were muffled by the isolation. When you returned to the outside everything was glaring, loud, a surprise. And you felt lighter and it was easier to breathe. I wanted to fly, to run, to dance, to shout, liberated at last from the suffocation.

The house hid nothing apparent, yet there was an invisible curtain that never went up. I had the feeling that everything was hidden behind the display.

Once inside, there was no way out, yet where you were was unclear, without dimensions or paths or entrances or exits.

It was as if everything was significant, but nothing a clue.

Mischa's voice enveloped you, seeped inside you through your skin and the surface of your eyes. No one would ever talk to you the way Mischa did, never in your entire life. Rather than him seeming strange, everyone else seemed strange after you were with him. Only now in Via Garibaldi, returning to the place of Mischa's former presence, do I feel that I truly had once been here. At the time, I felt I was not there.

I was uneasy at sensations that could not be smoothed out and from which there was no escape because no clarity.

One day while we were staying with Mischa, a small girl with quiet brown Arab eyes and red shoes appeared at the doorway. Now, she was still there, but transformed into a boy. The small girl I was remembering was the mother of this small boy I now encountered. The mother still wore red shoes (and a red dress), and her eyes were still silent.

She remembered Mischa and the half light of his flat.

On the terrace, just before the sun disappeared, its rays and light still present, an extraordinary light illuminated the cupolas and palazzi of the Roman skyline in the direction of Trinità dei Monti and the Villa Medici beside it. It had been a clear, warm, June day. In the evening, dark clouds formed behind us and a ridge of clouds with pink edges cut across the sky above the view. The particular combination of time, of cloud, of temperature, and the pink ochre of the buildings produced a light of improbable clarity and tone that I have seen only in paintings of Rome, never in Rome, never in reality.

The light was unique and familiar.

Bowles wonders in The Sheltering Sky *how many sunsets we shall see before we die.*

Not many.

Eight

Delacroix was already an established painter when he came to photography. He used it as an aid to painting, an *aide-mémoire,* or as a tool to capture an instant of movement.

Degas grew up with photography. Sometimes he, like Delacroix, used it as a reference for his paintings. On the whole, this was not the case. Photography was an independent pursuit. He was interested in its instantaneity of vision and the play of light effects. The light of photography seemed mysterious and, though rendered by the apparent objectivity of the camera, it unhinged in its mystery, something subjective. Photography furnished unaccustomed visions, a direct inspiration for sight.

Degas shared something with photography. His paintings often resembled photographs; he sought to translate the light effects of the photograph and its possibilities for intimacy in his paintings, as well as to render these effects in the photographs he took. Degas's attitude to photography was experimental, as it was towards gravure and other methods that related to the printing of images and their diffusion, some of which pre-dated the invention of photography.

For Delacroix, photography was used for its objectivity in order to serve painting; Degas, with a different sense of painting and having come to maturity when photography had become more pictorial and more technically developed, was interested in the photograph because it dealt with problems also inherent in painting, that is, general problems of the image and representation. The practices were aesthetically complementary, not one a subordinate aid to the other.

Delacroix's work comes closest to photography in his lithographs, in areas of the definition of line and the rendering of tonal shades. His lithographs were primarily illustrations for books. Degas was not an illustrator.

Between 1895 and 1896, the year of the invention of the cinema, Degas was an active photographer. The photographs he took are beautiful. They are of friends and family, largely in interiors where light could be controlled and used as a modelling or painterly device. He applied light to an existing subject to further model it, as you might apply paint, with the difference that the play of light was upon an objective subject, whereas painting, though it might deploy a model, had to recreate it in paint. It was a different kind of modelling and a different relation of subject to object in the image.

Light and time are at the heart of Degas's paintings and his photographs. The photographs seem more intense, possibly because they lack colour and are on a smaller, more hermetic scale and because the reality of light in a photograph made it seem more not less secret. In a painting, light is created artificially. In a photograph, it is registered. The fascination in Degas's photographs is in the relation of registration to perception, the objective to the subjective.

Photographs decompose reality; paintings create them.

I went to an exhibition of Degas's photographs at the Bibliothèque Nationale (August 1999).

The subject of these photographs was light. Family and friends were brought to light in a light that also blurred them, made them fragile and evanescent. They were there and not there, solid and passing in a light touched by time. Line and outline were of the slightest substance. Rather than defining, they were permeable, invaded and suffused by light, an exquisite sadness.

Degas accomplished this with gentleness and delicacy.

Degas achieved what few photographers ever do, photographs without rhetoric, not even that of modesty, still less that of realism, and not that of art. The lack of statement is a total blankness, approaching abstraction.

The images have been stripped of everything until they reach the essence of the material that composes them.

Fellini models light in his films.

Nine

Memory in Fellini's films is fabricated. The fabrications multiply locations. No location is firm, secure or reliable. Each place opens to another, and another in turn, embedded, circular, passing, vertiginous. These are shots, sequences of shots, parts of a narrative. They do not line up as linear, successive displacements.

Each origin reveals itself as a reflection in memory and in light. What you think is an origin, which will progress and advance, becomes a reflection of an origin, a false origin, itself reflected. This origin returns, as in a labyrinth.

The elements of memory, of reflection, of light, thicken and coalesce in repetitions, variations, returns, fadings, but no continuity, no beginnings, nor ends, nor directions, no advance, nor progression, no inevitability.

In the films of Welles, we know the consequences of actions at the beginning of the film: in *Othello*, for example. Nevertheless, *Othello* astonishes us with its inevitability and the unavoidable.

Touch of Evil begins with a foreseen, senseless act of revenge for an action in the past. Like most of Welles's films, it is haunted by memories: the murder that occurred years ago of Quinlan's wife transposed, like guilt, into the present on to Vargas and his wife, further played out, in a counterpoint of memory, with the bullet that Quinlan carries in his leg from his past when he protected the life of his friend Menzies, now betraying him. The wound gives Quinlan a twinge as an intuition of danger and truth, the truth of Menzies's betrayal which Quinlan guesses.

Tanya (Marlena Dietrich) is like an ancient Greek chorus who recalls the past, comments on the present, foretells the future.

The sense of the action in the film is a future-past, the tense of a return.

The opening scene of death and the closing one of death echo each other and are echoes of echoes from the past, from out of the dead.

Welles's sounds superimpose, echoing from a depth, as in the last scene of *Touch of Evil*, as if voices are already dead, remembered, echoes from another world, entering this one as memory, and having memory as their subject.

'*Rosebud*'.

The Wellesian past haunts the present.

Characters die in Welles's films with memories on their lips, which they have spent their lives seeking to recover. These memories are their life, life as a labyrinth, a circle, an enigma, a mirrored emptiness.

The opening of *Citizen Kane* is in a past-future tense.

The close is in a present-past.

Light is the form and substance of Fellini's films.

And light, which vanishes, clarifies, illuminates, is the substance of Fellinian memory. The substance of memory is the substance of film, an 'as if' memory, imitating memory, like memory, a theatre of memory, not false memory, but the truth of what memory is, an impossible reflection.

Often one dreams the nature of dream in dreams.

In Fellini's films, the films are the mirrors of film in which the dreams in the films are an instance of the mirror.

Ten

Dreams of disappearances are not uncommon.

You may lose someone, or a thought, or some person that had been at your side an instant beforehand in your dream. The loss in the dream resembles the loss of the dream when you awake.

The dream is a field where you search what had been present a moment ago and is now lost (for ever?). It happens in writing as well. The dream calls the presence up then erases it. These images are flickerings of light in your darkness. To find the lost presence whose remnants and traces you can still sense forces you to retrace your steps. The retracing is a hopeless search for origins and for yourself, hopeless because the operation of the dream is to confound these paths, multiplying them so you lose your way, or obliterating the steps. Origins proliferate in the labyrinth of the dream you seek to follow in order to arrive at the true beginnings of yourself. The dream is the labyrinth in which you are lost and the only means given you to find yourself.

The dream dreams you as writing writes you.

The fragments in which dreams appear are the remnants of what has disappeared and which you dream to re-encounter the losses that come back to you

as half-realised partial appearances, dim presences. Later, you may try to piece these fragments together, in an analysis, but they seldom fit.
This disconnection is you.

Eleven

Deleuze likened Fellini's films to crystals: multi-faceted, shimmering, reflecting light and projecting its reflections, like the moon. Such light creates corridors, entrances, exits, tunnels, through which you travel to nowhere in particular. The reflected light is a maze of shadows and false paths.

Andare a luna (to go to the moon) is to be *lunatico* (a lunatic), *être lunatique*.

Twelve

Stromboli is a volcanic island off the coast of Sicily. It is said there that the *meduse* (jellyfish) retreat out to sea as the moon waxes and they advance towards the shore as the moon wanes.

It may instead be a matter of light.

At dawn and at dusk there are fewer *meduse* in the water.

Tahar said that large tortoises had been common around Stromboli. They had fed on the *meduse*. But they were slaughtered and made into soup, with the result that the *meduse* have now returned.

Seen under water, the *meduse* are transparent, not light (*luce*), but having lightness (*leggerezza*). You see them by seeing through them. Their bodies, diaphanous and fragile, a faded blue, frame and filter light, as if they were made of it. The *meduse* look like radiographs. They have a permeable, not reflective, surface.

They are oblong, rounded at one end. They float vertically in the water, head up.

From the body of the *meduse* long filaments extend that waver in the current, like a dance. With these filaments they sense and sting their prey.

Fellini's films caused me to think of Marey's chronophotographs of strands of light that contain in every present the trace of its pasts and the premonition of its futures as itineraries of light.

Watching the *meduse* was a similar experience.

Borges thought of time in terms of water, as flow.

Fellini's time belongs to light, sparkling and vibrating.

The *meduse* live in both elements, light and water, subject to the tides and the moon, and to stories and myth.

Fellini derealises his images, points them away from reality towards dream and light.

The feigned life and feigned memories in his films are sad because they have the scent of death and disappearance. And they are also sweet because they have the joy of play, of make-believe, of the moment.

It is in the nature of make-believe to announce its future disappearance and dissolution, when reality will appear and sweep it away. It is like the appearance of an adult to disrupt your game.

Make-believe is tenuous, hence the joy of it. It has been snatched from time, and thereby from necessity. It exhibits. Light is a metaphor and substance for the exhibition. Each moment is precious because it is momentary.

This is the delight of the dream, and its terror.

Thirteen

I recall a theatre performance in London nearly thirty years ago. I cried at its beauty, courage and joy. It was a feigned circus performed by the Leningrad Theatre of the Young Spectator on a small stage. The actors were young, elegant, passionate. There were hardly any sets, or props, in fact, hardly anything at all, only these graceful Russians making believe, with an intensity that created the visions of things that were not there.

The intensity caused you to imagine and make present what was only desire. It drew you into the beauty of make-believe: the flying trapeze, horses at a gallop, a terrifying tightrope walk, a man slowly inflated, about to burst, then the air was let out.

He spluttered back to shape.

This theatre without words came closest to writing.

Fourteen

On a bien inventé, pour me distraire les soirs où on me trouvait l'air trop
malheureux, de me donner une lanterne magique, dont, en attendant l'heure
du dîner, on coiffait ma lampe; et, à l'instar des premiers architectes et
maîtres verriers de l'âge gothique, elle substituait à l'opacité des murs
d'impalpables irisations, de surnaturelles apparitions multicolores, où des
légendes étaient dépeintes comme dans un vitrail vacillant et momentane.
Mais ma tristesse n'en était qu'accrue, parce que rien que le changement
d'éclairage détruisait l'habitude que j'avais de ma chambre et grâce à quoi,
sauf le supplice du coucher, elle m'était devenue supportable. Maintenant je
ne la reconnaissais plus et j'y étais inquiet, comme dans une chambre d'hôtel
ou de 'chalet', où je fusse arrivé pour la première fois en descendant de
chemin de fer.

Au pas saccadé de son cheval, Golo, plein d'un affreux dessein, sortait de
la petite forêt triangulaire qui veloutait d'un vert sombre la pente d'une
colline, et s'avançait en tressautant vers le château de la pauvre Geneviève de
Brabant. Ce château était coupé selon une ligne courbe qui n'était autre que
la limite d'un des ovales de verre dans le châssis qu'on glissait entre les
coulisses de la lanterne. Ce n'était qu'un pan de château et il avait devant lui
une lande ou rêvait Geneviève qui portait une ceinture bleue. Le château et
la lande étaient jaunes et je n'avais pas attendu de les voir pour connaître
leur couleur car, avant les verres du châssis, la sonorité mordorée du nom de
Brabant me l'avait montrée avec évidence. Golo s'arrêtait un instant pour
écouter avec tristesse le boniment lu à haute voix par ma grand-tante et qu'il
avait l'air de comprendre parfaitement, conformant son attitude avec une
docilité qui n'excluait pas une certaine majesté, aux indications du texte; puis
il s'éloignait du même pas saccadé. Et rien ne pouvait arrêter sa lente
chevauchée. Si on bougeait la lanterne, je distinguais le cheval de Golo qui
continuait à s'avancer sur les rideaux de la fenêtre, se bombant de leurs plis,
descendant dans leurs fentes. Le corps de Golo lui-même, d'une essence
aussi surnaturelle que celui de sa monture, s'arrangeait de tout obstacle
matériel, de tout objet gênant qu'il rencontrait en le prenant comme ossature

et en se le rendant intérieur, fût-ce le bouton de la porte sur lequel s'adaptait aussitôt et surnageait invinciblement sa robe rouge ou sa figure pâle toujours aussi noble et aussi mélancholique, mais qui ne laissait paraître aucun trouble de cette transvertébration.

Certes je leur trouvais du charme à ces brillantes projections qui semblaient émaner d'un passé mérovingien et promenaient autour de moi des reflets d'histoire si anciens. Mais je ne peux dire quel malaise me causait pourtant cette intrusion du mystère et de la beauté dans une chambre que j'avais fini par remplir de mon moi au point de ne pas faire plus attention à elle qu'à lui-même.[3]

Je trouve très raisonnable la croyance celtique que les âmes de ceux que nous avons perdus sont captives dans quelque être inférieur, dans une bête, un végétal, une chose inanimée, perdues en effet pour nous jusqu'au jour, qui pour beaucoup ne vient jamais, où nous nous trouvons passer près de l'arbre, entrer en possession de l'objet qui est leur prison. Alors elles tréssaillent, nous appellent, et sitôt que nous les avons reconnues, l'enchantement est brisé. Délivrées par nous, elles ont vaincu la mort et reviennent vivre avec nous.[4]

Fifteen

Fellini turns memory into spectacle, stages and films it. Memory is invisible, interior, cast on a screen by the uncertainty of light and the fleetingness of dream.

It is not to be relied upon.

In *Intervista*, Marcello (Mastroianni), playing himself, and dressed as Mandrake the Magician for an advertisment, and Anita (Ekberg), bloated and ghastly, watch their shadows of twenty-five years ago from *La dolce vita* in the scene at the Fontana di Trevi before dawn after a terrible party. Marcello is fascinated with Ekberg, her mythical, voluptuous stature on to which he projects his desire and perhaps has formed her stature from his desire. The cinema for Fellini is a woman projected.

The image of them in the present watching their past brought back to life is an image that will pass and be extinguished. The present is not real (already an image) and the past is an image restored. Both are imitations.

The film plays on the passing and the passage of the image of Fellini inside the film he directs, an image multiplied and feigned.

Disappearance and reappearance are in the nature of images in the cinema. In Fellini's films, there are no displacements, rather metamorphoses of images, an engendering.

Scenes come into light then disperse in its glare, in the indifference of incandescence or in the absence of light, in a void.

Colours fade. Sounds are attenuated.

Prova d'orchestra is a film that quivers in the fragility of articulation and uncertainties of difference.

In *Fellini's Roma*, the excavations underground for the Rome *metropolitana* bring to view Roman frescoes that have been buried for two thousand years. As the frescoes come to light, and are revealed by it, at that instant they fade, disappearing into the light from which they came.

There is almost always a party in a Fellini film. The party begins at night in hope and ends at dawn in boredom and disillusion. Sometimes, his film is coextensive with a party and the party is the metaphor of the film.

E la nave va begins as a film of a memory that is a remembered film and closes on the reality of the set. *E la nave va* is dream invented to appear like film, memory invented to appear as dream, and dream invented to appear as memory.

Fellini films stage spectacles of papier mâché, of light and sound, of painted moons, cardboard elephants, and puffs of smoke, nothing substantial. The spectacles, like the party, mirror the film.

There is no other world for Fellini. There is nothing else more important than this nothing, this make-believe.

Sixteen

Borges's tiger, whose tongue caressed him, was not a reality that he then represented. His writing was not the image of the real tiger. There is no original tiger in Borges. Instead, there are tigers in different places, one no less real than another. Or, there is one tiger, but in multiple locations, each different, and the same. Borges's sameness is not a generality, like a classification, but a presence, which is its specificity.

That presence is tigerness.

Representation is about absences and realities lost.

Borges never represents. His writing causes a disturbance because we have become accustomed to the image as a referent for a reality that he denies us. Rather than confirming reality, he doubles it.

His is a writing and philosophy of astonishment.

Seventeen

I felt happy in Stromboli living with its gentle, puffing volcano.

At night, pink-red clouds form from out of the crater. Sparks shoot up into the air. In the morning, I walk on the black lava beach. From the stones, you can smell the volcano's scent. I live in a beautiful house. It is called 'Casa Araba'.

On a large chest there is a pink-yellow putty baby Jesus with an imploring gesture and a tiny broken penis. He is framed by a flower arrangement of false cloth flowers in two inverted glass jars. The flowers are faded and in different shades of grey.

Behind these, hung on the wall, is a Moroccan rug. To the side of the chest is a door that opens to the terrace. The door frames a glass panel and through it, from my bed, I can see the sea and the rose-blue-green of dawn.

This room had been the room of Gigi.

I feel the volcano as a comfort, something old and good, protecting you, always there, alive, rumbling, like a loved uncle.

It is the sound you make when I bring you orange juice in the morning in bed and you are still an animal and feel secure.

I went down to the beach just after seven o'clock as the three boats, practically rowing boats, the Stromboli fishing fleet, came in with their catch.

I bought two small aragoste *to steam,* scòrfano *for soup, and an* orata *to fry. I bought them from two brothers, who were exactly alike. Their faces were framed by masses of grey, curly hair. They wore the same faded pink T-shirt, short trousers, and no shoes. One began a sentence, the other concluded it, in perfect accord.*

Gigi was in the courtyard watering the plants in the early-morning sunshine. He greeted me with his soft, gentle smile.

Tahar cleaned the red, sharp-finned scòrfano. *'Tu sei brutto come uno scòrfano' ('You are as ugly as a scòrfano') is a saying in Italy. Tahar was beautiful to watch, graceful and elegant. He seemed to caress the fish, carefully circling its gills, as if not to hurt it.*

The courtyard was shaded with light-green grape vines. There was a wall fountain at one end.

The day was still fresh.

Notes

1   'It is entirely possible that, in disavowing my past, I establish a continuity with the past of someone else.'

2   Before you write, you don't know what you will write. And that with complete lucidity.

   If you knew something of what you would write before doing it, before writing, you would never write. It would not be worth it.

   To write is to try to know what you would write if you wrote – you only know it afterwards – before, it is the most dangerous question you can ask yourself. But it is also the most commonplace.

   Writing arrives like the wind, it is naked, it is ink, it is the written, and it passes like nothing else in life, nothing more, save itself, life.

3   'Someone had had the happy idea of giving me, to distract me on evenings when I seemed abnormally wretched, a magic lantern, which used to be set on top of my lamp while we waited for dinner-time to come; in the manner of the master-builders and glass-painters of gothic days it substituted for the

opaqueness of my walls an impalpable iridescence, supernatural phenomena of many colours, in which legends were depicted, as on a shifting and transitory window. But my sorrows were only increased, because this change of lighting destroyed, as nothing else could have done, the customary impression I had formed of my room, thanks to which the room itself, but for the torture of having to go to bed in it, had become quite endurable. For now I no longer recognised it, and I became uneasy, as though I were in a room in some hotel or furnished lodging, in a place where I had just arrived, by train, for the first time.

'Riding at a jerky trot, Golo, his mind filled with an infamous design, issued from the little three-cornered forest which dyed dark-green the slope of a convenient hill, and advanced by leaps and bounds towards the castle of poor Geneviève de Brabant. This castle was cut off short by a curved line which was in fact the circumference of one of the transparent ovals in the slides which were pushed into position through a slot in the lantern. It was only the wing of a castle, and in front of it stretched a moor on which Geneviève stood, lost in contemplation, wearing a blue girdle. The castle and the moor were yellow, but I could tell their colour without waiting to see them, for before the slides made their appearance the old-gold sonorous name of Brabant had given me an unmistakable clue. Golo stopped for a moment and listened sadly to the little speech read aloud by my great-aunt, which he seemed perfectly to understand, for he modified his attitude with a docility not devoid of a degree of majesty, so as to conform to the indications given in the text; then he rode away at the same jerky trot. And nothing could arrest his slow progress. If the lantern were moved I could still distinguish Golo's horse advancing across the window-curtains, swelling out with their curves and diving into their folds. The body of Golo himself, being of the same supernatural substance as his steed, overcame all material obstacles – everything that seemed to bar his way – by taking each as it might be a skeleton and embodying it in himself: the door-handle, for instance, over which, adapting itself at once, would float invincibly his red cloak or his pale face, never losing its nobility or its melancholy, never showing any sign of trouble at such a transubstantiation.

'And, indeed, I found plenty of charm in these bright projections, which seemed to have come straight out of a Merovingian past, and to shed around me the reflections of such ancient history. But I cannot express the discomfort I felt at such an intrusion of mystery and beauty into a room which I had succeeded in filling with my own personality until I thought no more of the room than of myself.' (Translation: C. K. Scott Moncrieff)

4   'I feel that there is much to be said for the Celtic belief that the souls of those whom we have lost are held captive in some inferior being, in an animal, in a plant, in some inanimate object, and so effectively lost to us until the day (which to many never comes) when we happen to pass by the tree or to obtain possession of the object which forms their prison. Then they start and tremble, and call us by our name, and as soon as we have recognised their voice the spell is broken. We have delivered them: they have overcome death and return to share our life.' (Translation: C. K. Scott Moncrieff)

Chapter Seven
Portraits

A nos yeux, un individu, si complexe qu'il soit, a pour caractère primordial et essentiel d'être un. S'il ne l'était pas, ce ne serait plus un individu, ce serait un composé de plusieurs. Mais, chez le primitif, le sentiment vif interne de sa personne ne s'accompagne pas ainsi d'un concept rigoureux de l'individualité unie. Non seulement les frontières de celle-ci demeurent vagues et imprécises, puisque les appartenances de l'individu sont lui, puisque son double, son image, son reflet sont encore ici. Il y a plus: le *tjurunga* de l'Australien, le *kra* de l'Ewe, le *ntoro* de l'Achanti, l'homonyme des Ba-ila, etc., sans se confondre entièrement avec l'individu, ne se distingue pas non plus de lui. A défaut de cet élément qui fonde l'individualité en l'unissant aux ancêtres de qui elle provient, elle ne pourrait pas exister. L'individu n'est lui-même qu'à la condition d'être en même temps autre que lui-même. Sous ce nouvel aspect, loin d'être un, comme nous le concevons, il est encore un et plusieurs à la fois. Il est donc, pour ainsi dire, un véritable 'lieu de participations'.

Les Aino de Japon ont une curieuse croyance: d'après eux, 'les morts regardent les personnes qui n'ont pas encore traversé le fleuve de la mort comme des "esprits" (*ghosts*), et considèrent que les hommes naturels et réels, c'est eux-mêmes. Ils pensent de nous ce que nous pensons d'eux.'[1]

Lucien Lévy-Bruhl

One

I am in a place where people sign the visitors' book saying what a wonderful time they had and how gracious their host and hostess had been and how they looked forward to coming back. These repetitious banalities I find moving. They are sincere, yet empty because they are overcoded. They say nothing because there is no possibility for the specific. The remarks are clichés but the feelings, I think, are not. The cliché is simply a failed attempt to be particular.

The remarks are already memories of a time that has been spent and projections of memories in a future that can be envisaged as having been, which creates the need to promise to return to that past so that it, now gone, can be renewed.

The projected future is nostalgia. Some of the memorialists were here on their honeymoon. The written remarks of the guests are an accumulated memory for their hosts, for whom these inscriptions are precious. Yet everything was known in advance, including the accumulation.

Before I leave I shall be invited to add my remarks to the book of memories.

Two

Rossellini relates a story of visiting an Indian holy man when he was in India.

They sat together. The old man smoked cigarettes incessantly. He slowly massaged Rossellini's neck.

Rossellini began to cry, then he sobbed, out of control.

Three

I met Mara at the house in Via Garibaldi.

Some weeks later we had dinner.

She walked through Rome as if it belonged to her, including the stars and the moon and the gulls diving down at night at the Vittorio Emmanuele monument who perhaps thought it was a ship at sea. Their wings were reflected in the searchlights.

Mara flung open the windows in her flat and took possession of the Colosseo. 'Mine,' she said.

Mara astonished herself with her inventiveness and was immensely pleased. She was her own seduction.

She pointed to antique columns in the Foro Romano as if it were she who had made them materialise, like a magician. In the instant before the moment when she shouted 'Look,' they were not there.

They would cease to exist in her absence.

'Remember me,' she insisted.

Of all the things she said, this surprised me the most.

Mara lived in a present without a past. The function of her present was to obliterate all pasts.

Bertolucci's films seemed to frighten her.

In Bertolucci's films, couples relate to each other, and their gestures relate to each other, filtered through memories of a past. These pasts are not held in common. They are perspectives which cross and create gaps. The past makes the couple lonely and is the solitude of each within it.

Bertolucci's characters are their past that they seek and the past that eludes them.

In the present they search to refind the past. But the present is the place in which they hide from the past. The past accompanies them, pursues them, causes them to flee from it even as they seek it.

Regressive returns are flashed, like a neon sign, intermittent and fragmentary. The afterglow remains and accumulates, grows more intense as if the light of the past had coagulated or clotted by superimpositions, a layering.

The past for Bertolucci, and thus the present, are sexually and erotically charged. Sexuality is the source of pure energy that drives the characters. It also drives the film that invents these characters and tells their stories. The film is like a character, its own story mirrored inside the film.

The events of the story, in the sense of what happens, reflect the shape and structure of the story as if every event in the film is an event of the film. As the characters navigate through memory, trying to understand their desires, the film traverses a similar itinerary in search of its desires.

The film is a lens to bring into focus and a glass to reflect, at once transparent and casting light.

The light is flat, opaque, not luminous.

Four

Gigi, like all of us, has made his life out of the circumstances that have been given him. What he has done with what has been given him has also created his circumstances. This is Gigi's story.

Yesterday he told me, with great sadness, the story of his last fifteen years, much of which he regrets. His general mien of happiness and contentment is a masquerade, he said. The regret, and the masquerade, also belong to his story.

The sadness is when he sees the story as closed.

Sometimes we create a make-believe love, because not to have it can seem terrible.

Five

Caterina is an actress. She writes plays in which she is the sole player. In these plays she is multiplied and proliferates, each self out of reach of the others.

The stories are comic and sad. They are about her wanting and not being wanted, this gap.

She is rejected and left in her stories. What she recounts is what is left over, herself. This being left over urges her to write and perform.

In the stories she is a victim of incomprehension. The incomprehension is a motive to act out the incomprehension that she might thereby be understood, a way for her to be recognised and loved.

On stage, in masquerade, in a guise and multiple-faceted, she is herself by making believe she is not.

Caterina's truth is as a storyteller and actress, when she loses herself and creates the possibility of being found.

Six

In Rossellini's films, the existences of characters are shattered against their will and without their knowledge. The shattering of identity appears to be without sense because no prior steps account for it, either of events or in the structure of persons. It suddenly comes.

Characters become other than they once were, strangers to themselves. What is shattered are their previous steps *(trace de pas)*, gone without a trace *(pas de trace)*.

The ends of Rossellini's films, or of episodes within them, come as a surprise because they are unprepared. The itinerary that has brought characters to a new consciousness is erased as they approach their own conclusion, of which they have been unaware and which nothing of what they had been seems to have led.

The conclusion is like a conversion. It scandalises by overturning a past. There is one world, then suddenly it is different. Everything is different. Nothing of what had been remains.

Therefore there must be no prior steps, no prefiguring, no easy way.

Rossellini radically employs the ellipse to short-circuit usual narrative procedures of continuity and motive: that is, of a reason, a logic, therefore an interpretation. Instead, you have actions between points that cannot be satisfactorily joined. Between them is a blank where consequence is ordinarily inserted and which it fills. What appears instead is emptiness.

The Rossellinian ellipse is visual as well as temporal. He strips down images to essentials, emptying, abstracting them, unlike Visconti, whose detailing and finishing is excessive. The paring down prepares characters for what will come to them, suddenly and explosively. He divests characters of their connectives, what holds them together, preparing them for something different only possible when they face it in their nudity.

The disconnection is their nakedness and desperation.

They encounter another reality from the one they had lived with incomprehension, then illumination.

Nothing is in between.

Jean Narboni plays on the words *trace de pas/pas de trace* in a short note on *Germania, anno zero*. I am borrowing his insight.

Edmund, in *Germania, anno zero*, commits suicide. The suicide is his recognition (in an instant, a flash) of a former self. The flash illuminates the past and obliterates it. The recognition occurs in a situation of interior devastation.

Rossellini takes everything from the character, then waits for the consequences.

When Edmund jumps to his death nothing has anticipated this act. Yet, when it comes, and at that instant, it makes sense. The leap is the making of sense, the finding of lost and hidden connections.

Rossellini's films are headlong flights towards a place of light away from darkness and the past. He calls it '*choses telles quelles sont*', '*choses dans leur réalité*'.[2] This light, reality 'as it is', is a revelation.

It is what you find in desolation.

The ruins of Berlin, of Naples, of Pompeii, of Stromboli, are interior ruins though not symbolic nor abstract.

Rohmer remarked to Truffaut that Rossellini's greatest virtue was his lack of imagination.

Seven

Oscar Wilde's Dorian Gray is young, innocent and beautiful. Because he is beautiful, and his beauty includes an inner grace, he is beloved. Out of love an artist paints his portrait. This portrait Dorian Gray keeps.

It is a perfect likeness of the model, as beautiful as he.

Various events change Dorian Gray's character. He loses his innocence and with it his grace and sincerity. Inside, he becomes ugly. Outside, remarkably, he remains as he always was. He is not even touched by the ruin of age.

His portrait rather than his appearance assumes the ugliness and decay of his interior. Dorian Gray hides this portrait away as one hides one's soul.

In effect, the portrait *is* Dorian Gray. It is his reality. His real appearance is his falsity.

The event that leads to this disaster is a love affair.

Sybil Vane is common and ordinary. Dorian Gray finds her by chance playing Juliet in a dreary London theatre. Her Juliet transfigures her and trans-fixes Dorian Gray.

On stage, Sybil Vane turns the mundane into the sublime, herself into a Juliet, the stage into a garden in Verona.

Sybil Vane comes to love Dorian Gray completely (as he loves her) so that she no longer has reason to make-believe that she is Juliet, no longer feels the necessity to transform reality. She can at last become herself by virtue of feeling truly loved. She can be, unashamedly, Sybil Vane.

Sybil Vane had enthralled Dorian Gray by her surface, now he could have her substance.

But for him, the purity of Sybil Vane resides in her masquerade, in her theatrics, her make-believe, her appearance not her truth. It is aesthetic beauty, the reverse of banality, of the everyday and ugliness. For him, she is most herself when she is not herself. When she renounces her make-believe, because she is in love with him, really and truly in love, he renounces her because he can no longer love the her who is only herself, therefore no longer beautiful, because she has become part of the world whose nature necessitates theatre as its contrast and opposition.

Beauty is the contrary of the world; it is artifice. Purity has no place in vulgar reality without changing its substance, risking becoming vulgar and common, what Sybil Vane becomes to him by virtue of her most pure act of love for him.

Can you ever really be yourself in love? Love is suited to fiction, which is always by nature deceitful.

Gray's punishment is that he becomes the imperishable work of art whose surface and appearance is beautiful and eternal while the painting of him is ugly and disgusting.

It is the portrait of his soul and ruin.

The Picture of Dorian Gray is not this portrait, nor the other.

It is the gap.

Sybil Vane could no more recognise Dorian Gray than he could her.

Wilde's story is echoed in Poe's *The Oval Portrait*, re-echoed in Godard's *Vivre sa vie*, which cites it. Godard's love stories – stories of deceit, incomprehension, betrayal and loss – are modelled on the stories of Rossellini, especially his *Viaggio in Italia*, and more generally they are love stories from films.

Eight

The character of the painter in Jacques Rivette's *La Belle noiseuse* struggles to find truth in an image he paints of a woman: the truth of himself, his model, his marriage, his past, his present, his everything.

The quest for truth in representation, including the film that presents this quest, is diabolical.

Towards the end of the film, the painting finished and, with the help of a small girl, he walls it up behind a brick wall. No one can see it, not even and not especially, the audience.

The conclusion is an out of sight, unspeakable, unseeable.

The film is complicit with the character. It duplicates its own fiction.

What you most want to see, the true image, is denied you.

But to what can an image be true? What is the *image juste*?

In the film, you are given images in abundance. Yet, whatever you are given, you want to know what is behind it, what is hidden, what it means, and so on. This desire can never be satisfied. No sign is completely adequate.

The painter presents to the other characters and to us not the true painting but its substitute, a false painting. This painting is anodine and conventional and hides nothing.

He painted this painting in an instant.

Let me try to remember a story. A few details of which may not be accurate, but it should not matter.

In Calvino's *Lezioni americani*, to illustrate a lesson on swiftness and slowness, Calvino tells a tale of the artist and the Chinese emperor. The emperor calls on the artist, the greatest in the empire, to draw him a picture of a duck. The artist consents, on condition that he has five years, a stipend and a house with servants. At the end of the term, nothing apparently has been done. The artist requests a further five years under the same conditions. It is granted by the emperor, though grudgingly. Moments before the end of the second five-year term, when still nothing has been drawn, the artist picks up his brush and in a few seconds draws the most sublime picture of a duck that was ever done.

Could there have been, I wonder, another drawing? One not for the emperor but for the artist, which the artist could not show to the emperor because it would not have been acceptable or because the artist simply did not desire to do so? And if this was the case, would Calvino's lesson (his lessons) – namely that one term can beget the contrary and that the play of fiction is a play of language that cannot be stilled and which migrates – hides another lesson, one he dared not pronounce and which if he had might have revealed the falsity, the cleverness of the lesson he did pronounce?

Had Calvino been hiding something from us? An impossible paradox? A more profound contrary?

Nine

Michel Leiris's journal of his voyage from Dakar to Djibouti in 1931–3 was published as *L'Afrique fantôme*.

The journal entries are daily. They include details of dinners, discomforts, hours of sleep, meetings, encounters with animals, dreams, erotic fantasies, gossip, letters to his wife, the need to masturbate, reflections on the erotic, his aversion to physical contact, his loneliness, his desire for the Ethiopian, Emawayish, his irritation with ethnography, the annoying presence of his colleagues, comments on the Parisian avant-garde, troubles at border crossings, reflections on masturbation ('you are never alone'), descriptions of Africa and Africans.

The Africa through which he travels is saturated by African spirits, ghosts and phantasms, all part of the African everyday. For the Africans, life and death, the spiritual and the real, dreaming and waking, are continuous and interconnected. Every aspect of life is symbolic, a sign of a beyond, a spirit world that is present and palpable. Nothing is insignificant as it is in a scientific/secular universe. The most humble action is filled with meaning. The sacred touches everything and everyone.

In Ethiopia, Leiris became fascinated with the Ethiopian cult of the *zars* and its possession rituals. The *zars* inhabit a parallel world to the ordinary one. The two worlds intertwine. The sacred is inside the profane, inflecting it. The other, sacred, world is inside the profane world, not exterior to it in a distant heaven. In times of stress, such as illness or a rite of passage, Ethiopians believed themselves possessed by their *zars*, some of which are personal to them. Established rituals govern possession and its exorcism. There is an ordered round of determinations and established ways to annul these.

Daily life is negotiated by maps of signs, imprints, traces of the *zars* and prescribed itineraries for avoiding or invoking them.

I imagined these maps to be like early medieval maps, those which might have guided Marco Polo and provoked his imagination, maps terrestrial and celestial illustrated with imaginary beasts and monsters, rising from out of the sea, blowing up a storm from the heavens.

Leiris wondered at the theatricality of possession. To what degree was it a masquerade (bad faith)? Were the Ethiopians possessed, or were they making believe they were possessed? If possession was not falsely enacted, but real, how was it experienced? Was it the performance that generated the feeling of possession, or was it the fact of possession that resulted in the feeling being manifest? Did fictions lead one to truth?

Leiris's loneliness in Africa and his physical isolation from others – he recoiled from physical contact – made him wonder all the more at the genuineness of Ethiopian rituals, the connections that were experienced. He observed the Africans, but he could not participate. Witnessing possession, he was witnessing his own exclusion, and not only as ethnographer. On the other hand, the ethnographic choice, to observe, is a choice for exclusion.

The experience of exclusion troubled Leiris: to be aloof, to be uninvolved, to gather evidence, to take photographs. Professionalism was a self-imposed exile for him, permanent separation.

His sense of exclusion informed his ethnographic method. Or rather, his method began with the fact of that exclusion. By including himself, his own distress at exclusion and his instinct for sensing corruption, including the consciousness of exclusion and the agony of distance from others in his viewing of them, it enabled him better to see, even to bridge, the gap, not by denying his feelings, but by admitting them and putting them to good use. Subjectivity was not a defect to be overcome or effaced, but an instrument to be used.

His sensitivity to bad faith and his desire for purity caused him not only to question possession rituals and wonder at their truth, but to question himself and thereby ethnography, thus changing a professional relation towards the Africans from one of observation to that of dialogue, though not quite one of empathy.

The problem of being on the outside before an otherness to which he did not belong was not confined to Leiris. It was a central fact of ethnography and to travelling in a strange land.

The Africans often hid things from the ethnographer and dissembled. They provided misleading information and false representations. They made false images for the ethnographer, constructing a fake parallel world for their observers in order better to hide the one they wished not to be observed.

This irritated Leiris immensely. It irritated him even more when the Africans wanted money to tell him the truth and to provide him with the genuine performance, not the performance made-for-ethnography. They were not simply falsifying to protect their culture, but falsifying to sell it at a higher price.

This corruption troubled Leiris, more than the ethnographic consequence of false evidence. It compromised an ideal of purity and his suspicions of bad faith, including his own and the bad faith of ethnography.

Diogenes of Sinope, the greatest of the Cynics, went about Athens with a lantern looking for an honest man and never finding one.

L'Afrique fantôme is filled with accounts of Leiris's dreams as journal entries or in fragments of letters to his wife. The dream, like possession, required interpretation to discover what was being buried and hidden. He called dreams 'feigned life'. He called theatre, 'feigned death'. In these feignings, where references were blurred and distorted, truth had a chance.

Ethnography, true also for most travel literature and geographical/travel films, turns the native into spectacle, theatricalised by the traveller or ethnographer – it is the 'exotic'. The native, translated into a language not his own, taken over by it, is reinvented, written from one culture into another that we might identify an identity which to the native makes him a stranger to himself.

In the translation, fragments of experience take on the colour of unreality, feigned life (because it is like a dream), and feigned death (because it is a shadow play).

Make-believe was a thin line for Leiris between good and bad faith and between life and death. The issue was an issue of verisimilitude, truth-seeming, life-seeming, thereby an ethnographic issue of how to represent, how to deal truly with an other and an other who had a complex system of spirits, shadows and theatrical possession, a system of otherness in fact, and how to deal with yourself in this situation.

In both instances, identity is uncertain.

In Africa, Leiris approached something more troubling, more mysterious than bad faith. It was an experience of a severe split that went beyond Sartrian philosophical reflection.

Leiris sometimes doubted his own presence in Africa (he tried to annul his presence by attempting suicide). He also came to doubt the reality and sense of the expedition, as if it were a *fantôme*, a dream, a groping in the dark. Perhaps, in these feelings, he was closest to the Africans and their experience of a fantasmagoric world. By that fact, by what he shared in common with them of terror and unease, the Africans were no longer other to him and he less other to himself. He had found a way to understand that involved him so that he was no longer alone, on the outside. It provided the foundation of his ethnography and the impulse for his journal.

He interrogated African phantoms, and by their means and with their help he interrogated his own.

Leiris tried to dispel the sense of unreality and disconnection he felt by accumulating banal, concrete, irreducible, 'real' details: 'the truck broke down and we were mired in the mud'.

And there were photographs, hyper-realism, to attest to the solidity of things.

Ten

How can you, dispossessed, comprehend possession?

The stability of the existence of the other for Leiris and of his own existence vacillated because relations were difficult. He was not in the same space of the same world as they, but looking in, locked in a cage at the reverse side of the bars.

The Ethiopians were not the only ones haunted by spirits. Leiris's ghosts tracked him, relentlessly, through Africa, as he questioned his desires and as he encountered the desires of others, other systems.

Literally, he felt dislocated.

His obsession with distance, separation, therefore with the erotic, masturbation particularly, and with possession, became a method.

Later, he extended it to African art.

To become engaged by becoming other than oneself, to become possessed by the other to become oneself, and to go beyond oneself into the other in order to transform the ethnographic experience and its exteriority, became the boundaries within which Leiris defined his ethnography. It enabled him to touch others and understand, to realise, not simply intellectually, but as daily practice and experience, the experience of regarding as a subjective experience. The consciousness inflected and modified his seeing.

It brought him from outside in, from an exclusion that he endured as inadequacy, to a comprehension of the experience of distance, so that it might bring him close.

Distance is a condition of representation.

It was a condition central to all of Leiris's work. He understood that to enact what he felt required a writing that went beyond representation and its disconnections to what he called poetry and theatre, and sometimes wrote: poetry as a theatre of words, writing as performative, a re-experiencing, a poetic ethnography.

Leiris's diary is beautiful. The coming close, the redefinition of himself, is a daily affair, composed of trivia, often directionless, incoherent, nothing high-sounding, or profound, simply this awareness, an attentiveness like the Ethiopians attentive to their *zars*, a stepping hesitantly, carefully through a field of *fantômes*, dreams, emotions.

Leiris wondered whether, if he had made love to the Ethiopian, Emawayish, would he have been successful? She had been circumcised. How would he have given her pleasure? A massage with perfumed oils, perhaps?

'Si j'avais couché avec Emawayish, sait-on jamais? Je l'aurais peut-être fait jouir ...'. [3] *Peut-être.*

With the gulfs of race, history, the profession of observer to observed, the gap of outside and in, how can you reach out? Leiris seemed cold sometimes, but also sorrowful, tender.

From Leiris's African journal:

> Mais aussi je suis trop seul. Je ne reçois plus de lettres. Il n'y a personne à qui je puisse, du fond du coeur, parler. Des fantômes engendrés par cette espèce d'internement, je suis victime; petits fantômes à vrai dire, qu'il suffirait de moins d'un chant de coq pour faire crouler mais qui, malgré leur vanité, restent terribles, car ils sont un doigt mis sur la blessure mal cachée. Paroles d'Emawayish cet après-midi quand, lui parlant du manuscrit, je lui disais qu'il serait bon surtout qu'elle écrive des chansons amoureuses, comme celles d'autre nuit: *Est-ce que la poésie existe en France?* Puis: *Est-ce que l'amour existe en France?*

Jamais la science, ni aucun art, non plus qu'aucun travail humain n'atteindront au prestige de l'amour et ne pourront combler une vie si le manque de l'amour l'anéantit. Et tout cela si épouvantable en même temps que si beau! Parures précieuses à en pleurer ... . L'amour, qui nous unit et nous sépare, qui nous fait nous condenser en un seul objet et creuse un précipice entre nous et le reste; l'amour, qui nous fait haïr *les autres*, puisqu'il n'est qu'une éclatante confirmation de notre singularité, de notre solitude; ...[4]

Eleven

The means that enabled Pasolini to reach out from beyond his loneliness, solitude and isolation was the text: the poem, the book, the film. To create was an act of solitude and a yearning for solidarity.

The texts were interpositions, the establishment of distance, and attempts to close the distance, the signs of separation from the otherness of others and from the otherness of oneself, and the signs of belonging.

Leiris could feel the outline, the border of death, in every phrase he wrote. That is why he had to break with procedures of seeming-true and procedures of objectivity to find the truth of the illusions within them.

Theatre acknowledged the illusion, a feigning that was not illusory and could be terrifying.

You had to be possessed.

Twelve

'I had been grey, grey in pallor, and hesitant, afraid, tremblingly so, and for years, in despair, at the edge of non-existence.

'My security and dependability was smoking.

'One day, some months ago, an old woman from France rang, here on some official visit. She was a friend of my ex-lover from the time I had begun my mourning and my greyness. I realised, as I put down the phone, that this woman was the last trace of a love affair I had clung to, but which had no presence. In the realisation that its presence had long been gone, though I had imagined it had not, it was no longer there.

'I could see my imagination.
'I crushed out the cigarette that I had been smoking during the phone call.
The colour of years ago flowed back to me, instantly. I could feel it from inside
me.
Nothing that happened then or now belonged to my will.
Since the beginning of September I had dreams of loss and of death (of my ex-
lover, my mother, and my father). Those dreams were extremely painful, and in
the state between sleeping and waking I told YOU these dreams.
'Today, was the first time I did not tell you anything.'

Thirteen

'Space seemed unobstructed, and the unhurried wind, which carried us
along as on a slow river, caressed our foreheads, our cheeks, the backs of
our necks. I believe we all felt the same felicity, a felicity almost physical. I
say almost, for there is no happiness or pain that is solely physical; the past
always interposes itself, as do the circumstances, surprise and other ingre-
dients of consciousness. The excursion, which must have lasted an hour
and a half, was also a voyage through the lost paradise that is the 19th century. To travel in the balloon dreamed up by Mongolfier was to return to
the pages of Poe, of Jules Verne, of Wells. It will be remembered that the
"Selenites" who inhabited the interior of the moon travelled from one
gallery to another in balloons similar to ours – and felt no vertigo.'

Notes

1   'In our eyes, an individual, however complex he may be, has the primordial
    and essential character of being a singular unity. If he was not that, he would
    not be an individual, but rather composed of a plurality. In the primitive,
    however, the feeling of an internal life is not matched by a strict notion of
    singular individuality. Moreover the boundaries are vague and imprecise,
    since the individual includes his various loyalties, and as well his double, his
    image and his reflection. And there is more: the *tjurunga* of the Australians,
    the *kra* of the Ewe, the *ntoro* of the Ashanti and the namesake of the Bai-ila,
    etc., without being completely confounded with the individual, is not either
    distinguished from him. Without this element that constitutes individuality

by linking one to one's ancestors from which you come, it would have no existence. The individual is only himself on condtition that at the same time he is other than himself. Under this novel aspect, far from being a unity as we conceive, he is at once singular and plural. He is therefore, let us say, a veritable "location of identities".'

'The Aino of Japan have a curious belief: according to them "the dead regard those who have not yet crossed the river of death to be 'shades' (ghosts), and consider actual and natural persons to be themselves. They think of us as we think of them." '

2   'things as they are', 'things in their reality'.

3   'If I had slept with Emawayish, who knows? Perhaps I would have given her pleasure ...' . *Perhaps.*

4   'But also I feel very much alone. I no longer receive letters. There is no one to whom I might intimately speak. I am the victim of fantasms engendered by this kind of internment; indeed, the slightest of fantasms, so that it would take no more than the cry of a cock to make them disintegrate, despite their vanity remain terrible because they are like a finger stuck into a badly hidden wound. The words of Emawayish this afternoon when, speaking of the manuscript, I said to her that it would be very good if she could write some love songs, like the ones of the other night: *Does poetry exist in France?* Then: *Does love exist in France?*

'Never will science, nor any art, nor any human endeavour attain the prestige of love nor could it ever fill a life if the lack of love, extinguished it. And that is so horrible and at the same time so beautiful! Precious loveliness to make you weep ... . Love, which unites and separates us, which causes us to concentrate everything in a single object and digs a precipice between us and everything else; love, which makes us hate *others*, since it is a dazzling confirmation of our distinctness, of our solitude; ...'

Chapter Eight
Xanadu

Lord! what a strange world in which a man cannot remain unique even by taking the trouble to go mad.

G. K. Chesterton

One

An encyclopedia entry for 'Marco Polo' concludes: 'Some scholars ... question whether Polo actually journeyed to China.'

The written account of Marco Polo's voyage to China appeared at the turn of the 13th century, first published in French as *Les Voyages de Marco Polo*. It was received with amazement, not being taken as credible.

Marco Polo was the captain of a Venetian galley. In a battle with the Genoese in 1298, he was defeated and taken prisoner. In prison, he met a professional writer, Rusticello. Together they wrote *Les Voyages de Marco Polo*, part dictated, part concocted, or perhaps all of it was concocted.

The *Voyages* relate that Marco Polo was in China from 1275 to 1292. He left Venice in 1271 with his father and uncle, who were Venetian merchants. He was then seventeen years old. They reached the summer capital of Kublai Khan at Shang-tu in 1275. The Mongol emperor was impressed with the young man, who he appointed to his diplomatic service. For three years Marco Polo held the post of governor of Yang-chou.

The *Voyages* is a literary work. It was meant to astonish. It was a memorial, not a journal. The voyage was altered by time, memory, fantasy, egotism, convention, dreams, literary ingenuity, the boredom of prison, the inventiveness of Rusticello, the opportunism of Polo and the exigencies of language.

In Calvino's *Le città invisibili*, Marco Polo invented cities the Khan believed (feigned to believe?) existed.

They had names like *Eufemia*.

Two

Rusticello's writing certainly had textual precedents.

During Marco Polo's voyages, it is hard to see how the exotic realities he encountered would not have provoked his imagination. Even the most banal occurrences can suggest fabulous visions. One cannot prevent literary models and the suggestiveness of writing from transforming reality, thus loosening the hold of language on its referents and giving language a life of its own – *la sortilège des images*.[1]

According to Borges, Kublai Khan dreamt his palace in Xanadu. He had it built according to his dream. Five hundred years later Coleridge dreamt a poem of the palace, a beautiful, sublime poem. His dream was interrupted. The poem is a fragment of what it would have been had the dream been complete. Charles Foster Kane built his Xanadu in California, equally left unfinished.

Citizen Kane, after we hear and see spoken Kane's last word, 'Rosebud', opens with the spoken and the written first lines of the Coleridge poem: *'In Xanadu did Kubla Khan a stately pleasure dome decree ...'*.

Citizen Kane is labyrinthine. You are led to an empty conclusion that clarifies nothing. The film has the quality of a dream from the moment it begins, not only because the film is fragmented and tangled, nor because every vision is distorted, but because its sounds are hollow and resounding, sounds from a depth, like the beyond of dream and of death from where Kane's voice issues.

I felt it was Othello in Welles's *Othello* who had dreamt the story of his murderous jealousy just as Joseph K dreamt his absurd trial in Welles's *The*

Trial. I like to think that *Citizen Kane* is Kane's dream, dreamt at the moment of his death. It is Kane, and we, who see the sled consumed in the flames of Kane's possessions, as he himself will be consumed in a finality that his dream foretells and concludes.

Three

Borges remarked that Xanadu was an archetype first manifest in the palace, then in a poem. Its latest manifestation is in film. Whoever compared them would have seen that they were essentially the same.

Is China the dream of Marco Polo, as Calvino suggests, in whose dream Kublai Khan is an accomplice in the dreaming?

Four

Calvino's *Le città invisibili* seems perfectly ordered, yet arbitrary.

The succession of Marco Polo's descriptions could have been different and each description different.

Calvino, I am sure, came upon his cities as his writing encountered them, leading him from city to city, narration to narration, arriving like the wind, as Duras said of writing.

The novel *René Lys*, by Victor Segalen, takes place behind the walls of the Forbidden City. The city cannot be penetrated or seen. It is a city of secrets that gather and congeal. The interior of the city is a labyrinth of incomplete visions. The writing is clear, lucid, but what is written is not.

The writing densifies, accumulates, overlaps, extends, but goes nowhere.

Segalen's China, like Calvino's, is unpeopled. It has spaces and monuments, but these are metaphysical, as in a De Chirico landscape, and equally unstable, out of true. Each object (monument) in the same space of writing or of a picture plane is in a different world with its space and time.

The monument is blank.

Five

I prefer to believe that Marco Polo never went to China.

Calvino's *Le città invisibili* are geographies of cities the Khan does not know and will never know. They are no longer what they were. As they are being described, description alters them. Besides, they never were in fact.

Polo advances into unknown territory as he speaks. To narrate and to explore is the same act, one that Conrad reiterated and whose writing travellers to Africa, such as Leiris and Gide, took as their models.

There is no such thing when you narrate as pure description. The unknown you come across is what you are bound to invent as you go forward, pushed by the necessity to narrate what has never been before.

These narrations are not fancies, even though they find what was not there.

What you find when you narrate turns out to be nothing definite except an opening to an unknown, including the places you have not yet been and have not yet written and which may never be written, but which you can only find in writing. Writing extends the expanse of the unknown, including its pain and loneliness. It puts into words what no one knows and tries to make it recognisable.

Polo's China is created in a prison cell.

Six

The nomadic Mongols of the northern steppes, who invaded and took possession of the agricultural civilisation of China to the south in the 13th century, came to control a vast territory as far west as Budapest, north beyond the Himalayas, south to Canton and east of Beijing.

The effectiveness of Mongol rule brought peace to central Asia. It made travel and commerce safer and easier. The conditions created by the Mongols under the Khan encouraged the journey of the Polos to the Mongol court from Venice. The Mongol court was filled with foreigners at the time, Europeans and Muslims, doing business. Their presence was encouraged for the skills they could bring, the trade they could encourage and because, not being Chinese, the Khan felt secure with them.

The Khan appointed foreigners as his advisers, emissaries and administrators.

Marco Polo, among other foreigners, was appointed a Khan provincial administrator.

In China, from the 3rd century, geography had been an important pursuit and became an established science. It was linked to military needs and the needs of administration to control large territories and, within them, to recruit labour, to impress soldiers, to collect taxes, to build roads, to construct bridges, to control flooding, to dig canals and open navigable waterways. Many of China's cartographers and geographers were famous, like Wei Hsiu, at the end of the 3rd century, and the geographer Chang Chu, who compiled a geography of parts of Shanxi and Sichuan in the 4th century.

Chu's geography, which was topographical, and also included the biographies of notables in the region, listed local monuments, described local customs, catalogued fauna and flora, not excluding the birds, and provided information on resources and commodities, iron as well as honey and bamboo. Geography from the outset was unavoidably ethnographic, a human geography for reasons of administration, of economy, of science and of power.

Seven

There are two phases to geography.

The first is that of exploration, to discover the unknown. The second, that of description, classification and study, to order what has been discovered. The second phase is also affected by the unknown, but differently.

The world once covered by exploration threatened to disappear as it was uncovered. Writing and description, later painting, drawing, photograpy and film, remembered what had not been known and before it would disappear and not be known again when it had disappeared. These representations were classified in the album and in the archive, marked as representations, a time already past.

Representations are fundamentally memories.

The *Archives de la planète* and its geography were like this.

Discovery introduced time as anxiety and a historical sense haunted by disappearance. The century that instituted the historical narrative instituted progress. Progress provided the tools and sciences for remembering and recording. It also provided the tools that changed the world rapidly and drastically, and caused what was recorded to disappear and gradually instituted amnesia and fantasies.

Progress necessitated technologies of memory, like the gravure and the photograph to make memory seem real and hence what it represented as not lost.

The *Archives de la planète* are haunted by the threat of disappearance induced by the progress it embodied.

Lévi-Strauss beautifully evoked this situation and that of the ethnographer in *Tristes tropiques*, which is its *tristesse*.

Eight

The ruins of a Portuguese fort, 16th century, perhaps earlier, along the Ghana coast, west of Accra, near Cape Coast. Cape Coast had been a trading port. A local bourgeoisie of middlemen merchants grew up there at the end of the 19th century, spawned by free trade and British colonisation. Many adopted British costumes and manners: gold-headed walking sticks, pocket fobs, panamas and boaters, clubs, tea-parties, soirées, English accents. Their sons, some of whom went to Oxford and Cambridge, were the intelligentsia, the elite. Among them, between the world wars, were radicals expressing a new nationalism, flavoured with Bovril, tempered by cricket bats.

Some time ago, I wrote about one of these young men. He was called Kobina Sekyi. Comintern policies were reversed in the mid-30s as the threat of Fascism began to be better appreciated. The Comintern no longer identified the enemy as the bourgeois capitalist state, but rather as Fascism. It called on national Communist parties to co-operate with bourgeois parties in a popular front against Fascism. The Comintern equally extended its support to anti-colonial bourgeois nationalism in the European colonial empires. Sekyi was courted by the Comintern, though to little immediate effect. Nevertheless, the global situation and the activities of the Comintern added a different and socialist taste to African nationalism, especially after the Second World War. Anti-colonial radicals, such as George Padmore from the West Indies, had gone to the Soviet Union. Padmore met a young Kwame Nkrumah in London; he had a considerable influence on him and, through him, on the post-war independence movement in Ghana.

I knew Padmore's widow in Accra. She had a privileged place in Ghana but was completely isolated.

Some of the cells in the fort were relatively intact. There were rows of iron rings in each to chain the slaves brought to the coast by African traders dealing with chiefs up-country and the Portuguese and Dutch along the coast. Later, they dealt with the British. The Africans were packed into slave ships specially designed with space-saving ingenuity. Inevitable losses in the cargo were calculated: so many bodies to be packed, a certain percentage of waste estimated against the profits of transporting so many so far.

The design drawings of the period of the hull interiors of slave ships and later drawings evoke the horrors of the voyage to the Americas, and reminded me of Joseph Cornell boxes and the miniature worlds he formed within the space of a few centimetres.

The bodies in the drawings resembled small, animated dolls. They were stacked as one would books in a long hall of a library. The design of the hulls of the slaving ships and the needs of economy in packing were conceived on a shelving principle. The design of the interior of ships for the transportation of slaves from Africa and of convicts to Australia were not dissimilar to the design of eighteenth-century libraries.

It was in the long hall of the Old Library at Trinity College, Dublin, that I remembered Cape Coast and the slave ships.

Africans who died on the way to the Americas – the numbers were considerable – were tossed overboard.

Nine

You cried at the fort, were inconsolable with sadness.
The fort was mournful for you, closed in on you, like a pressure.
Our relation had only begun then and it was already ending.

I recall an afternoon we spent in Liverpool.

We went to a Chinese restaurant in a broken-down Georgian quarter of the city. We ate dim sum for the entire afternoon, brought to us in steam baskets which were never removed. We were indefatigable eaters, or I was. The presence of what we ate was stacked one on top of the other, new ones to one side, consumed ones to the other.

Later, I went to the same restaurant with someone else, full of expectation, and was disappointed, as so often happens with tastes. Sensuality is the moment of it. After that it is sustained in memory.

This loss, also a proliferation, Borges celebrated (and Pasolini mourned).

Borges was content to create the labyrinth of loss as a journey without regrets.

Your tears irritated me as they comforted you.

I recall the sounds belonging to the beach and of the waves inside the fort, sweeping and thudding, marking the ruins as they slipped away.

Ten

Kafka's stories begin with the banal of the everyday. These events and experiences are excessively ordinary and the writing is blank. Kafka's eloquence is the absence of it, an astonishing neutrality that provides no view. It is not simply the events that are banal, but the writing of them is banal.

Kafka's style is not to have one.

It is a writing that strives for nothing. These stories literally go nowhere. The banality accumulates and blankness is sustained. What we read is absurd, senseless, insignificant and for these reasons unpossessable, and for that reason, terrifying. Unable to identify even the most common things can cause a loss of self-identity. It is not knowing where you are, a displacement without a system to guide you, or boundaries to confine you. The writing does not approach meaning nor does it accept it.

Nor, strictly speaking, is there anything so strong in it as a refusal of meaning. Quite simply, meaning is absent, but the strangeness is an effect of assuming that meaning is present and proceeding to write (Kafka) and to act (his characters) as if it is, when it is not. It is the reverse of a verisimilitude where the reader (or spectator) is complicit in believing something is true which is make-believe. In Kafka, the concreteness of the ordinary is everywhere (you cannot help but believe it), but it nevertheless seems unbelievable because it is stripped of everything but its ordinariness.

Eleven

Jean Collet: *Vous avez placé dans Le Mépris une réplique troublante qui va beaucoup faire réfléchir les spectateurs. C'est la citation de Hölderlin dans la bouche de Fritz Lang. Il y a plusieurs interprétations possibles de ce texte, et Fritz Lang ajoute: 'Ce n'est plus la présence de Dieu, c'est l'absence de Dieu qui rassure l'homme ...'*

Jean-Luc Godard: Oui, c'est un texte très étrange de Hölderlin parce qu'il est incompréhensible.

J. C.: *Pourquoi l'avez-vous mis?*

J.-L. G.: Parce que c'est un texte qui s'appelle *La Vocation du poète,* et que Lang symbolise dans *Le Mépris,* le poète, l'artiste, le créateur. C'était bien, donc, qu'il dise une poésie sur la 'vocation du poète'. Que ce texte soit étrange, c'est certain, je ne le comprends pas. Et Lang ne le comprend pas non plus. Il a rajouté: 'Etrange, mais vrai.' Ça, c'est lui qui le dit, ça le regarde ...

L'ennui, c'est qu'on croit que les mots doivent toujours signifier quelque chose. Et on croit par contre qu'un tableau ne signifie pas. Ce qui rend les peintres furieux. Une peintre est capable d'écouter de la poésie sans dire: 'Qu'est-ce que ça veut dire?' Ici, il y a des mots qui jouent entre eux. Il n'y a qu'à rêver, penser sur ces mots. Moi, je trouve que c'est beau, on est là, au coin du feu, on voit ces mots et on leur trouve des significations, ou on n'en trouve pas, mais c'est une activité de l'esprit, c'est excitant. Il n'y a qu'à écouter, regarder. Mais le poète ne cherche pas les significations. Il n'y a qu'à comparer les poèmes d'Éluard enregistrés par Gerard Philipe ou par Éluard. Gérard Philipe quand il dit 'sur les oreilles de mon chien', prend une voix larmoyante. Au contraire, Paul Éluard donne l'impression que les mots sont des objets sculptés. Ils sont comme ça ...

J'ai choisi Hölderlin parce que Lang est allemand, et aussi parce que Hölderlin a fait de nombreux poèmes sur la Grèce. Les trois quarts des gens ne le savent pas. Mais je voulais par là sous-entendre *L'Odyssée*, la Grèce. J'ai choisi Hölderlin à cause de cette fascination que la Grèce, la Méditerranée exercent sur lui. Mais il faut accueillir ce poème comme un poème. On ne demande pas à Beethoven ce que signifie sa musique.[2]

Godard's remarks on Éluard reminded me of Cunningham.

Cunningham taught that words were sculpted forms, hence the absence of rhetoric in his readings of poetry.

It was like that ...

Notes

1   the spell of images.

2   Jean Collet: *You have set out in Le Mépris an unsettling line that forces the audience to reflect upon it. It is the quotation from Hölderlin spoken by Fritz Lang. There are many possible interpretations of the text, and Fritz Lang adds: 'It is no longer the presence of God, but the absence of God which reassures man ...'*

Jean-Luc Godard: Yes, it is a very odd text of Hölderlin because it is incomprehensible.

J. C.: *Why did you put it in?*

J.-L. G.: Because it is a text called *The Poet's Vocation* and in *Le Mépris* Lang symbolises the poet, artist, creator. Thus, it was right that he speaks poetically about the 'poet's vocation'. Certainly, the text is strange. I don't understand it. And Lang does not understand it either. He has to add: 'Strange, but true.' That is what he says, its up to him ...

The trouble is that people believe that words must always mean something. And on the other hand they believe that a painting doesn't have a meaning. This makes painters furious. A painter can listen to poetry without saying: 'What does that mean?' In this instance words are playing with each other. One only has to dream to think of these words. I find this beautiful. One is there, in front of the fire, sees the words and finds meanings for them, or not, but it's an activity of mind and it's exciting. One has to listen, to look. The poet does not seek meanings. Just compare the poems of Éluard recorded by Gérard Philipe or by Éluard. Gérard Philipe, when he says 'on the ears of my dog', assumes a tearful voice. Paul Éluard, to the contrary, gives the impression that the words are sculpted objects. They are like that ...

I chose Hölderlin because Lang is German and also because Hölderlin wrote many poems about Greece. Three quarters of the audience won't know that. But I wanted to suggest *The Odyssey*, Greece. I chose Hölderlin because of the fascination that Greece, the Mediterranean had on him. But the poem needs to be taken as a poem. One doesn't ask Beethoven what his music means.

Chapter Nine
Interlude

He opened the geography to study the lesson; but he could not learn the names of places in America. Still they were all different places that had different names. They were all in different countries and the countries were in continents and the continents were in the world and the world was in the universe ... .

What was after the universe? Nothing. But was there anything round the universe to show where it stopped before the nothing place began? It could not be a wall; but there could be a thin thin line there all round everything. It was very big to think about everything and everywhere. Only God could do that. He tried to think what a big thought that must be; but he could only think of God.

James Joyce

One

The volcano on Stromboli constantly bubbles, sometimes more, sometimes less. It is always active. I found the constancy comforting. I looked to the volcano when I got up in the morning and before I went to sleep at night.

The crater has a high side and low one. The lava naturally flows from its lowest point into the sea. The lava hisses when it touches the sea and steam is given off. It is most visible from the other side of the island. If you dive down into the water, you can sometimes hear Stromboli murmuring and rumbling. I felt that the meduse *too were listening to the volcano. Their dancing filaments of light were like antennae to capture sounds. The rhythms of their dance were choreographed by the volcano.*

Beneath you, and you feel it, the earth explodes and rumbles.
Rather than this making me uneasy, I found it made me secure.

Two

According to Lévy-Bruhl, in primitive societies, men can assume multiple identities. These identities are not successive, nor alternate, but co-existent. Nor are they simply images, nor phantoms of a reality. They are independent realities simultaneously present. Neither is the source of the other, neither one *the* reality, the other its trace or representation. Nor is there a hierarchy of doubles. Neither is primary, none is the first from which the second derives. Co-extensive, they are co-equals.

A person can be in two places at once, both real, neither imaginary. In one place, he murders an enemy in the bush. In another, he is at home with his family. Independent witnesses can verify that he was at home, other witnesses that at that moment he was murdering someone. Both sets of witnesses are believed to be correct. This is not seen as contradictory nor as incompatible.

The truth lies in the improbable.

The man at home is as guilty of murder as the man who had been seen to be the murderer. They are the same person.

On the other hand, this same is different. It is not impossible for the man at home and the man who is murdering to encounter each other as one might meet oneself in the same time in diverse spaces, or in diverse times in the same space.

This meeting of yourself is the meeting Welles contrives as Kane meets his death in *Citizen Kane,* hence the circle.

Three

You meet yourself, your paths cross, in another universe.

A man might be a man and an animal, a crocodile or a hippopotamus, and still a man. His double identity is simultaneous. Such beliefs reveal a theory of identity and of the individual different from those in advanced societies except among artists.

When these beliefs were encountered by missionaries, it was difficult for the missionaries to make sense of them without altering them. The improbable to the missionary was natural to the primitive. Such reasoning seemed unacceptable, uncivilised.

To make sense of the primitive required the missionary to convert the thought of the primitive into the thought of the missionary as if sense and non-sense were either side of a divide of power and value.

In a Western and colonial situation it is not for the missionary to change his thought. The primitive has to be converted to missionary reason. The missionary accomplished the conversion even before he met his first African.

The missionaries found an African soul where none existed. They found an afterlife whose resemblance to the hereafter was merely superficial. This was serious, devastating business.

Nevertheless, it is odd that a missionary, who believed in the Immaculate Conception, could not understand African doubling as non-representational.

Were these doubles, the missionary hopelessly asked, a nascent soul?

Four

African realities are not images, nor phantom extensions, but concrete realities in diverse locations. A statue does not represent a god. It is one.

This is not a mistake or foolishness. A man in one time can see himself as a man in another time being killed, but he sees that scene even when he was then, at that instant, a child.

This is what occurs in *La Jetée*.

The Africans, for whom Livingstone projected a magic lantern show, ran out of the hall in fright as Abraham raised a knife about to sacrifice his son, Isaac. It was perfectly sensible for the Africans to have done so.

Our religions are representational and symbolic. Compared with African beliefs, they are secular.

Some missionaries who had come to Africa to convert the primitive

encountered in African societies an ideal sacredness that they felt had been
lost in their own. Coming to Africa was not a matter of bringing religion
but of finding one.

   This discovery was a disturbance.

Chapter Ten
Dahomey (I)

Nous sommes laïcs d'une manière effroyable devant ces animistes
convertis ou non. Nous nous accommodons de ce que nos chefs
politiques ne soient pas en même temps des chefs religieux. Nous avons
laïcisé les professions comme celle de médecin qui est un art sacré pour
les africains. Nous avons laïcisé la nature entière: la foudre qui est de
l'éléctricité, les ténébres de certains jours qui sont des éclipses. Nous
avons laïcisé nos mérites que nous nous attribuons, nos fautes et nos
malheurs que nous imputons à notre prochain. Laïcisé encore notre vie
extérieure qui, excepté à l'église, ne donne lieu à aucune prière au travail,
dans la rue ou en voyage. Nous délibérons sur toutes choses sans prières.[1]

Père Francis Aupiais

All invitations must proceed from heaven perhaps; perhaps it is futile for
men to initiate their own unity, they do but widen the gulfs between them
by the attempt. So at all events thought old Mr Graysford and young Mr
Sorley, the devoted missionaries who lived out beyond the slaughter-
houses, always travelled third on the railways, and never came up to the
Club. In our Father's house are many mansions, they taught, and there
alone will the incompatible multitudes of mankind be welcomed and
soothed. Not one shall be turned away by the servants on that veranda, be
he black or white, not one shall be kept standing who approaches with a
loving heart. And why should the divine hospitality cease here? Consider,

with all reverence, the monkeys. May there not be a mansion for the monkeys also? Old Mr Graysford said No, but young Mr Sorley, who was advanced, said Yes; he saw no reason why monkeys should not have their collateral share of bliss, and he had sympathetic discussions about them with his Hindu friends. And the jackals? Jackals were indeed less to Mr Sorley's mind, but he admitted that the mercy of God, being infinite, may well embrace all mammals. And the wasps? He became uneasy during the descent to wasps, and was apt to change the conversation. And oranges, cactuses, crystals and mud? And the bacteria inside Mr Sorley? No, no, this is going too far. We must exclude someone from our gathering, or we shall be left with nothing.

E. M. Forster

One

Père Francis Aupiais was a missionary of *La Société des missions africaines de Lyon*, the leading French missionary society in Africa.

The *Société* was founded in 1856 and began its mission in Dahomey (now Benin) in 1861. Père Aupiais was born in 1877. He went to Dahomey as a missionary in 1903. In 1930, he made a missionary propaganda film, *Le Dahomey Chrétien*, describing the work of Christianisation and civilisation by the mission. The film was made for a French audience. It is not evangelical. It was principally financed by Albert Kahn and first presented at a private showing at Kahn's house in Boulogne-Billancourt late in 1930.

Except for brief visits to France, Père Aupiais remained in Dahomey until soon after the first showing of his film.

The Church felt that the film showed African customs and beliefs too favourably. The Christianisation it displayed was syncretic, not pure, not the total conversion of the pagan, but a partial accommodation.

After viewing the film, the Church banished Aupiais to a small parish in the Landes. He was not allowed to return to Africa again.

Two

In 1916, Albert Kahn formed the *Comité national d'études sociales et politiques* (CNESP), an elite grouping of intellectuals, writers, artists, academics and politicians, who met each week at Boulogne-Billancourt to address the problems of the world. The CNESP was liberal-conservative. It discussed how best to maintain humanist ideals, social order, traditional ties in a world about to come apart in war, revolution and economic distress. *Le Dahomey Chrétien* was presented to the CNESP.

Aupiais had earlier studied *la géographie humaine* with Jean Brunhes. He visited Paris in 1926, again in 1927, where he attended lectures in anthropology at *L'Institut d'ethnologie* given by Marcel Mauss and Lucien Lévy-Bruhl. Mauss and Lévy-Bruhl attended the CNESP meetings. In 1927, Lévy-Bruhl had published his *L'Âme primitive,* which tried to make sense of the religious/social ideas in primitive societies. Lévy-Bruhl presented Aupiais to Albert Kahn and the CNESP.

By then, Kahn's interests had shifted from geography to social and political studies, which included anthropology, in part for its link with colonialism. *Géographie humaine* had itself shifted its bias, becoming less geographical and more social or, in other words, interpreting the geographical less with biological and physical models and the social more with historical and sociological ones.

Kahn and Brunhes became interested in Aupiais's film project.

To Aupiais, African beliefs were reflections of a profound religious consciousness, not error, savagery or darkness, as the Church maintained.

He discovered a sense of sacredness among Africans that he found lacking in the irreligiosity and secularism of France. He was ambiguous about the French civilising mission in Africa and about a Christianising mission intent to destroy what the Church regarded as evil, but which he found sublime.

Aupiais was in love with Africa. It was his Utopia of sacredness.

For Aupiais, the task of the mission was not to tear away the fabric of social beliefs in Africa, but to build on these and seek to conserve them. As a student of anthropology, he understood the cultural/social unity of African societies, that African religion was not separate from the secular, a category which did not exist as such in Africa, everything belonging to the sacred. To sweep away African religious beliefs and impose in their place

Catholic ones would disrupt the foundations of African society and would, Aupiais believed, have damaging social consequences.

Aupiais's social/anthropological response to Africa was echoed in the anthropology of Mauss and Lévy-Bruhl, in the regionalist assumptions of Brunhes's *géographie humaine*, and the elitist politics of Kahn and the CNESP, stressing gradualism, social adjustment, the importance of tradition and the need for social order.

The CNESP wanted change without the risk of social and political upheaval. The CNESP mechanism for social change was that it be directed by elites. It was technocratic and class-based, inherited from nineteenth-century positivism and French republicanism: the belief in reason and science to bring progress and happiness, a limited notion of democracy, not to be extended to everyone and avoiding the risk of socialism and worse. Its positivism was tempered by a new conservative spiritualism, by philosophical positions, like those of Bergson, that sketched the limits of reason, and sociological positions, like those of Bruhnes, that stressed the importance of regional and local institutions.

These notions would later be central to Christian Democracy.

The Church's insistence on an exclusive single religion without a wider sense of spiritualism in part was a defence of its own institutional power. Aupiais had no doubt about the truth of Christianity. But he saw that truth in a going-beyond of institutional arrangements. He saw it thus, not only because of his aversion to the secular in France, but because his anthropological training allowed him to perceive a spiritual world in plural terms.

Aupiais combined an intellectual modernism derived from sociology with a profound sense of religiosity. And, rather than arguing for the imposition of Christianity by the Church in Africa, he argued for the maintenance of African religious structures within a broad sense of faith by pointing to the social basis of religion, a social science view that relativised the Church yet universalised the notion of the sacred, and beyond that touched upon egalitarian positions of the equality of all persons.

The Church had universalist claims for the particularity of its faith. Aupiais, by universalising the sacred, undermined universalist claims based on particularity.

His position, evident in his film, disturbed a Church seeking to hold on to a past that was already slipping away.

Le Dahomey Chrétien is a key to many things.

Three

L'Institut d'ethnologie was founded in Paris in December 1925 by Lucien Lévy-Bruhl and Marcel Mauss.

> Il est à la disposition des gouvernements et protectorats coloniaux pour tous renseignements concernant les missions (françaises et étrangères), l'étude des races indigènes, la conservation et l'étude des faits sociaux. (1925)[2]

> Au point de vue colonial pur, il est un axiom reconnu que l'on ne peut administrer que les peuples que l'on connaît ... . Chaque jour qui s'écoule sans qu'on recueille ces fragments d'humanité est un jour perdu pour la science des sociétés, pour l'histoire de l'homme. Et ce, dans l'urgence: la France a charge d'âmes et est responsable devant les groupes humains qu'elle veut administrer sans les connaître. (1913)[3]

L'Institut d'ethnologie offered its services to the French colonial authorities, not to make colonial rule more effective but to ensure that colonial rule was less destructive of African societies and thereby more effective.

There were two aspects to this.

One was professional. Anthropologists were concerned to preserve primitive societies as much if not more for the sake of anthropology, as document and field, than for the sake and well-being of the societies studied. Primitivism, as an idea, and anthropology and geography as practices, were shaped by evolutionism and its contrasts of primitive/advanced, backward/civilised. Africa was invaluable, indeed precious, as a record and trace of earlier forms. The threat that primitive societies would disappear meant not only that fragments of humanity would disappear, but with it invaluable knowledge, knowledge important for everyone.

The other aspect was social and ideological. Anthropology looked backwards, to preservation, to keeping things together, to protecting threatened institutions. It had little interest and few concepts for dealing with change, and little sympathy with development and modernisation.

The African, who had to endure a new situation, had different interests from anthropologists. African attitudes were ambiguous towards colonialism, not necessarily negative or defensive. The new, seen as a threat by anthropologists interested in knowledge, was received by Africans more positively, interested as they were in survival under new conditions.

Built into anthropology was a nostalgia for simpler, more whole forms of social existence. Anthropology implicitly stood out as a criticism of modernisation.

Without colonialism the existence of anthropology would have been impossible. Colonialism was the necessary condition for anthropology. But it was also the reason for its necessity, its need to gather traces of social/ cultural knowledge before colonialism caused them to be lost forever.

Four

The radicalism of Leiris's diary and his anthropological work are in his recognition of the anthropological dilemma.

Leiris exposed the illusion of an objective scientific position, and stressed not only the subjectivity of the observer and the uncertainty of observation, but the productivity of that uncertainty, the fact that subjectivity and desire were tools, instruments of knowledge. Otherness was not to be gathered up, shelved and catalogued as irreducible and fixed, but was a problem and a relation. It was dynamic, part of change. The direction of Leiris's anthropology took him to surrealism, to which he was already sensitive, and to possession rituals, to theatre, the imaginary, and to sculpture and psychoanalysis.

It also took him to politics, that is, to a relation to Africa that was current, not academically restricted or aloof. It was a way to be *engagé*, not the academic, but the committed intellectual.

There is no paternalism in Leiris. Africa was not only a source of knowledge, but of joy, pleasure, adventure, possibility. He was interested in what was, but not in its preservation as such. He loathed colonialism not because it was changing things, but because it was exploitative. Unlike the positions of Aupiais, of Lévy-Bruhl, of Mauss, still less that of the CNESP and Kahn, who seem genteel, antique, conservative, hopelessly of the 19th century, musty, Leiris could see not only the service that Africa might provide for anthropological knowledge, but Africa's own independent contribution to knowledge, its thought, its art and thereby its real and unquestioned claim to independence. He had freed himself from the evolutionism of the now no longer new social sciences.

Leiris, with Bataille, and in their journal *Documents*, sought to redefine the artistic and anthropological object and thereby art and the primitive within an anthropology inflected by surrealism and recent achievements of the avant-garde in painting, particularly of Braque and Picasso.

Modernism in this area was sympathetic to the primitive. It understood primitivism as within the modern and one of its conditions, not an exotic object to be regarded from afar, or from above as an immutable backwardness.

To Leiris and the modern movement and its avant-garde, primitivism was not backwardness. On the contrary. And it was seen as a source of liberation and a way to understand what makes all of us human, a suppressed and unconscious otherness within us, as Freud had revealed.

Anthropological work in France was an aspect of the modern movement in the arts. It was in cultural/art journals and in writings such as those of Leiris, rather than in scholarly articles and academic books, that anthropology became a source of crucial *documents* for the avant-garde. And it was within that modernity of subjectivity and the unconscious, of hidden and plural perspectives, that the artistic modern embraced Freudian psychology as well as anthropology.

Five
The 1920s were years of opportunity for French anthropology, especially in Africa.

L' Institut ethnographique international de Paris had been founded in 1910

by Arnold Van Gennep and Maurice Delafosse. *L'Institut français d'anthropologie* was founded in 1911. Both were similar to institutes established at *l'Ecole pratique des hautes études* and at *l'Ecole des langues orientales*.
L'Institut d'ethnologie was founded in 1925.

The demand by anthropologists for knowledge and documents was voracious and self-justifying.

Anthropologists could be as competitive over a burial ground as slave traders had been for slaves.

They looted African villages and minds and shipped the booty back in crates to metropolitan France. They took possession of Africa in writings, in journals, in notes, in sketches, in photographs. The photographic image was the principal visual means to represent Africa in scholarship and in popular culture: magazines, newspapers, postcards, photograph albums, illustrated lectures, the cinema.

Sometimes, anthropologists directly called on colonial force to extract what was necessary to them from reluctant, unco-operative villagers, who wanted to keep what was theirs unseen and unsullied.

The collection and the catalogue were central to anthropology.

Collecting could often be aggressive because the sense of the imminent social ruin hastened by the European presence created the urgently felt need to collect before it was too late.

African time was circular, repetitive, rural. Colonial time was linear, progressive, historical, evolutionist.

Anthropology was in a race with time, whose tempo it had hastened. The African was the prize of the race and the obstacle in it. The Africans were seldom a passive field. They too resisted.

Many museums in Paris were established in the 19th century by private collectors who shared in the enthusiasm for orientalism and the exotic, stimulated by travel and exploration. The *Archives de la planète* belong within a tradition of the museum collection of the exotic and the exotic detailed in photograph albums in vogue from the 1850s.

Le Musée d'ethnographie du Trocadéro was established in 1878 by Ernest-Théodore Hamy (1842–1908). After the death of Hamy, the museum and its collection were neglected. It formed the basis of the anthropological *le Musée de l'homme* established in 1929 on the Trocadéro site, a *'fantastique magasin de bric-à-brac'*.[4]

It was *le Musée de l'homme* that sponsored an anthropological expedition from Dakar to Djibouti in 1930–31, spanning the French African colonial empire from west to east, to collect objects and artefacts for the museum. The expedition was headed by the anthropologist Marcel Griaule, whose later work was among the Dogon in Mali. Leiris was the expedition's secretary.

Leiris's ambiguity to anthropology included an ambiguity to its mania to collect. Much of his journal relates the everyday, banal activity and difficulties of finding objects, collecting them, recording them, crating and arranging them for shipment to the museum in Paris.

Today (1999), at its old site in Trocadéro, the African collection in *le Musée de l'homme* (about to be rehoused) substantially consists of the material collected by Griaule's 1930–31 expedition. To visit the *Musée* is to journey back to 30s France and the anthropological vision then of Africa, a France and a modernism immobilised like antiques in cases and shelves, and not the primitive.

Six

Griaule had a theory of fieldwork. In it you did not first impose a structure, which would then determine what you collected, but you collected whatever you could, whatever you encountered, whatever came to hand, from which, it was assumed, pattern and structure would emerge. Selection came after the act of collection, after facts and evidence were gathered, not before. Photographs belonged to the same classification of facts.

You could not determine in advance, according to Griaule, what was significant and what was not significant.

The document was not, thereby, the consequence of a prior interrog-

ation, but the field of a subsequent one. The documentariness of the document, its purity and value as fact, was the greater the less it seemed to be
the consequence of interpretation, and instead to have existed before significance was assigned to it, as if reality uninterpreted was more purely
itself, thus more real, and more objective.

According to Griaule, if collecting were theoretically self-interested it
would distort the collection to its scientific detriment and compromise the
anthropological value of the objects collected. Collecting must be open, not
closed by theoretical predeterminations.

To predetermine what you would gather would spoil the value of what
you had found. You would be faced with your own image, the object plus
interpretation.

In Griaule's view, a storage pot was as anthropologically significant, if not
more so, than a finely worked bronze sculpture or an elaborate mask.

Value could not be assigned in advance, nor assigned by a cultural scale
of values. All objects were documents, all equally facts. This approach
included facts gathered from interrogations of informants. Griaule had a
complicated means to force informants to reveal tribal secrets and hidden
objects, and, as a last resort, he called in the troops or threatened to.

The absence of written documentation in the *Archives de la planète*, the
reliance on the *autochrome* as fact, and the obsessive collecting by the
Archives may seem connected to Griaule's view of the document and
beyond it to that of Leiris's and Bataille's view of the document in their
journal *Documents*.

But this was not the case.

Griaule's position is particularly modern. It is related to Bazin's phe-
nomenology and his ontology of film where reality is identified and set free
by film, unencumbered by interpretation, not reduced to the singularity of
a linear narrative of events, a thin line of causation. It relates also to the
Rossellinian revelation of *'choses dans leur réalité'*, the harsh presence of the
real to which he leads his characters, and which Bazin and the *nouvelle
vague* celebrated.

The modernity of this view is not a naive representational realism. It is
a view of the muteness, silence, grandeur and terror of reality, its obscurity
and mystery, to be left open, to be there in openness and presence as opportunity, through which meanings and interpretation might pass but may
never be fixed.

There is a clear contrast and gap between Griaule's documentary reality
and Brunhes's representational one. Brunhes emphasised facts as objects
to be fixed in place by a structure in advance of their presence, of any gathering up of fact, to be used to determine what was gathered.

First interpretation, then reality.

Griaule proposed the unfixed object extracted, by force if necessary, then
put into play, not to signify this or that, but given its freedom, allowed to
migrate and to reveal its multiplicity and mystery.

This view has religious, sacred overtones. It is a point of intersection
between the primitive, anthropology, psychoanalysis, spiritual Catholicism,
the avant-garde, and it includes the realisms of Bazin, Bresson, Rohmer
and Rossellini.

Notes

1 'In contrast to the animists, whether converted or not, we are secular in an
appalling way. We adapt to political leaders who are not religious leaders. We
have secularised the professions such as medicine, a sacred art for the
Africans. We have secularised the whole of nature: lightning as electricity, the
darkness of days as eclipses. We have secularised our merits, which we
attribute to ourselves, and our faults and misfortunes, which we blame on
our neighbours. We have secularised the whole of our exterior life, except at
church, not making room for prayer at work, nor on the street, nor in our
travels. We think of things without prayer.'

2 'It is at the service of governments and colonial protectorates for any
information relevant to French and foreign missions, the study of native
races and the preservation and study of social facts.'

3 'From the point of view purely of colonialism, it is a recognised axiom that
one cannot administer peoples whom one does not understand ... . Each day

that goes by without gathering up these fragments of humanity is a day lost for the science of societies and for the history of man. And it is a matter of urgency: France is in charge of souls and is responsible for groups of people whom it wishes to administer without understanding them.'

4   'a fantastic junk shop'.

Chapter Eleven
Dahomey (2)

L'abus de l'individualisme crée le socialisme; l'abus de l'industrialisme donne naisssance au syndicalisme; l'abus du socialisme-syndicalisme engendre le soviétisme, le soviétisme le terrorisme; du terrorisme au despotisme, du despotisme à l'anarchie, de l'anarchie à la licence, de la licence à la débauche, de la débauche à l'épuisement, de l'épuisement au fléau, à l'épidémie, à l'invasion, la lutte sans fin.[1]

Albert Kahn

The soul is born, he said vaguely, first in those moments I told you of. It has a slow and dark birth, more mysterious than the birth of the body. When the soul of a man is born in this country there are nets flung at it to hold it back from flight. You talk to me of nationality, language, religion. I shall try to fly by those nets.

James Joyce

One

You peered at me from behind the shower screen, wet hair in front of your eyes, a look that seemed to last for ever.

The water dripped from you in a slow motion. At that moment everything was frozen, suspended beads of moisture that washed away time, the photo of an athlete in flight taken at high speed.

I found you beautiful.

I sensed the fragility.
And you said, 'Oh, you're so delicate.' Your eyes touched me as if I were a
precious porcelain.
You looked at me intently. I felt you were imagining the time when I would
no longer be there. It made me already memory, like a figure in a photograph. I
did the same, holding on to your beauty in the fear of the future of your absence.
You too were already past, projected into anticipated memory and forgetting.
I felt the loss.

That night you curled up against me. I heard your sobs. Your body twitched.
You imagined when we would be forgotten.
You said, it was as if nothing would have existed, not this moment, nor you,
nor I, nor anything, only the sensation of fading, and the mourning of it in
advance.
Without the passing of moments and the passing of the memory of them, there
would be no future.
'How can you keep hold of things?' you asked, in tears.

Two

Jean Brunhes taught geography at the *Université catholique de Fribourg* in
Switzerland near Berne from 1896 to1912, when he was appointed director of the *Archives de la planète*.

Fribourg had been a Catholic stronghold during the Reformation. The
Catholic tradition of the city and the importance of the *Université
catholique* were current during the time Brunhes was there. At the *Université* there was a current of thought trying to reconcile faith with the secular
world and its sciences and learning.

There was a strong opposition Social Catholic movement that was anti-
liberal, anti-socialist, anti-bourgeois and anti-capitalist, attitudes which
strengthened a traditional Catholic anti-Semitism. Social Catholicism
identified secular values, especially those associated with economic development and capitalism, as eroding faith and social and moral authority. The
line between Social Catholicism and a more enlightened, open and liberal
Catholicism was not always clear.

Père Aupiais embraced modern ethnography, in part for its inherent criticism of modern society and its valorisation of primitive, particularly sacred, forms. The modernism of ethnography was his weapon against the modernity of current society whose secularism he condemned.

Brunhes was a modern Catholic with ties to a spiritualist movement seeking to accommodate secular currents of thought of which *la géographie humaine* was an example. Yet in other respects, like Aupiais, he was a traditionalist and *géographie humaine* an ideological tool on behalf of his social and political conservatism. It was the principal reason for Kahn's support of Brunhes and geography.

Faith, for Brunhes, could only be sustained on condition that the world as it was changing, and whose changes he favoured, would not destroy the structures that sustained belief. Modernity without a soul was not worth the candle. But the soul cut off from the modern could only flicker and die.

A major documentary project of the *Archives*, recorded on film and *autochromes*, was at Angkor Wat in Cambodia. The *Archives* catalogued the Angkor Wat site and its monuments in minute and exhaustive detail. There are other, similar examples of documentation and documentary method in the *Archives*: Japanese temples, clutches of Buddhist monks, Vietnamese villages, Afghan cavaliers, Yugoslavia untouched by time, Ireland without a history, without troubles, picturesquely poor, photographed by young French women on a holiday of sorts.

Every *autochrome* was a step backwards from the time and culture of those who created its images. The images were constructed perceptions of a time already lost though still present, like Ireland, or having been lost with only fragments attesting to it, like Angkor Wat, beautiful for its mystery and lostness.

The *Archives* were an archaeology of living remains, the *autochromes* the memories of a memory. Though what was recorded was indisputably real, existent, actually there, it was photographed as being already memory or in the process of becoming a memory in a future that was to cause it to erode and disappear.

Every *Archive* image is an image of the ruin.

To regard the images of the *Archives* now is not to see them as they would have been seen at the time when they were gathered. The images then were traces of a present passing, memories for a future, and already memories then, already of the past, and, because frozen, because stilled in the momentariness of the *autochrome*, easily catalogued and stored for sciences that were founded in evolutionism with its progressive but nevertheless conservative implications.

The photographic image is a trace of the real and the imaginary of the real. No matter how concrete a photographic image may be, it inevitably evokes the sense of the passing of the object of which it is evidence, and by that fact takes the object from out of the real and delivers it into the imaginary, in a moment that you can touch, because it is realistic, and a moment not there, because it has passed, celebratory and mournful at once.

The *Archives de la planète* recorded a present that would be a past in the future and a present that was already a past in the present.

The social sciences were fascinated by the coexistence of times even if they inflected coexistence with a nostalgia for the passing of the past that served an ideology of conservatism. The *Archives* had both positions, the simultaneity of time that enabled it to collect its photographic samples in a past still present, and the sense of the passing of time that urged upon it the necessity to collect before the present-past would disappear.

It was the coexistence of times, no longer linear and progressive, that was the time-movement of the avant-gardes. Cubism used the forms of African and Oceanic art not only as citation, as an element in a heterogeneity of elements, but as forms of heterogeneity, of spatial and temporal overlaps. The surrealists played with memory, eroticism, primitivism, desire, dream, interweaving these between a past, the personal, the social and the archaeological, bringing out the hidden, the unconscious, the secret, and bringing them forward in time, juxtaposing levels, disrupting homogeneities.

Three

In a Visconti film, his melodramatic tragedies are matters of bad timing.

You arrive too late when what you wish for is already gone, or you arrive too soon and you are not met, not appreciated.

Desire in Visconti is a flickering trace whose object is never quite attained. The gap between desire and realisation intensifies the passion of longing, hysterically, operatically. Visconti's women are divas.

What you seek you cannot have. There is a lack of join between what you imagine and wish for, the reality you invent of reality, and the reality that is and is all you can have (but not want). The insufficiency of reality provokes the desire and dream to go beyond it and invites, thereby, destruction.

It is not only time that is at stake for Visconti, but a living by his characters in different times, in different realities but at the same time.

Visconti describes everything. He obsessively fills in details to fix objects and complete spaces, as if they threaten to escape him. The detailing is an attempt at possession, at fixing. What is fixed are not objects or scenes, but images of them, their remains, the signs of their passing. It provokes the need for detail, as if to insist on a real while acknowledging it as the image of it, and thereby temporality and lack of substance. This struggle, and the gap and passions it engenders, is encompassed by every Visconti image, every scene, every moment. It is a condition of existence.

Built into Visconti's films is a nostalgia that belongs to the construction of his objects. His realism is evidence, like a clue, of bad timing, of arriving a moment too late after the reality you seek has passed and all that remains is a tattered memory.

It is the images of other imagined worlds, better worlds, worlds in accord with desire, that Visconti's characters try to impose upon the world in which they live. The result only widens the gap between what reality is and what you are. It is a melodrama of time and imagination out of phase with the real.

What is imagined does not conform to reality and reality cannot be transformed by imagination, except in films where imagined worlds can be made to seem real and where make-believe, including the make-believe of melodrama where characters long for the impossible, is the only means to escape the melodramatic tragedy.

Visconti's characters live in images consumed by memories and wishes that include what the characters see coming, threatening to erase their present when all they cling to and caress will be gone. The drama of the stories in the films are mirrored by the films. The films are their mirrors.

Visconti makes the mirror visible in his images, the effect of the mirror at the core of images, of images of a reality that is not.

Visconti's excessive and obsessive concern with realistic details, combined with a sensibility where reality is a determinant and is out of reach, creates a cinema not of realism but of colour, movement, sound, where detail becomes a detail of composition, of the image, choreographed like dance and concert, operatic. The real belongs to the image for which reality is pretext and opportunity.

Four

Rainer Werner Fassbinder inverts the melodrama while retaining its forms.

His characters dream the dreams of society. They are conformists. They do not wish for more than society promises them. They rush, hasten, grasp, sacrifice, die for the promises promised them, making them seem absurd, then grotesque for the immensity of their desire and the paucity of the substance they desire.

His characters often have and get everything. They win the lottery. They capitalise on German reconstruction. They move forward. They succeed. They become something. It is the reverse of decadence and yet appears as the very heart of it. It is the winning that destroys them and kills them as absurdly as it has rewarded them, because it is empty.

Visconti's characters lose everything. Fassbinder's characters gain everything, which turns to nothing.

To dream the social dream is to dream the parody of it, its excess and caricature, its essential corruption.

Fassbinder can enjoy the art of corruption while using it to condemn the social fact of it. In this manner his films resemble the early novels of Joseph Roth, disliked by Walter Benjamin as 'left melancholy'.

Where Visconti details a realism that is passing, Fassbinder theatricalises a reality that is current, that does not pass. Theatricality and artificiality cause it only in part to become an image since the image turns back against itself, back as its mirrored caricature, revealing it to be falsely theatrical and thereby, for that reason, truly instructive.

Fassbinder's images confront you. There is no nostalgia.

A Visconti image is an image to love. It is filled with regret, an exquisite, near painful beauty, delicious loss.

Fassbinder jeers.

Five

Henri Bergson's philosophy centres on time and memory and the uncertainties these imply for identity, the subject and objectivity. All of modernism was touched by Bergson. He was an immensely popular figure. His lectures at the *Collège de France*, open to the public, were enthusiastically received.

Bergson created a new philosophical narrative of an uncertain, fragmented, plural world afloat in time. It was different from the cohesive master narratives proposed earlier by positivism and evolutionism.

Bergson had an interest in the occult like Marey and attended séances as Marey did. He sought traces of an other, nether world, not visible nor palpable, a world of movement-memory like the filaments of light in a Marey chronophotograph, the flickering shadows left behind by movement. You literally entered memory in his images, leaping into it, plunging, diving into a simultaneity of times, of overlapped temporal depths.

Bergson's stress on the uncertainty of reason, the insertion of the subject into philosophy, and of philosophy into the uncertainties of time and the non-linearity of memory, despite its radical philosophical implications, and its importance for the arts that were becoming obsessed with time and the forms of a new subjectivity, also brought Bergson into conservative favour, recommending him to tendencies in Catholic thought, among which was the spiritualism important to Jean Brunhes and the stress on an interiority rather than the exterior of the material world.

For some, Bergson was socially conservative, politically retrograde, especially where his thought supported conservative social thinking in the new social sciences such as geography and ethnography. His attack on objectivity and positivist sureties seemed to go to the core of republican ideals, its progressist sentiments, its pragmatisms.

Despite repeated attempts by Bergson to secure an academic appointment at the predominantly republican Sorbonne, he was unsuccessful. His ideas were instead accepted within the *Collège de France*, which is not a teaching institution nor an award-giving institution, where Bergson was a professor and to which he was instrumental in having Jean Brunhes appointed in geography and financed by Albert Kahn.

Six

The French Third Republic legislated the separation of Church and State over a range of social institutions, notably educational.

The Church had not only lost influence as a result of the economic and social changes linked to industrialisation and capital, but the condition of secularisation was politically and legally codified by the French state. As a result, and for its survival in a civil secular society, the Church began to involve itself directly in secular politics. Even as it condemned secularisation, it was forced to voice its condemnation in a secular context of power in order to be effective as a religious force.

The Catholic response to secularisation and modernisation was not uniform within the Church, nor among Catholics. By the 1890s, the Church began to seek an accommodation with the state and its institutions. It tried to redirect the Church towards civil society, seeking to inflect modernity with Christian values and infiltrate secular institutions, including political ones.

The positions of accommodation and compromise were actively promoted under the pontificate of Leo XIII. When Leo died in 1903, the year Père Aupiais arrived in Dahomey, these positions were again threatened by a revived conservative, anti-modernist and anti-Semitic fervour.

The Church, on the defensive in metropolitan France, was on the offensive in the French colonies. There, the state and civil society, which the Church criticised at home for irreligiosity, gave the Church the support it needed to evangelise Africa. Excluded from institutions of education in France, it was included in the structures of institutional power in France overseas.

Overseas, the Church, through missionary societies, was a part, and sometimes a crucial part, of colonial rule.

It administered education, industry, agriculture, marketing, thrift, savings, health, welfare. It influenced codes of behaviour, codes of dress, attitudes of mind, social gestures.

It was a force of French *civilisation*.

Le Dahomey Chrétien is three hours long, divided into three one-hour films. The whole of the film is further divided into eight sections under headings that catalogue the work of the mission. It was shot between January and the end of May 1930 by Frédéric Gadmer, an *opérateur* from the *Archives de la planète* on loan to Aupiais.

The film celebrates the role of Catholic missionaries in the framework of colonialism, that is, the promotion by the Church of secular activities Christianised in an indissoluble unity of France, Catholicism, *civilisation*.

The success of the palm-oil industry in Dahomey in one sequence of the film is attributed to the conversion of the African manager to Christianity, to civilised, modern habits of mind, and to the formation of agricultural scientific school-farms in which the Christian faith is combined with agricultural skills and French expertness as mutual natural allies.

Every soul saved was a potential French franc earned and step forward in *civilisation*.

Kept out of modernising institutions at home, the Church re-entered these through the door of imperialism, in the frame of which it proclaimed the Gospel.

The colonial frame was the condition for the effectiveness of the Church's religious mission, as it was for the effective functioning of anthropology.

In the colonies, the Church indulged itself in French patriotism, loyalty to the state, a reintegrated State and Church in which the libertarian ideals of the Revolution and of the Third Republic were absorbed and Christianised. The secular and sacred unified were brought among the savages, and, if you can believe the tales of the kingdom of Dahomey, among one of the most savage of savages.

The mission to Dahomey was a dream come true.

As is the nature of dreams, it was not wholly consistent.

A central sequence in *Le Dahomey Chrétien* concerns an African village fête for Jeanne d'Arc, orchestrated by Père Aupiais. It is patriotic and Christian.

The French national heroine is played by a village girl astride a horse in the spirit of medieval village mystery plays. The villagers play at the make-believe of being French. The play is an African playing. The Africans whoop it up, ear-to-ear smiles, wiggle, grin, laugh, a spontaneous mimicry and masquerade, the eruption of bodies.

Young black girls sashay.

They wear the white wings of angels with polka dots and the white grins of Africa shining against blackness, full bodies fluttering wings in a rhythm and beat to which no Christian wings had ever fluttered before. The bodies were not symbolic, not instruments to express a sacred. They *were* the sacred, the literal embodiment of it, possessed, taken by rhythm and movement, representing nothing, instead *being* something.

How was this to be understood?

Notes

1 'The abuse of individualism creates socialism; the abuse of industrialism gives birth to syndicalism; the abuse of socialism-syndicalism results in sovietism, sovietism in terrorism; from terrorism to despotism, from despotism to anarchy, from anarchy to licentiousness, from licentiousness to debauchery, from debauchery to exhaustion, from exhaustion to plague, to epidemics, to invasion, struggle without end.'

Chapter Twelve
Dahomey (3)

Ces danses sont des prières. Il faut nous mettre dans l'esprit que la danse là-bas est une prière. D'ailleurs c'est une prière dans un état d'inconscience, dans un état second. Les tams-tams qui battent ont une espèce de vertu magique grâce à laquelle ils mettent les danseurs dans un état d'inconscience … .

Ces danses ne sont peut-être pas très harmonieuses, il y a d'ailleurs moins harmonieuses encore. Mais elles ont une certaine gravité et on voit qu'elles sont faites sous le signe de la gravité de la religion. Ce qu'il faudrait pour nous rendre l'impression ce sont les tam-tams, et les chants … . [1]

Père Aupiais

Mais comment s'y prendre pour aborder par le commencement – l'étude des Religions Africaines? Il nous a paru que l'on devait recourir, pour ce travail à la méthode de la géographie humaine, c'est-à-dire, que l'on partirait de ce postulat: s'il est vrai que les religions sont une réalité a marqué d'une forte empreinte les hommes qui en vivent, comme le fait la terre, suivant les conditions du sol, du climat, de la végétation, etc., auxquelles elle soumet l'être humain; il n'est pas moins vrai qu'en face de la religion, les hommes comme ils l'ont fait pour le sol de leurs plaines, ou de leurs montagnes, se sont portés spontanément à des adaptations, à des manifestations d'activité, à des transformations adventices qui doivent

constituer un beau terrain d'étude des hommes dans l'observation de leur
habitation, de leurs procédés de culture, de leurs instruments de travail,
de leurs réactions devant les nécessités de la vie. L'étude des religions
pourra aussi comprendre l'observation de l'activité à la fois spirituelle et
matérielle des hommes dans leur prise de possession des cultes qu'ils ont
hérités de leurs ancêtres. [2]

Père Aupiais

L'ethnologie est une discipline qui est à la fois surannée et militante. Elle
est surannée parce qu'elle est exotique, qu'elle a un parfum colonialiste:
n'est-elle pas issue en grande partie des conquêtes coloniales? Et aussi
parce qu'elle étudie de préférence des traditions en voie de disparition.
Elle se penche davantage sur les manifestations religieuses, les techniques
dites primitives que sur l'évolution des problèmes actuels.

Mais c'est également une discipline qui est militante en ce sens que, si
des gens s'adonnent à l'ethnologie, quittent leur pays pour aller étudier
d'autres groupes, ce n'est pas simplement par curiosité: c'est en fait parce
qu'ils contestent leur propre civilisation.[3]

Jean Rouch

One

If 1913 is taken as a base year, increase in production in French Africa by
1925 was 135 per cent in chemical products, 325 per cent in colonial products, 155 per cent in oil products and 1120 per cent in metals. In France's
Asian empire the figures were 155 per cent for metals, 783 per cent for rub-
ber and 228 per cent for chemical products.

Labour shortages in Africa were acute. The French authorities resorted
to forced labour to maintain production. The methods used to induce
Africans to work were often brutal. The Africans were badly paid or not
paid at all.

Albert Kahn had 4 million francs invested in mining in the French
Congo.

His initial fortune was made on speculation in gold and diamonds in South Africa.

Two

Aupiais, despite his idealisations of the sense of the sacred among Africans, was in Africa to convert the Africans to Christianity. He thought of this work not as a displacement of religious sensibility, but as a continuation of it in a new direction within new forms. Issues of transformation and conversion, though confused and often vaguely thought, involved cultural and social questions, as well as intellectual and political ones of considerable moment.

Some of the assumptions in the geographical regionalism of *la géographie humaine* formed part of Aupiais's ideology and his missionary activities. To convert Africans and sustain their religious sense of the world, he needed to understand their world. To understand their world, he needed to observe it carefully, not through faith and hope but as it was, as understood by the Africans. His task was not to interpret, but to comprehend as objectively as possible. The African world could only be known, he believed, as it was lived by the Africans, in their terms, not how he would have liked things to have been or in order to make what he saw into something else. He had to free himself from what he expected of Africa in order to receive from it what it was. *La géographie humaine* and ethnography provided him with a methodology and an attitude.

The colonial geography of Dubois had regarded the colonies as a field for radical transformation. In its way, the Church did not have a dissimilar position: Africa needed to be transformed (saved) by the truth of Catholicism. The false pagan, animist and devilish religion, the false gods of paganism, to which Africans were hopelessly devoted, needed to be erased. Their destruction was the mission of the Church, its struggle against evil.

The Church believed itself to be not only a force for good in Africa, but of the modern, the benefactor of progress and civilisation, positions that the Church embraced or rejected according to circumstance.

That the Church was unhappy with the views expressed by Aupiais is as comprehensible as the unhappiness of Brunhes and Vidal with the geography of Dubois. Aupiais adopted a way of being in Africa that, despite his missionary vocation, was informed by the social sciences, the perspectives of ethnography and *géographie humaine*.

For the Church, Aupiais's sympathy for African religion was worse than inappropriate. Such sympathy and scientific attitude could end by accepting pagan religion as merely another religious manifestation, part of a universal sociology, and thereby would relativise all religions, including Catholicism. There would then be no true, one religion, no scale of values, but instead, a variety of religious practices and and an equality of beliefs.

Truth for the sciences was a truth irrespective of value or interpretation. The idea of truth as objective, multiple and relative, outside morality was, for the Church, the distinguishing mark of secularism.

Yet, as Aupiais knew and practised, to understand and recognise the truth of African religion as a universal sacredness required a passionate objectivity, not the passionate particularity of the Church.

The differences between the Church and Aupiais were crucial. They went to the heart of a modernist dilemma that had implications for geography and ethnography. Aupiais was committed to a scientific methodology in order to preserve and value in Africa a religiosity that a rationalist/scientific culture was undermining. Such religiosity could only be seen and appreciated for what it was by means of a morally neutral, ethically relativist and objective social science. The Church rejected science and its findings to proclaim instead a religious truth that it justified because it was truth and revelation, and because it had the benefits of civilisation on its side. In the colonies it had power on its side.

This too was part of a contradictory step forward.

Aupiais's idealism, and his belief that Dahomey was an ideal society, if not the Promised Land, combined with a social science methodology that was not without its own idealisations, had recommended Aupiais to Kahn.

Aupiais's path may have recalled for Kahn his own voyage to Japan and China, his own idealisations of a new society and new social order that the *Archives de la planète* at first embodied.

Three

A humanist, rationalist, modern Catholic, like Rossellini, who politically supported the positions of Italian Christian democracy, made a series of films with religious subjects for television of the early history of the Church (*Atti degli Apostoli* [1969], *Agostino d'Ippona* [1972], *Il Messia* [1975]). These films located the Church in a tradition of modernity, as contributing to Western thought and rationalism, as part of progress. It does not take away from the brilliance of these films to observe that they are ideologically positioned within a Catholicism trying to balance modernity with tradition and seeking political power to achieve that balance by ordering society in a certain direction.

Rossellini made the astonishing claim for his films that he simply showed things the way they were. He showed things for what he wanted them to be, all the more necessary and doggedly held because what he wanted coincided with what he insisted was true, thereby beyond debate.

Rossellini could be very testy with others for not seeing that he was right.

Four

Sometimes, like last night, I have dreams that seem to last the entire night, one succeeding another. There is no evident setting that connects these dreams.

One dream is in an operating theatre in Hong Kong. The surgeon is having lunch, chatting to me about what he will do to me, his instruments before him, as I lay watching, unable to change the course of what will happen.

Another dream, in Belfast, involves me sitting in my new car, watching in slow motion another car coming towards me, about to collide.

Another dream is in New York. I look for people and they are gone. I try to arrange meetings and they are cancelled.

In these dreams, in various places and of varied incidents, there is a common theme of helplessness regarding a future in which I know what will happen, and which I want to avoid, but can do nothing about.

In dreams, you are the spectator of yourself, the dreamer dreamt, astonished at a course of events beyond your will, out of your control. It is the nature of dream to be involuntary, concerning you, which you are inside and the subject of, but can only watch, unable to influence, the dream taking you along, despite you.

Last night, I suppose, these dreams were particularly vivid because during the day I had seen Fellini's Otto e mezzo, *a film of a dream as a nightmare of non-resolution and failure until the main character, Guido, the film director, realises that to succeed one needs to enter the dream and accept it, reinvent it, not regard it in a Freudian manner, to bring one to a cure. Instead, dreams need to be thought of as a way to deal with reality by entering into the fictions that reality provokes, becoming a character in one's films, as such, an invention in which you know that it is an invention and not thereby real, and that is the pleasure of it.*

But I did not dream a Fellini dream.

I dreamt a dream of no escape.

Five

The Dahomey film project, as it was sketched out, was, I presume, the result of discussions between Aupiais, Kahn, Bruhnes, and with others, possibly Lucien Lévy-Bruhl and Marcel Mauss.

It was decided to film six types of subjects or themes. These were to be

1. hospitals, schools, plantations, ceremonies, religious instruction;
2. picturesque scenes: hunting, fishing, agriculture, crafts, etc.;
3. moral aspects: manners, politeness, decency, personal dignity, family ceremonies, marriages, funerals;
4. African customs of child-rearing and caring for the sick;
5. examples of variations of the similar ceremonies among different tribal groups;
6. esoteric ceremonies of the fetishists, hypnotism, cataleptic fits, levitation, divination, exorcism, pacts with the devil, judicial ordeals.

The nearly seven hours of rushes are in accord with these categories, which are close to Brunhes's *géographie*. It was agreed between Kahn and the missionary society that the society would retain the material of the first three categories (pertinent to Christianisation *civilisation*) and that the *Archives* would retain the scientific material of the other three categories. There was some overlap.

Two films would be produced: *Le Dahomey Chrétien* for the mission (realised) and *Le Dahomey religieux*, for the *Archives* (not realised). It is probable that *Le Dahomey religieux* was not made because Aupiais was in difficulties with the Church. That film would have created worse problems.

Nevertheless, it is not difficult to see what *Le Dahomey religieux* would have been from the rushes.

The two films, actual and not, present two distinct realities conceived, however, as complementary.

The ethnographic filming of native life, *Le Dahomey religieux*, was intended to reveal the religiosity of African society pervading all aspects of African life from the most ritualised to the most everyday and functional. If the Africans erred in their beliefs, these nevertheless were presented in their religious spirit which might then be channelled towards the true faith. In other words, what linked Christianity and paganism was a universal sense of religiosity, the basis for a coming together.

Between *Le Dahomey religieux* and *Le Dahomey Chrétien* there is a logical continuity of pagan religious sentiment in the one directed into a new Christian path in the other. Christian conversion, the films suggest, was only a possibility because of a prior African religious sensibility. Such syncretism figured in the early history of the Church and in part guaranteed its success, of which the Jeanne d'Arc sequence is a perfect example of a religious blend and of religious populism.

Without the social/religious reality seen in the rushes for *Le Dahomey religieux* there would not have been the reality shown in *Le Dahomey Chrétien*. Only ethnography and *géographie humaine*, not the Church, were able to perceive and imagine *Le Dahomey religieux* and to perceive the social price and mechanisms that belonged to the experience of colonialism, social change and the French Catholic mission.

Six

Aupiais's originality rests in the permeability between two positions: one, that of progress and *civilisation*, and which was made evident; the other, of pagan religiosity, primitive sincerity, sacredness without hierarchy *and which was not permitted to appear.* It was the difference between a colonial/missionary reality and an African one. The latter was a Church and colonial nightmare.

The permeability raises questions of interest having to do with religion, modernity, the Church, and Africa, and with the cinema and its means, including its history.

Why did Père Aupiais choose to film this material? If he is presenting an argument about conversion and sacredness, why argue these in the film? Is there something about the cinema that accords with his argument?

African religiosity, the African sense of the sacred, as Aupiais understood it and as he learned it from Lévy-Bruhl, adhered to everything in African life and was within everything Africans did. What they did was physically expressed, in movement, primarily in dance. *'Ces danses sont des prières.'*

Film, able to capture movement, could alone capture, Aupiais believed, the African sacred made manifest in action.

African religion was performative and visible, not silent, solitary, not a matter of words, not of writing.

It was bodily, physical, concrete, suited to the cinema and to sciences of observation, alongside whose birth the cinema was born.

To film, for Aupiais, had nothing to do with ordinary language, nor narratives of events. It had to do with presenting the real in its object-ness, as it was, uninterpreted, the real as reality, the document of the real. The documentary ideal was an ideal of ethnographic fieldwork and of *géographie humaine.* The cinema shared with the new sciences, from which it had come (anatomy, optics, mechanics), a perspective and ideological frame, exactly what Aupiais required for his religious mission. It strengthened the mission because the cinema could render the real and thus reach the true. That true was served by the suppressed *Le Dahomey religieux* as modernism would be served by the substance of its content, which the Church, at every manifestation of modernism, opposed and where it could, censored.

It is in religiosity where Aupiais meets, if not Picasso, certainly Breton.

The Church maintained that sacred truth was not in the world of appear-

ances, but in the Word, in Scripture, in the Spirit. In Africa, Aupiais shock-
ingly found it in the body, in action, in the fête, in societies with a deficiency
of writing and an excess of the corporeal.

The Africans, for Aupiais, were religious in their *being in the world*.
Religion was an *embodiment*, not symbolic, not a representation, not the
gap but the overlap, the inclusion.

What Africans did and created, all their acts, were religious. The gap that
representation assumes, of writing standing for something else not there,
not seen, the image for an absence, did not belong to their universe. The
religious world was coextensive with *the* world. The absent was present. The
spirit was manifest. Religion was not an outside, a separation, which might
occasionally be entered or beckoned towards, invoked in religious representations and signs.

It was an everywhere.

It was in the contrast with Africa that it was possible to understand the
representational/symbolic Western aspect of Western art and of Western
Christian belief, and to see the partiality of Western thought and Christianity as a belief system, a way of conceptualising. Not only was religion
relativised but all cultural practices were causing them to lose their centre,
their universality, their legitimacy, their exclusivity and their hold, exactly
the fear of the Church and the danger it correctly sensed from Aupiais's
work.

African objects shared in a religiosity of being. Statues were not signs of
gods; they *were* gods. The tools that fashioned them, the wood and metal
from which they were fashioned, were not instruments to construct a religious object but belonged to the sacred.

Voodoo, for Aupiais, and what he believed was central to the religious sensibilities of Africans in Dahomey, was not to him superstition, the work of
the devil, but a constant, perpetual living-in-the-sacred. It included divination, incantation, communions, sacrifices (including human), cannibalism,
rituals of possession, that is, the dispossession of self and the manifestation
of possession within the community as a sacred community to be celebrated
in dance, theatre and ritual.

Aupiais condemned nothing of this, not even its apparently shocking aspects of ritual murder and cannibalism.

Africa was Aupiais's ideal world in harmony with itself because in harmony with the universe and the sacred, a world best apprehended by the sciences with their attention to the concrete, their reservations about interpretation, and by cinema, the means to re-embody and realise the concrete.

Aupiais believed that only the camera could see and make manifest the movement of social cohesion in religious possession and ritual. In sharing in the physical the camera could touch the spiritual *in* reality. He did not depict the act of praying (prayer is invisible), but prayer as movement, gesture, dance, the-being-the-reality-of-prayer, which the cinema was able to register, and record almost for the first time, a palpable sacred reality. You could touch it. It was made of flesh. And it was mysterious.

Le Dahomey religieux, though not fully constituted as a film, is one of the important documents of the modern cinema and evidence of the cinema's modernity.

In *Le Dahomey Chrétien*, a film of missionary propaganda, significance was what you added to images in a narrative stream as their interpretation. Added significance is absent from the unrealised *Le Dahomey religieux* and, I believe, would have been absent even if the film had been finished.

In *Le Dahomey religieux* the images are self-sufficient, as close as possible to the duplication of what is seen, the thing itself, the mirror of itself. The images touch the unspeakable, the superfluity of speech.

In that sense and to that degree they recall the splendid, directly ethnographic films of Jean Rouch.

Aupiais called African religion *cérémonialisme*, the fact of religion in the activity of it, the act of being religious in all actions only possible in Aupiais's Promised Land, discovered by Aupiais, as other explorers have, with modern instruments to guide him.

Notes

1   'These dances are prayers. We need to understand that dance is a prayer.
    Moreover, it is a prayer in a state of unconsciousness, a second state. The
    drums that beat have a magical quality thanks to which the dancers enter a
    state of unconsciousness ... .'
    'These dances are not always very harmonious, but there are others that are
    still less harmonious. But they have a solemnity and one can see that they
    are done under the sign of religious solemnity. We need to make ourselves
    aware of the impact of these drums, and the songs ... .'

2   'How does one begin to approach the study of African religion? It seems to
    us that one must have recourse to the methodology of human geography,
    that is, that one ought to proceed from this postulate: if it is true that
    religions have strongly marked human beings, as the earth too has been
    marked by soil conditions, climate and vegetation to which human beings
    have submitted, then is it no less true that, faced with religion, men, as they
    have done for the soil of plains or of mountains, have spontaneously
    adapted it, by their actions, by merely fortuitous changes, which, taken
    together, constitute an excellent field for the study of human beings by
    observing their habitation, agriculture, tools, in short, their responses to the
    necessities of life. The study of religion may also thereby include the
    observation of actions, both material and spiritual, as men take possession of
    the beliefs they have inherited from their ancestors.'

3   'Ethnology is a discipline both outdated and politically committed. It is
    outdated because it is exotic, scented with colonialism. Did it not issue in
    great part from colonial conquests? And also, because by preference it
    studies endangered traditions, and tends to favour religious manifestations,
    techniques thought to be primitive, rather than concentrating on current
    problems.
    But it is equally a discipline that is politically committed in the sense
    that if those who devote themselves to ethnology leave their own country in
    order to study other groups, it is not simply for the sake of curiosity, but
    because they contest their own culture.'

Chapter Thirteen
Congo

Il me parle de l'hypersensibilité de la race noire à l'égard de tout ce qui comporte de la superstition, de sa crainte du mystère, etc. – d'autant plus remarquable qu'il estime d'autre part le système nerveux de cette race beaucoup moins sensible que le nôtre – d'où résistance à la douleur, etc. Dans la subdivision du Moyen-Congo où d'abord il était administrateur, la coutume voulait qu'un malade, à la suite de sa convalescence, changeât de nom, pour bien marquer sa guérison et que l'être malade était mort. Et lorsque Morel, non averti, revenait dans un village, après une assez longue absence, pour recenser la population – telle femme, à l'appel de son ancien nom, tombait comme morte, de terreur ou de saisissement, dans une crise nerveuse semi-cataleptique si profonde qu'il fallait parfois plusieurs heures pour faire revenir à elle.[1]

André Gide

One

I shall be leaving for Belfast soon and you will remain in Hong Kong. This time being away is not like other times, however long the absences. This time I won't be returning.

To leave things behind is ambiguous. I am sorry (and find things to miss) and I am glad (because there are things I want to forget). The ambiguity is what lies between. I think myself glad, or make myself believe I am glad, because I can't handle the missing and see departing therefore as liberation, even when I know it is not. At least it will be definite.

Such fooling oneself can be a way to exist.

One can dislike what one needs and even what one loves. Dependence, even as you cling to it, is difficult to accept. I wonder, when I left A, if that was the time I loved her most. Leaving was a protest to make her sit up, force her to realise how desperate I had become in a relation that had grown stupid and empty. But she didn't notice. She only felt her own hurt, or perhaps felt nothing very much at all.

At this moment we are not getting on. The atmosphere is of mutual irritation at what we say or don't say to each other. Words, and silences, are equally empty. We are silent and we talk for the same reason, the inability to speak.

I recall the novels of Natalia Ginzburg.

I love her novels.

In them, all sentences are simple, direct. Each word and phrase, numbingly everyday, point to a universe of the not-said, and it is in this not-said, a terrible overwhelming unexpressed, in which everything is said, and which is the silent saying of her writing and its beauty.

Ginzburg says less than is meant, as James Joyce says more than is meant.

Meaning, in either case, is outside language, what it cannot reach.

Writings of absence and writings of excess are not that different. The trick is to find a writing that is exact, nothing more, nor less. Meaning is what is left out in Ginzburg and cannot be reached in Joyce. But their writing has need of this lack. Meaning conditions their writing because it is poignantly, sometimes dizzingly, absent. An exact writing would have no need of meaning, not even its absence.

Our words to each other have no meaning now, a kind of babble, too much and too little. We speak banalities that have nothing to do with us. Only a few days earlier everything we said seemed significant, as everything now is not.

The difference was in being happy and in not being happy.

How can this have come about?

Just as I have already left Hong Kong, though am not yet in Belfast, we are leaving each other too, now, before we have to.

We have made promises of a future in which we will be together once again.

But we are acting out the present with another future in mind. It is a way to get ready to leave. Leaving is to be nowhere, not yet.

I frighten and comfort myself with imaginings and frighten and comfort you with them. I suppose you must be doing the same, but only to yourself, not to me.

It is your generosity.

Two

André Gide documented forced-labour practices in his journal *Voyage au Congo* (1927). Gide dedicated *Voyage au Congo*, '*À la Mémoire de Joseph Conrad*'.[2]

Gide was 58 when he travelled to the Congo. He was accompanied by Marc Allégret. Marc Allégret was 27. Allégret made a film during the trip, *Voyage au Congo*, to which Gide lent his name. The film celebrates African bodies. Allégret became a film-maker when he returned from the Congo, making the kind of films the French *nouvelle vague* loathed.

Truffaut parodied Allégret in *La Peau douce*.

Allégret went to the Congo as Gide's secretary and lover. During the voyage he discovered the joys of pre-pubescent African girls, cheaply purchased. He was the son of a Presbyterian minister, Élie Allégret, who had been a father figure and spiritual guide to Gide, though only five years older than him.

The Gide and Allégret families were close. Élie Allégret had been to the Congo to establish a Presbyterian mission between 1889 and 1891. He returned to the Cameroons and Gabon during 1892 and 1903.

When Gide undertook his voyage to the Congo, it no longer existed in name. It had been absorbed in 1910 into *l'Afrique équatoriale française*. The French divided their African empire into two zones, *équatoriale* (AEF) and *occidentale* (AOF). The choice of the title *Voyage au Congo* referred to a complex past, literary, sentimental and psychological, dense. The past keeps the journal alive. It included Conrad, Gide's relation with Élie Allégret, his liberation from Allégret's religious/paternal influence. Gide first expressed this liberation in voyages he made to North Africa in 1893 and

1895, both erotically charged for him. The *Voyage* is a re-evocation of a past set of relations made poignant by Gide's consciousness of growing old as he is writing with Marc by his side.

In the Congo Marc Allégret liberated himself from his relation with Gide. Marc's relation to Gide mirrored Gide's earlier relation to Marc's father. Sometimes, Gide registered his regret at seeing things not shared with Marc, as if, without Marc as a witness, what he saw lacked substance.

The events reported by Gide were often transpositions of earlier events that Gide recalled. The journal is shadowed by a past not completely reconciled for which the journey is made to effect a reconciliation, a laying to rest of disturbances from the past. It was also shadowed by a sense of termination in a future: ageing, the last journey, the end of an affair.

Gide is divided between the writer who writes and the subject written. The gap is played out in memories, each step forward tracked by the past.

Gide and Allégret were transported through the bush on litters by African bearers. The litters were like hammocks serving as sedan chairs, made available to Gide, and made possible, by the colonial authorities whose forced labour Gide condemned while availing himself of it. Travel by other means was not feasible.

African boys carried trunk loads of Gide's books. This had been a way of travel to French writers in the 19th century who brought their libraries with them. Chateaubriand, during his travels in the Near East, had donkeys bearing the burden of his erudition. Perhaps one was called 'Balthasar'.

Scattered through Gide's journal are comments on Corneille, on Latin poets, on other writers that he consulted. Africa is a literary site for him, often classical, variants of ancient Greece and Rome. This was a convention and cliché of travel diaries that transformed primeval landscapes into literary and classical ones, for example those of Virgil and Pindar.

What Gide saw was familiar because it evoked images from books. And it was familiar because it evoked memories. The familiar was made unreal because it was made part of a stream of images to which every event returned and into which it was absorbed.

Gide himself was an image of his writing. He belonged to writing, to which the journal delivered him and to which he delivered himself on a daily basis. The journal creates him, a literary figure journeying through references.

Three

Gide and Allégret arrived at Cotonou, in Dahomey, by ship towards the end of 1926. There was no deep-water harbour. Like Père Aupiais, they disembarked in a small lighter. The lighter was rowed close to the shore, to which they were hoisted in a basket held by a crane and which the film records. In *Le Dahomey Chrétien* there is a similar sequence of nuns brought ashore, their winged white habits fluttering in the breeze like exotic birds.

Gide and Allégret crossed the Belgian Congo and the AEF (the Cameroons, Gabon, the Middle Congo, Oubangui–Chari, Chad) to Bangui by rail, boat, car, foot and litter.

In Allégret's film, Africans dance, work, walk, flirt, court, make love, hunt, gather, play push-ball, wrestle, bathe. The emphasis is on their bodies. The film has images of the exotic, as in the first films of the cinema. It capitalised on the vogue for the exotic which it embellishes. It authenticates a fantastic, serving itself by the capacity of the cinema and its images to make the real fantastic.

Allégret's exotic is vulgar and oversimple.

Four

Voyage au Congo begins with two initiations.

One, the initiation of Allégret into Africa which brings him to a situation, figuratively and literally, of liberation: growing up, desire, power, coming to manhood. Allégret had come to Africa in the shadow of Gide. To make a film was to make something his own.

The other, the sexual initiation of young Africans into adulthood in rites of circumcision which Allégret films. In this scene, Allégret moves to a fiction centred on a courtship and marriage.

The African bodies are beautiful. Shiny, black, smooth, muscled, graceful, shy. The girls are exquisite. Young, full-bottomed, full-breasted, long-legged, caressed by the camera.

The subjects are carefully posed, each gesture worked and staged.

Gide complained that Allégret struggled to find natural gestures and postures that never were natural because they were posed. Nothing was ever found, he said, or spontaneous. The natural existed only when the camera no longer turned.

Gide describes a scene of a baby resisting being breast-fed, feeling satiated after a series of takes and refusing the breast. When Allégret had given up, the baby peacefully suckled the breast, the real lost forever.

Writing could recall this loss by duplicating it in words. Film lacked this power, being dependent on the object. Gide insists on the distinction.

Inside the settings of landscape, village, and the dailiness of African life, a courtship is staged between Djimta and Kaddé. The marriage celebration is ethnographic and fictional, each lending itself to the other. The ethnography authenticates the fiction, the fiction dramatises the ethnography. The ethnography is made of images of the real; the fiction is the narrative of it which signifies.

Reality appears more real because it is narrativised. The narrative appears real because it is documentarised. There is a double dishonesty because doubly denied.

Allégret achieved a scenic naturalism, a make-believe in the guise of a seeming-true, a consistency where the real blends with the contrived. This was not a reality that would disturb but an illusion of the real to give comfort from which all edge had been erased.

Posing the Africans was posing them in order that they might seem true. This truth was entirely conventional. The Africans act out a role given to them in conformity to the images of Africa that Allégret believed to suit

Africans and which others might thereby best appreciate as genuinely and realistically African.

Gide negotiated his understanding of Africa with a literary past he brought with him, not in order to make Africa conform to literature, but rather to transform Africa by the literary. Allégret sought out a conformity to the vulgar. When Gide came across an African site, he seized upon it in its immediacy, something which surprised him, disturbed him, and thereby provoked a reflection. Allégret brought images with him, not to negotiate, but to confirm.

No surprise. No reflection.

Had Gide's suggestions on spontaneity been heeded, consistency would have been sacrificed. Because then there would have been more than a single reality. The reality filmed would have been faced with the reality of its filming. There would have then been multiple worlds and perspectives, the uncertain positions of the subject filming and subjects filmed, not this smoothness that cheapens everything, including the erotic.

In *Voyage au Congo*, the two families of Djimta and Kaddé dance in an illuminated night. The camera dwells on the sensuality of the spectacle. The dancers form a circle for Djimta and Kaddé to dance a dance of love. There is a scene of intimacy between them. They touch, stroke each other, fondle, caress.

They are shy, passionate, giggly, aroused.

Gide's *Voyage au Congo* was published in 1927. Allégret's film was presented the same year.

This was a period in Paris when African art was fashionable and *négro* and black culture celebrated. Black and African cultures were used to redefine modernity, a going towards an interior heart of darkness seen to be at the heart of a new art and a new freedom. Nightclubs, drugs, jazz, sex, rhythm, Joséphine Baker.

'la négromanie ... jazz déchirants ... charlestons épileptiques. Dans nos music-halls, au théâtre, la noire vaut deux blancs.'[3]

Five

Could it be that the *Archives de la planète* is the creation of an ideal world in miniature, an extensive diorama, cities built to a small scale, the world shrunk for storage in the space of a room?

This world is ordered (because you can choose its elements), but left uninterpreted (because each element is a simulacrum of the real). The order is the key. You may claim that the order has been dictated to you by what is, as you might say a dream comes to you.

Some things you leave out that might disturb order, unlike a dream which is always a disturbance, which you cannot shape and is the shape of you.

The planet created by the *Archives* consists of regions. The regions are composed of nations, their traditions, landscapes and features. The traditions have their peoples and their priests. And the traditions and the priests help to form a life in accord with a geography and a region.

Only postage stamps are lacking.

Life does not escape beyond the borders of this world. It is hermetically sealed, an imaginary with impermeable borders because the world is in *autochromes* and the *autochrome* is fixed because it is an image, and real because it seems to be and is wanted to be.

The *Archives* are a way to possess an ideal without having to face that it no longer exists. Each *autochrome* traces a disappearance. Like ethnography, the geographical–photographic collection accumulates fragments of a passing. By means of it one can insist on an ideal, not as reality, but as that set against it, a form of reality, reality against time, reality as imagination, as dream, as fantastic.

It is the temptation of the *Archives*.

It invites you to journey not by its consistencies, but by its lack of them. These gaps are its opportunity.

Notes

1   'He speaks of the hyper-sensibility of the black race as regards everything that has to do with superstition, their fear of mystery, etc. – which are all the

more remarkable because he thinks, on the other hand, that their nervous system is much less sensitive than ours – whence their resistance to pain, etc. In the subdivision of the Middle Congo, where he was at first stationed, custom demanded that a sick man on his recovery should change his name, to make it quite clear that he was cured and that the person who had been ill was dead. And when Morel, who was unaware of this, came back to a village after rather a long absence, to make a census of the population, a woman's terror and shock at hearing her old name would often be so great that she would fall down as if she were dead, in a semi-cataleptic fit, which it would sometimes take hours to get her out of.' (Translation: Dorothy Bussy)

2   'To the Memory of Joseph Conrad'.

3   'negro mania ... agonizing jazz ... epileptic charlestons. In our music halls, in our theatres, a black is worth two whites.'

Chapter Fourteen
The Promised Land

... slouching towards Bethlehem to be born.

W. B. Yeats

One

I was sent to live with my grandmother almost as soon as I was born. Except for a few troubled years, I never lived at home. When I did, it never felt like home, whatever home was supposed to feel like.

Home was something I missed, but seemed never to reach.

Sometimes, when I am in new places, I imagine them as possible homes, since I have not arrived there from any place in particular. I think, rather I project, 'I shall buy a house here.' In Stromboli, perhaps, or Paris, or Gaillac, or Rome, or Ascoli Piceno, even places I have never known. Kerala, for example, or Madagascar.

When I was in London in 1960, I took a job teaching in a school in Nigeria, in a small village. On the flight out to Nigeria, I stopped in Rome, where I had never been before. As with other places, before and since, with which I have no connection, Rome seemed wonderful. I was there for about a fortnight. In the last week, I fell in love with an American girl called Diana who I befriended in the Villa Borghese.

We were very innocent. She spoke Italian and I did not. We had dinner in a small trattoria near Piazza Navona. Every night I was in love with Diana and ate mussels in the trattoria and felt nothing was real. She had auburn hair to her waist. Her eyes were brown and she always laughed at me and I always lied to her.

I have been back to Rome each year since then. Each year I have looked for the trattoria and never found it, as if it was never there.

I don't know what happened to Diana.

Perhaps it was the fact of looking for something that was not and was only remembered as it should be that duplicated my sense of home. Italy, more particularly Rome, became an adopted home. I am not sure who adopted who, but Rome was where I always returned, just as one returns to home.

Eventually, I found friends in Italy and I created one of them and his children as a fictitious adopted family.

That relation no longer exists.

Two

Almost as soon as I began this book, I knew its ending.

It would be a quotation from a book of the end of a journey which is a book of a (perilous) journey.

The journey is a search for home. Home is found by its characters at the end though it is a fictional place, imagined (the Promised Land), and in the wrong place. They arrive at home inadvertently. It needs someone to tell them they have arrived, that this place they never knew existed was their home.

What was home to them? Home was where they would no longer be strangers, where there would be no gap.

I held to this ending from the beginning of the book without, during the entire time of writing, returning to it. I knew the ending well. I had cried over it. It had moved me enormously. It was my ending. I could not imagine a time when I would feel any different as I did when I first read the book.

When I read the ending, I felt I had come home too.

I returned to it now, and the ending was gone. It had become something else, weaker than my feelings, not at all as I remembered, flat, irrelevant to me, another home lost.

At first, I decided to put it in the book anyway. I had held on to it for so long and it had guided me, I thought. It has not been easy to write this book. It had no form to follow, no place to arrive at, no centre to hold things together. I wrote the passage out from the book in translation. It was more flat in English than in Italian. I put it aside and restored it to the original Italian. But it simply did not work. It meant very little to me.

The ending would have come from near the close of Primo Levi's first novel, Se non ora, quando? (If Not Now, When?).

It is the story of a Russian–Polish guerrilla unit of Jews during the war who make their way across the Soviet Union, into Poland, Germany, Austria, eventually reaching Italy on their way to Palestine, the Promised Land. For the entire, miserable journey, they have experienced everything, including death and killing.

When they arrive in Italy, almost at the end of the war, they are on a train, in a box car exactly like those that carried the Jews to the death camps, and like the one that carried Primo Levi to Auschwitz, from which he returned to Turin, where he later killed himself. They alight from the box car and meet with four Jewish soldiers from Palestine who had joined with the British forces when the British invaded Italy with the Americans in 1943.

One of these soldiers speaks Yiddish and thus the Russian and Polish Jews and the assorted Jews from Palestine can converse in a language and culture virtually extinguished by the Nazi German final solution.

The Russian–Polish guerrillas want to know where they are, what Italy is, and Chaim, the Jew from Palestine, tells them.

What he tells them is a tale of tolerance.

'Italy is different,' he says.

What I remembered was the rose-pinks of Italy, the smells of the trattoria where I had been with Diana, a noisiness, the casual, nonchalant, effortless beauty of Italian taste, dusk in the Borghese Gardens, a sensuality that enveloped me everywhere, a warmth that was maternal but allowed me to breathe.

Home indeed. It was that loss and that refinding that had made me weep.

But I had made it up.

Nothing of it was there.

Chapter Fifteen
Of Exactitude in Science

From Jorge Luis Borges:

In that Empire, the craft of Cartography attained such Perfection that the Map of a Single province covered the space of an entire City, and the Map of the Empire itself an entire Province. In the course of Time, these Extensive maps were found somehow wanting, and so the College of Cartographers evolved a Map of the Empire that was of the same Scale as the Empire and that coincided with it point for point. Less attentive to the Study of Cartography, succeeding generations came to judge a map of such Magnitude cumbersome, and, not without Irreverence, they abandoned it to the Rigours of sun and Rain. In the western Deserts, tattered fragments of the Map are still to be found, Sheltering an occasional Beast or beggar; in the whole Nation, no other relic is left of the Discipline of Geography.

From *Travels of Praiseworthy Men* (1658) by J. A. Suarez Miranda

Bibliography

Les Archives de la planète

Beausoleil, Jeanne (ed.), *Villages et villageois au Tonkin 1915–1920* (Paris: Collections Albert Kahn, 1986).

—— (ed.), *Irlande 1913* (Paris: Collections Albert Kahn, 1988).

—— (ed.), *Albert Kahn et le Japon. Confluences* (Paris: Collections Albert Kahn, 1990).

—— (ed.), *L'Auvergne au quotidien 1911–1917* (Paris: Musée Albert Kahn, 1992).

—— (ed.), *Pour une reconnaissance africaine: Dahomey 1930* (Boulogne: Musée Albert Kahn, 1996).

Berthier, Gilles Baud, *Commerces d'Asie: Autochromes & Noir et Blanc 1908–1927* (Boulogne: Musée Departmental Albert Kahn, 1994).

Brunhes, Jean, *La géographie humaine: essai de classification positive* (Paris: Alcan, 1910).

—— 'Ethnographie et géographie', *L'Ethnographie,* nouvelle série, n.1, 1913, pp.29–40.

—— *Human Geography* (abridged) (London: George G. Harrap, 1952).

Brunhes, Jean et C. Vallaux, *La Géographie de l'histoire: géographie de la paix et de la guerre sur terre et sur mer* (Paris: Félix Alcan, 1921).

Gendrot, Carine, *Le Renouvellement du regard sur le monde à travers les Archives de la Planète: analyse du fonds photographiques sur l'Indochine* (Thèse), Université de Paris I Panthéon-Sorbonne, 1996.

Mattera-Corneloup, Marie, *A l'ombre d'Angkor: Le Cambodge années vingt* (Boulogne: Musée Albert Kahn, 1992).

Musée Albert Kahn, *Autour du monde: Jean Brunhes, regards d'un géographe, regards de la géographie* (Boulogne: Musée Albert Kahn, 1993).

—— *Albert Kahn: réalités d'une utopie 1860–1940* (Marseille: Musée Albert Khan, 1995).

Cinema

A Vicious Motive, Despicable Tricks – A Criticism of Antonioni's Anti-China Film 'China' (Beijing: Peking Foreign Languages Press, 1974 [an eighteen-page pamphlet that reproduces an article that appeared in *Renminh Ribao*, 30 January 1974]).

Agel, H., *Un Art de célébration, le cinéma de Flaherty à Rouch* (Paris: Éditions du Cerf, 1987 [*BIFI 26 AGE u*]).

Anon., *Robert Flaherty, photographer/filmmaker. The Inuit, 1910–1922* (Vancouver: Vancouver Art Gallery, 1979–80).

Andrew, Dudley, 'L'Afrique vue par le cinéma français pendant l'époque coloniale' in C. W. Thompson (ed.), *L'Autre et le sacré: surréalisme, cinéma, ethnologie* (Paris: Éditions L'Harmattan, 1995, pp.283–305).

Anon., 'Les actualités reconstitués de George Méliès', *Archives* n.21, mars 1989, Institut Jean Vigo-Cinémathèque de Toulouse.

Aubert, Michelle, 'Cinéma d'actualité et institution militaire en France de 1914–1918' in Michel Lagny, Michel Marie, Jean A. Gili and Vincent Pinel (eds), *Les Vingt premières années du cinéma français* (Paris: Presses de la Sorbonne Nouvelle, 1995, pp.371–6).

Audouin-Dubreuil, Louis, *La Croisière jaune: Carnets de route de Louis Audouin-Dubreuil, 4 avril 1931–12 février 1932* (Boulogne-Billancourt: Éditions de l'Albaron, 1992).

Aumont, Jacques, *L'oeil interminable, Cinéma et peinture* (Paris: Librairie Séguier, 1989).

Aumont, Jacques, André Gaudréault and Michel Marie, *Histoire du Cinéma, Nouvelles approches* (Paris: Publications de la Sorbonne, 1989).

Baliikci, Asen 'Anthropologists and Ethnographic Filmmaking' in J. R. Rollwagen (ed.), *Anthropological Filmmaking* (Chur: Harwood Academic, 1988).

Baker, Steve, 'The Hell of Connotation', *Word and Image* v.1, n.2, 1985, pp.164–75.

Baudry, Jean-Louis, 'The Apparatus', *Camera Obscura*, n.1, 1976 pp.104–26 (originally published as 'Le dispositif', *Communications*, n.23, 1975, pp.56–72).

—— 'Cinéma: Effets idéologiques produits par l'appareil de base', *Cinéthique*, nn.7–8, 1979, pp.1–8.

Baudry, Pierre, 'Terrains et territoires. Cinéma documentaire–Cinéma de fiction', *La Licorne*, n.24, 1992 Université de Poitiers.

Bazin, André, 'Montage interdit' (1953,1957) in *Qu'est-ce que le cinéma?* (Paris: Les Éditions du Cerf, 1981, pp.48–62).

—— 'Le Cinéma d'exploration' (1953,1954) in *Qu'est-ce que le cinéma?* (Paris: Les Éditions du Cerf, 1981, pp.25–34).

—— 'Le Monde du silence' (1956) in *Qu'est-ce que le cinéma?* (Paris: Les Éditions du Cerf, 1990, pp.35–40).

Bellour, Raymond, 'L'Arrière-monde', *Cinémathèque*, n.8, automne 1995, pp.6–11.

Bensmaïa, Reda, 'Jean Rouch ou le cinéma de la cruauté' in Réné Prédal, *Jean Rouch, un griot gaulois* (numéro spécial de *CinémAction*), *CinémAction*, n.17, 1982.

Beylie, Claude, 'Compte rendu de Rouch: *Les fils de l'eau*', *Cahiers du cinéma*, n.91, 1959, pp.66–7.

—— 'La chasse à la vérité à l'arc' in Réné Prédal, *Jean Rouch, un griot gaulois* (numéro spécial de *CinémAction*), *CinémAction*, n.17, 1982.

Blakeway, Claire, *Jacques Prévert. Popular French Theatre and Cinema* (London and Toronto: Associated University Presses, 1990).

Blin, Roger, '*La Croisière noire*', *La Revue du cinéma*, v.II, 1930.

Bloom, Peter, 'A travers le miroir cinématographique' in *L'Autre et Nous* (Paris: Syros,1995).

Bordes, Raymond and Charles Perrin, *Les Offices du cinéma éducateur* (Lyons: Presses universitaires de Lyons, 1992).

Boulanger, Pierre, *Le Cinéma colonial de 'l'atlantide' à 'Lawrence d'Arabie'* (Paris: 1975 [*BIFI 10 BOU c*]).

Bousquet, H. (ed.), *Catalogue Pathé des années 1896 à 1914: Années 1907, 1908, 1909* (Paris: H. Bousquet, 1993).

Braun, Marta, *Picturing Time: the Work of Étienne-Jules Marey, 1830–1904* (Chicago: University of Chicago Press, 1992).

Breton, Émile, 'Mettre en circulation des objets inquiétants', *La Nouvelle Critique* n.82, 1975, pp.74–8.

Brigard, Emilie de, 'Historique du film ethnographique' in Claudine de France (ed.), *Pour une anthropologie visuelle* (Paris: Mouton, Paris 1979, pp.21–51).

Brunius, Jacques-Bernard, 'Le Cinéma et l'amour', *La Revue du cinéma,* v.I, décembre 1928.

—— 'Hallelujah', *La Revue du cinéma*, v.XI, 1930, pp.34–7.

—— 'Evolution des films nègres I', *Documents 33,* n.7, 1933, pp.6–8

—— 'Evolution des films nègres II', *Documents 33,* n.8, 1933, pp.4–8

Cahiers de la Cinémathèque, 'Cinéma et histoire, Histoire du cinéma', *Cahiers de la Cinémathèque,* nn.35/36, 1982.

Cardinal, Roger, 'Les Arts marginaux et l'esthétique surréaliste' in C. W. Thompson (ed.), *L'Autre et le sacré: surréalisme, cinéma, ethnologie* (Paris: Éditions L'Harmattan, 1995, pp.51–71).

Carné, Marcel, 'Le cinéma à la conquête du monde', *Ciné-Magazine,* octobre 1930.

—— 'L'exotisme au cinéma. En marge de l'Exposition coloniale', *Ciné-Magazine,* juillet 1931.

Certoni, Albert, 'Confrontation entre Sembene Ousmane et Jean Rouch', *France Nouvelle,* n.1033, 4–10 août 1965.

Chardère, Bernard, 'On commence quand?' in Michel Lagny, Michel Marie, Jean A. Gili and Vincent Pinel (eds), *Les Vingt premières années du cinéma français* (Paris: Presses de la Sorbonne Nouvelle, 1995, pp.377–84.)

'Cinéma documentaire, cinéma de fiction. Frontières et passages', *La Licorne,* 1992, Université de Poitiers.

'Le Cinéma et la vérité', *Artsept,* n.2, avril–juin 1963 (*BIFI*).

Cinémas et réalités, Travaux XLI: Université de Saint-Étienne (CIEREC): 1984.

Colleyn, Jean-Paul, *Le regard documentaire,* (Paris: Editions du Centre Pompidou, 1993).

Convents, Guido, *Préhistoire du cinéma en Afrique 1897–1918. A la recherche des images oubliées* (Brussels: OCIC, 1986).

Cooper, Merian C., *Grass* (New York: G. P. Putnam's Sons, 1925).

Cosandey, Roland and François Albera, *Cinéma sans frontières 1896–1918*
(Lausanne: Éditions Payot, 1995).

Crawford, Peter Ian, 'Film as Discourse: the Invention of Anthropological
Realities' in Peter Ian Crawford and David Turton (eds), *Film as Ethnography*
(Manchester: Manchester University Press, 1992).

Crawford, Peter Ian and David Turton (eds), *Film as Ethnography* (Manchester:
Manchester University Press, 1992).

Damisch, H., 'Au risque de la vue' in *Peinture–Cinéma–Peinture* (Paris:
Hazan/Direction des musées de Marseille, 1989).

De Heusch, Luc, 'The Cinema and Social Science: A Survey of Ethnographic
and Sociological Films', *Visual Anthropology* v.1, n.2, 1987, pp.99–156.

Delmeulle, Frédéric, 'Gaumont et la naissance du cinéma d'enseignement
(1909–1914)' in Michel Lagny, Michel Marie, Jean A. Gili and Vincent Pinel
(eds), *Les Vingt premières années du cinéma français* (Paris: Presses de la
Sorbonne Nouvelle, 1995, pp.67–76).

Desanti, D. and J. Decock, 'Cinéma et ethnographie', *Arts d'Afrique*, n.1, 1968,
pp.37–9, 76–80.

Deslandes, Jacques, *le Boulevard du cinéma à l'époque de Georges Méliès* (Paris:
Editions du Cerf, 1963).

Deslandes, Jacques and Jacques Richard, *Histoire comparée du cinéma*, 2 vol.
(Paris: Casterman, 1966–8).

Devarrieux, Claire and Marie-Christine de Navacelle (eds), *Cinéma et réel* (Paris:
Autrement, 1988).

Dieterlen, Germaine, 'Entretien avec Germaine Dieterlen à propos de Marcel
Griaule et du cinéma ethnographique' in C. W. Thompson (ed.), *L'Autre et le
sacré: surréalisme, cinéma, ethnologie* (Paris: Éditions L'Harmattan, 1995,
pp.433–41).

Domarchi, Jean, 'Présence de F. W. Murnau', *Cahiers du cinéma*, v.IV, n.21, mars
1953, pp.3–11.

Dubois, Philippe, 'Vue panoramique: l'affaire Marey–Lumière ou la question
cinéma:photographie révisée' in Michelle Lagny, Michel Marie, Jean A. Gili
and Vincent Pinel (eds), *Les Vingt premières années du cinéma français* (Paris:
Presses de la Sorbonne Nouvelle, 1995, pp.417–32).

Dumas, Marie-Claire (ed.), *Les Rayons et les ombres, cinéma* (Paris: Éditions Gallimard, 1992).

Dureau, G, 'Une exposition Coloniale à Marseille: la cinématographe coloniale', *Ciné-Journal,* n.257, 26 juillet 1913, pp.4–5.

Durgnat, Rayond and Scott Simon, *King Vidor, American* (Berkley: University of California Press, 1988).

Durosay, Daniel, 'Images et imaginaire dans le *Voyage au Congo*: un film de deux "auteurs"', *Bulletin des Amis d'André Gide,* n.80, octobre 1988, pp.9–30.

Earle, Edward W. (ed.), *Points of View: The Stereograph in America: A Cultural History,* (Rochester: Visual Studies Workshop Press, 1979).

Eaton, Mick, *Anthropology – Reality – Cinema. The Films of Jean Rouch* (London: British Film Institute, 1979).

Eaton, Mick and Ivan Ward 'Anthropology and Film', *Screen,* v.20, nn.3–4, Autumn–Winter 1979–1980.

Echard, Nicole and Paul Stoller, *The Cinematic Griot: the Ethnography of Jean Rouch* (Chicago: University of Chicago Press, 1992).

Edwards, Elizabeth (ed.), *Anthropology and Photography, 1860–1920* (New Haven: Yale University Press, 1992).

Elsaesser, Thomas, 'The New Film History', *Sight and Sound,* Autumn 1986.

Esien, Ingrid, 'Des identités marginales aux rites de possession dans les films de Jean Rouch' in C. W. Thompson (ed.), *L'Autre et le sacré: surréalisme, cinéma, ethnologie* (Paris: Éditions L'Harmattan, 1995, pp.349–68).

Feld, Steven (ed.), *Studies in Visual Communication,* 11, n.1, Winter 1985.

—— 'Themes in the Cinema of Jean Rouch', *Visual Anthropology,* n.2, 1989.

Ferro, Marc, *Cinéma et histoire* (Paris: Denoel-Gonthier, 1977, and a new edition published by Éditions Gallimard, 1993).

Fescourt, Henri, *La Foi et la montagne* (Paris: Paul Montel, 1959).

Fieschi, Jean-André, ? *Cahiers du cinéma,* n.168, juillet 1965.

—— 'Dérives de la fiction. Notes sur le cinéma de Jean Rouch' in Dominique Noguez, *Cinéma, théorie, lectures* (Paris: Klincksieck, 1973).

Flaherty, F. H., 'Setting up House and Shop in Samoa', *Asia,* n.25, 1925, pp.638–51, 709–11.

—— 'Behind the Scenes with our Samoan Stars', *Asia,* n.25, 1925, pp.746–53, 795–6.

—— 'A Search for Animal and Sea Sequences', *Asia*, n.25, 1925, pp.954–63, 1000–04.

—— 'Fa'a-Samoa', *Asia*, n.25, 1925, pp.1084–90, 1096–1100.

France, Claudine de (ed.), *Pour une anthropologie visuelle* (Paris: Mouton, 1979).

—— *Cinéma et anthropologie* (Paris: Maison des sciences de l'homme, 1984).

Frizot, Michel, *Avant le cinématographe: la chronophotographie* (Beaune: Association des Amis de Marey et Ministère de la Culture, 1984).

Gardner, R. G., 'Anthropology and film', *Daedalus*, n.86, 1957, pp.344–50.

Gaudenzi, Laure, *La Danse au cinéma des origines à 1906, Constitution et analyse d'une filmographie internationale* (Mémoire de maîtrise) (Paris: Université Paris III–Sorbonne Nouvelle, 1990).

Gaudreault, André, *Du littéraire au filmique, système du récit* (Paris: Meridiens-Klincksieck, 1988).

—— *Ce que je vois de mon ciné ...* (Paris: Meridiens-Klincksieck, 1988).

—— *Pathé 1900, fragments d'une filmographie analytique du cinéma des premiers temps* (Laval: Presses de l'Université de Laval, 1992).

Gauthier, Guy, *Le documentaire un autre cinéma* (Paris: Éditions Nathan, 1995).

Gianikian, Yervant and Angela Ricci Lucchi, 'Notre caméra analytique', *Trafic*, n.13, hiver 1995, pp.32–40 (in Italian in *Griffithiana*, nn.29–30, settembre 1987).

Gide, André, [a defence of the film] in *Les Nouvelles littéraires*, 23 juin 1928, p.1; reprinted in *Bulletin des Amis d'André Gide*, n.80, octobre 1988, pp.31–6.

Gili, Jean A. 'Les débuts du spectacle cinématographique en France' *1895*, *Bulletin de l'Association Française de Recherche sur l'Histoire du Cinéma*, n.3, 1987, pp.17–24.

Godard, Jean-Luc, 'Jean Rouch remporte le prix Delluc' in Alain Bergala (ed.), *Jean-Luc Godard par Jean-Luc Godard* (Paris: Cahiers du cinéma–Éditions de l'Étoile, 1985, p.155; reprinted from *Arts*, n.701, 17 décembre 1958).

—— 'Étonnant', *Arts*, n.715, 25 mars 1959; reprinted in Alain Bergala (ed.), *Jean-Luc Godard par Jean-Luc Godard* (Paris: Cahiers du cinéma–Editions de l'Étoile, 1985, pp.177–8).

—— 'L'Afrique vous parle de la fin et des moyens', *Cahiers du cinéma*, n.94, avril 1959; reprinted in Alain Bergala (ed.), *Jean-Luc Godard par Jean-LucGodard* (Paris: Cahiers du cinéma–Editions de l'Étoile, 1985, pp.180–2).

—— 'Un cinéaste c'est aussi un missionaire. Jean-Luc Godard fait parler Roberto Rossellini', *Cahiers du cinéma*, n.94, avril 1959; reprinted in Alain Bergala (ed.), *Jean-Luc Godard par Jean-Luc Godard* (Paris: Cahiers du cinéma–Editions de l'Étoile, 1985, pp.187–90).

—— *Introduction à une veritable histoire du cinéma* (Paris: Albatros, 1980).

Goldner, Orville and George E. Turner, *The Making of King Kong* (New York: A. S. Barnes, 1975).

Haardt, Georges-Marie and Louis Audouin-Dudreuil, *La Première traversée du Sahara en automobile* (Paris: Plon, 1923).

—— *De Touggourt à Tombouctou par l'Atlantide* (Paris: Plon, 1923).

Hansen, Miriam, 'Benjamin, Cinema and Experience: The Blue Flower in the Land of Technology', *New German Critique*, n.40, winter 1987, pp.179–224.

Iris, Pour une théorie de l'histoire du cinéma, v.2, n.2, Paris: Analeph, 2e semèstre, 1984 *(BIFI)*.

Jadot, J. M. 'Le cinéma au Congo Belge', *Institut Royal Colonial Belge Bulletin des Scéances*, v.XX, n.1, Brussels, 1949, pp.407–37.

Jordan, Pierre-L, *Cinéma* (Marseille: Musées de Marseille–Images en Manoeuvres Éditions, 1992).

Kramer, Robert, 'Pour vivre hors-la-loi, tu dois être honnête' in *Dans le réel la fiction* (Paris: GNCR, 1994).

Kuenzli, Rudolph (ed.) *Dada and Surrealist Film* (New York: Willis, Locker & Owens, 1987).

Kyrou, Ado, 'Amour-érotisme au cinéma', *Le Terrain Vague*, 1957.

—— 'Le Surréalisme au cinéma', *Le Terrain Vague*, 1963.

Lacassin, Francis, 'Machin', *Anthologie du cinéma*, n.39, novembre 1968, pp.433–96.

—— *Alfred Machin 1877–1929* (Paris: 1968).

Lagny, Michèle, *de l'Histoire du cinéma. Méthode historique et histoire du cinéma* (Paris: Armand Colin, 1992).

Lagny, Michèle, Michel Marie, Jean A. Gili and Vincent Pinel (eds), *Les Vingt premières années du cinéma français* (Paris: Presses de la Sorbonne Nouvelle, 1995).

Landay, Maurice, 'Propagande et cinéma. Le film colonial', *La Dépêche Coloniale*, 3 septembre 1918, pp.1–2.

—— 'Propagande et cinéma. Les leçons cinématographiques coloniales', *La Dépêche Coloniale,* 6 septembre 1918, p.1.

Lardeau, Yann, 'Un drame de la sauvagerie', *Cahiers du cinéma,* n.490, avril 1995.

Lebensztejn, Jean-Claude, *Zigzag* (Paris: Flammarion, 1981).

Lefèvre, Raymond, 'Le cinéma colonial' in Nicolas Bancel, Pascal Blanchard and Laurent Gervereau, *Images et colonies. Iconographie et propagande coloniale sur l'Afrique française de 1880 à 1962* (Paris: BDIC [Nanterre] and ACHAC [Paris], 1993 pp.170–73).

Le Men, S., *Lanternes magiques, tableaux transparents* (Paris: RMN, 1995).

Leprohon, Pierre, *L'Exotisme et le cinéma. Les chasseurs d'images à la conquête du monde* (Paris: Les Éditions J. Susse, 1945).

Leprun, Sylviane, *Le Théâtre des colonies: scénographie, acteurs et discours de l'imaginaire dans les expositions, 1855–1937* (Paris: Harmattan, 1986).

Leroi-Gourhan, A., 'Cinéma et sciences humaines. Le film ethnologique existe-t-il?', *Revue de la géographie humaine et d'ethnologie,* n.3, 1948, pp.42–50.

Levin, G. Roy, *Documentary Explorations. Fifteen Interviews with Film-Makers* (New York: Doubleday, 1971).

London, Jack, 'Le message du cinéma', *Profession écrivain,* 10/18, Paris, 1980.

Machin, Alfred, 'L'éducation par le cinématographe', *L'Arc-en-Ciel,* n.145, mars 1909.

—— 'Le cinématographe et la conquête du monde', *Ciné-Journal,* 23–28 avril 1909, pp.9–10.

—— 'Le Cinématographe dans le Désert', *Ciné-Journal,* 24 avril–5 mai 1909, pp.6–8.

—— 'Notes d'un globe-trotter cinématographique', *Ciné-Journal,* n.43, 11 juin 1909.

—— 'La chambre noire dans le désert', *L'Arc-en-Ciel,* n.148, juin 1909.

—— 'A coups de fusil et d'objectif à travers l'Afrique Centrale', in *Le Livre d'Or de la Cinématographie,* Éditions Ciné-Journal, novembre 1911.

Mannoni, Laurent, *Le Grand art de la lumière et de l'ombre – archéologie du cinéma* (Tours: Nathan, 1995).

Marbot, B., 'Mouvement et instantanéité' in *L'Invention d'un regard (1839–1918)* (Paris: RMN, 1989).

Marcorelles, Louis, *Eléments pour un nouveau cinéma* (Paris: UNESCO, 1970).

Marey, Étienne-Jules, *Le Mouvement* (1894) *(*Nîmes: Éditions Jacqueline Chambon, 1994).

Marsolais, Gilles, *L'Aventure du cinéma direct* (Paris: Seghers Éditions, 1974).

Matthews, J. H., 'Du Cinéma comme langage surréaliste', *Études cinématographiques,* nn.68–9, 1965.

—— *Surrealism and the Film* (Ann Arbor: University of Michigan Press, 1971).

Matuszewski, Boleslas, 'Une nouvelle source de l'histoire', *Le Figaro,* 25 mars 1898. Cited in: 'Le cinéma et l'histoire', *Cultures,* v.II, n.1, (Paris: Unesco, 1975).

Mead, Margaret, 'L'Anthropologie visuelle dans une discipline verbale' in Claudine de France (ed.), *Pour une anthropologie visuelle* (Paris: Mouton,1979, pp.13–20).

Mesguisch, Felix, *Tours de manivelle. Souvenirs d'un chasseur d'images* (Paris: Grasset, 1933).

Metz, Christian, *Le signifiant imaginaire: Psychanalyse et cinéma,* UGE, coll. 10/18, Paris, 1977.

—— *L'énonciation interpersonelle, ou le site du film* (Paris: Meridiens-Klincksieck, 1991).

Mitry, Jean, *Esthétique et psychologie du cinéma* (Paris: Éditions Universitaires, 1965).

—— *Histoire du cinéma: Art et Industrie I. 1895–1914* (Paris: Éditions Universitaires, 1967).

Morin, E., *Le cinéma ou l'homme imaginaire* (Paris: Les Éditions de Minuit, 1956).

Moullet, Luc, 'Jean-Luc Godard', *Cahiers du cinéma,* n.106, avril 1960 *(BIFI).*

Musée Marey, *La Passion du mouvement au XIX° siècle: Hommage à Étienne-Jules Marey* (Beaune: Musée Marey, 1991).

Musser, Charles, 'The Travel Genre in 1903–1904: Moving towards Fictional Narrative', *Iris,* v.2, n.1, 1984, pp.47–60.

'Ne visitez pas l'exposition coloniale (1931)' in *Tracts surréalistes et déclarations collectives 1922–1933,* v.I, Eric Losfeld, 1980, pp.194–5.

Nicolas, Alain, 'Entretien avec Jean Rouch' in Pierre-L. Jordan, *Cinéma*

(Marseille: Musées de Marseille–Images en Manoeuvres Éditions, 1992, pp.293–305).

Odin, Roger, 'Film documentaire, lecture documentarisante', *Cinémas et réalités,* Universitaires de Saint-Étienne (CIEREC), 1984.

Olivier de Sardan, Jean-Pierre, 'Où va le cinéma ethnographique?', *L'Ethnographie,* n.65, 1971, pp.1–11.

Ollier, Claude, 'Cinéma-surréalité', *Cahiers du cinéma,* n.172, novembre 1965, pp.50–52 *(BIFI)*.

Onclincx, G., 'Milieux coloniaux et cinématographie à l'exposition internationale de Bruxelles de 1897' *Cahiers Bruxellois,* 1958, pp.287–309.

Orlan, Pierre Mac, *'La Croisière noire',* *L'Intransigeant,* 4 mars, 1926.

Pagliano, J.-P., *En marge du cinéma français* (Lausanne: L'Âge d'Homme, 1987).

Pichon, Charles, 'Cinéma et missions', *L'Année missionaire,* 1931, pp.526–39.

Pinel, Vincent, 'Louis Lumière, la photograpie et le cinématographe' in Michel Lagny, Michel Marie, Jean A. Gili and Vincent Pinel (eds), *Les Vingt premières années du cinéma français* (Paris: Presses de la Sorbonne Nouvelle, 1995, pp.377–84).

Pinney, Christopher, 'The Lexical Spaces of Eye-Spy' in Peter Ian Crawford and David Turton (eds), *Film as Ethnography* (Manchester: Manchester University Press, 1992).

Poirier, Léon, *Pourquoi et comment je vais réaliser 'L'Appel du silence',* Comité d'action Charles de Foucauld, 1935.

Poirier, Leon, *24 images à la seconde* (Tours: Mame, 1953).

—— *À la recherche d'autre chose* (Brussels: Desclée de Brouwer, 1968).

Positif, 'Les maîtres fous et Tristes tropiques', *Positif,* 28 avril 1958, pp.54–5.

Prédal, Réné, *Jean Rouch, un griot gaulois* (numéro spécial de *CinémAction*), *CinémAction,* n.17, 1982.

—— 'Rouch, le film ethnographique et l'Afrique: l'espace, le temps, l'histoire', *Jean Rouch, un griot gaulois* (numéro spécial de *CinémAction*), *CinémAction,* n.17, 1982.

—— (ed.), *Le Documentaire français* (numéro spécial de *CinémAction*), *CinémAction,* n.41, 1987.

—— 'Jean Rouch, une inspiration surréaliste à l'épreuve du "direct"', in C. W.

Thompson (ed.), *L'Autre et le sacré: surréalisme, cinéma, ethnologie* (Paris: Éditions L'Harmattan, 1995, pp.333–47).

Ramirez, F. and C. Rolot, *Histoire du cinéma colonial au Zaïre, au Rwanda et au Burundi* (Tervueren: 1985).

Regnault, F.-L., 'Les attitudes du repos dans les races humaines', *Revue encyclopédique,* 1896, pp.36–46.

—— 'La locomotion chez l'homme', *Cahiers de Recherche de l'Académie,* n.122, 1896, p.401, and in *Archives de Physiologie, de Pathologie et de Génétique,* n.8, 1896, p.381.

—— 'Le grimper', *Revue encyclopédique,* 1897, pp.904–5.

—— 'Les musées des films', *Biologica,* n.2 (supplément 20), 1912.

—— 'Films et musées d'ethnographie', *Comptes Rendus de l'Association Française pour l'Avancement des Sciences,* n.11, 1923, pp.880–1.

—— 'L'histoire du cinéma, son rôle en anthropologie', *Bulletins et Mémoires de la Société d'Anthropologie de Paris,* nn.7–8, 1923, pp.61–5.

—— 'Le rôle du cinéma en ethnographie', *La Nature,* n.59, 1931, pp.304–6.

'Repudiating Antonioni's Anti-China Film', *Peking Review,* n.8, 22 February 1974.

Rittaud-Hutinet, Jacques, 'Le cinématographe Lumière et les autres: La concurrence en France en 1896 et 1897' in Michel Lagny, Michel Marie, Jean A. Gili and Vincent Pinel (eds), *Les Vingt premières années du cinéma français* (Paris: Presses de la Sorbonne Nouvelle, 1995, pp.399–416).

Rothenberg, Tamar Y., 'Voyeurs of Imperialism: *The National Geographic Magazine* before World War II' in Anne Godlewska and Neil Smith (eds), *Geography and Empire* (Oxford: Blackwell, 1994, pp.155–172).

Rothman, William, *Documentary Film Classics,* (Cambridge: Cambridge University Press, 1997).

Rouch, Jean, 'Renaissance du film ethnographique', *Geographica Helvetica,* n.8, 1953, p.55.

—— 'Cinéma d'exploration et ethnographie', *Connaissance du Monde,* n.1, 1955, pp.69–78.

—— 'A propos de films ethnographiques', *Positif, Revue de Cinéma,* 1955, pp.14–15.

—— *Essai sur la religion songhay* (Paris: Presses Universitaires de France, 1960).

—— 'Le Film ethnographique' in Poirier, Jean (ed.) *Ethnologie générale* (Paris: Bibliothèque de la Pléiade,1968).

—— 'Essai sur les avatars de la personne du possédé, du magicien, du sorcier, du cinéaste et de l'ethnographe', *Colloques Internationaux du Centre de la Recherche Scientifique,* n.544, 11–17 octobre 1971.

—— 'The Camera and the Man' in Paul Hockings (ed.), *Principles of Visual Anthropology* (The Hague: Mouton, 1975).

—— 'On the Vicissitudes of the Self: The Possessed Dancer, the Magician, the Sorcerer, the Filmmaker and the Ethnographer', *Studies in the Anthropology of Visual Communication,* n.5, 1978.

—— 'Jean Rouch talks about his films to John Marshall and John W. Adams', *American Anthropologist,* v.80, n.4, 1978, pp.1005–20.

—— 'Entretien avec Guy Hennebelle', Claudine de France (ed.), *Pour une anthropologie visuelle* (Paris: Mouton, 1979).

—— 'La Caméra et les hommes' in Claudine de France (ed.), *Pour une anthropologie visuelle* (Paris: Mouton, 1979, pp.54–71).

—— 'Introduction' in Claudine de France (ed.), *Pour une anthropologie visuelle* (Paris: Mouton, 1979, pp.5–11).

—— 'The Cinema of the Future?', *Studies in Visual Communication,* v.11, n.1, Winter 1985.

—— 'Entretien avec Jean-Paul Colleyn', *Demain le film ethnographique?, CinémAction,* n.64, 3ème trimestre, 1992.

—— 'L'autre et le sacreé: jeu sacré, jeu politique' in C. W. Thompson (ed.), *L'Autre et le sacré: surréalisme, cinéma, ethnologie* (Paris: Éditions L'Harmattan, 1995, pp.407–31).

—— and Enrico Fulchignoni, 'Conversation between Jean Rouch and Professor Enrico Fulchignoni', *Visual Anthropology,* n.2, 1989.

—— and Edgar Morin, '*Chronique d'un été*', *Domaine cinéma I, Cahiers trimestriels,* hiver 1961–2, Interspectacles, 1962.

Rouget, Gilbert, 'Un film expérimental: *Batteries Dogon*. Elements pour une étude des rythmes', in *L'Homme,* v.V, avril–juin 1965, pp.126–32.

Sadoul, Georges, *Louis Lumière* (Paris:Éditions Seghers, 1964).

Sardan, Olivier de, 'Où va le film ethnographique?', *L'Ethnographe*, n.65, 1971.

Scherer, Maurice, 'La revanche de l'Occident (*Tabou*)', *Cahiers du cinéma*, v.IV, n.21, mars 1953 pp.46–7.

Schivelbusch, Wolfgang, *The Railway Journey: Trains and Travel in the Nineteenth Century* (New York: Urizen Press, 1979).

Serceau, Michel, 'L'avènement du cinéma direct et la métamorphose' in Réné Prédal (ed.), *Le Documentaire français* (numéro spécial de *CinémAction*) *CinémAction*, n.41, 1987.

Simpson, Donald H., 'The Magic Lantern and Imperialism', *Library Notes, The Royal Commonwealth Society*, v.191 (NS), 1973.

Soupault, Philippe, *Écrits de cinéma, 1918–1931* (Paris: Ramsay Poche Cinéma, 1979).

Stoller, Paul, 'Artaud, Rouch and the Cinema of Cruelty', *Visual Anthropology Review*, v.8, n.2, 1992, pp.55–65; reprinted as 'Artaud, Rouch et le cinéma de la cruauté' in C. W. Thompson (ed.), *L'Autre et le sacré: surréalisme, cinéma, ethnologie* (Paris: Éditions L'Harmattan, 1995, pp.315–32).

—— *The Cinematic Griot: the Ethnography of Jean Rouch* (Chicago: University of Chicago Press, 1992).

Thompson, C. W., 'De Buñuel à Rouch: les surréalistes devant le documentaire et le film ethnographique' in C. W. Thompson (ed.), *L'Autre et le sacré: surréalisme, cinéma, ethnologie* (Paris: Éditions L'Harmattan, 1995, pp.263–81).

—— (ed.), *L'Autre et le sacré: surréalisme, cinéma, ethnologie* (Paris: Éditions L'Harmattan, 1995).

Toulet, Emmanuelle, 'Le Cinéma à l'Exposition universelle de 1900', in *Revue d'histoire moderne et contemporaine*, v.XXXIII, avril–juin 1986, pp.179–209.

Ungar, Steven, 'Narration et pratique spatiale dans deux récits surréalistes' in C. W. Thompson (ed.), *L'autre et le sacré: surréalisme, cinéma, ethnologie* (Paris: Éditions L'Harmattan, 1995, pp.93–110).

Véray, Laurent, 'Cinéma d'actualité et institution militaire en France de 1914 à 1918' in Michel Lagny, Michel Marie, Jean A. Gili and Vincent Pinel (eds), *Les Vingt premières années du cinéma français* (Paris: Presses de la Sorbonne Nouvelle, 1995, pp.87–104).

Virmaux, A. and O. Virmaux, *Les Surréalistes et le cinéma* (Paris: Éditions Seghers, 1979).

Williams, Linda, *Figures of Desire, A Theory and Analysis of Surrealist Film* (Berkeley: University of California Press, 1981).

Winston, Brian, *Claiming the Real: The Griersonian Documentary and its Legitimations* (London: BFI, 1995).

Witt, Mike, 'Godard, le cinéma et l'ethnologie: ou l'objet et sa représentation' in C. W. Thompson (ed.), *L'Autre et le sacré: surréalisme, cinéma, ethnologie* (Paris: Éditions L'Harmattan, 1995 pp.369–78).

Colonialism

Ageron, Charles-Robert, 'Gambetta et la reprise de l'expansion coloniale', *Revue française d'histoire d'outre-mer*, v.59, n.215, 1972 pp.165–204.

—— *L'Anticolonialisme en France de 1871 à 1914* (Paris: Presses Universitaires de France, 1973).

—— *France coloniale ou parti colonial?* (Paris: Presses Universitaires de France, 1973).

—— 'Jules Ferry et la colonisation', in François Furet (ed.), *Jules Ferry: Fondateur de la République,* (Paris: Presses Universitaires de France, 1986 pp.191–206).

—— et coll., *Histoire de la France coloniale,* 2 vols.(Paris: Armand Colin, 1991).

Andrew, C. M. and A. S. Kanya-Forstner, 'The French "Colonial Party": its composition, aims and influence, 1885–1914', *The Historical Journal,* n.14, 1971, pp.9–128 .

—— 'The French Colonial Party and French colonial war aims, 1914–1918', *The Historical Journal,* n.17, 1974, pp.79–106.

—— 'The "Groupe Colonial" in the French Chamber of Deputies, 1892–1932', *The Historical Journal,* n.17, 1974, pp.837–66).

—— 'French business and the French colonialists', *The Historical Journal,* n.19, 1976, pp.981–1000.

—— 'France and the Repartition of Africa', *Dalhousie Review,* n.57, 1977, pp.475–93.

—— 'France, Africa and the First World War', *Journal of African History,* n.19, 1978, pp.11–23.

—— *France Overseas: The Great War and the climax of French imperial expansion* (London; Thames and Hudson, 1981).

—— 'Centre and periphery in the making of the second French empire, 1815–1930', *Journal of Imperial and Commonwealth History*, n.16, 1988, pp.9–34.

Augagneur, Victor, *Erreurs et brutalités coloniales* (Paris: Montaigne, 1927).

Benoist-Mechin, Jacques G. P., *Lyautey l'africain ou le rêve immolé, 1854–1934* (Paris: Perrin,1978).

Betts, R. F., *Assimilation and Association in French Colonial Theory 1890–1914* (New York: Columbia University Press, 1961).

—— *Tricoleur: the French Empire Overseas* (London: Gordon & Cremonesi, 1978).

Binoche-Guedra, Jacques, *La France d'outre-mer (1815–1962)* (Paris; Masson, 1992).

Bouvier, J., 'Les traits majeurs de l'impérialisme français avant 1914', *Le mouvement social,* n.86, 1974, pp.99–128.

Brantlinger, Patrick, 'Victorians and Africans: the Genealogy of the Myth of the Dark Continent', *Critical Inquiry,* 12, 1985.

—— *Rule of Darkness: British Literature and Imperialism, 1830–1914* (Ithaca: Cornell University Press, 1988).

Broc, Numa, 'Nationalisme, colonialisme et géographie: Marcel Dubois (1856–1916)', *Annales de Géographie,* v.87, n.481, 1978, pp.326–33.

—— 'Les Grandes missions scientifiques Françaises au XIXe siècle (Morée, Algerie, Mexique) et leurs travaux géographiques', *Revue d'Histoire des Sciences et de leurs Applications,* n.34, 1981, pp.319–58.

Bruneau, Michel, 'Géographie française et empires coloniaux dans la première moitié du XX° siècle' in Michel Bruneau and Daniel Dory (eds), *Géographies des colonisations XV°–XX° siècles* (Paris: Éditions L'Harmattan, 1994, pp.35–49).

Bruneau, Michel and Daniel Dory (eds), *Géographies des colonisations XV°–XX° siècles* (Paris: Éditions L'Harmattan, 1994).

Brunschwig, H., *French Colonialism, 1871–1914: Myths and Realities* (London: Pall Mall Press, 1966).

—— 'French Exploration and Conquest in Tropical Africa from 1865–1898' in

L. Gann and P. Guignan (eds), *Colonialism in Africa, 1860–1960: the History and Politics of Colonialism, 1870–1914* (Cambridge: Cambridge University Press, 1969, pp.132–164).

—— 'Vigne d'Octon et l'anticolonialisme sous la Troisième République', *Cahiers d'Études Africaines*, n.14, 1974, pp.265–8.

Burrows, M., 'Mission civilisatrice: French Cultural Policy in the Middle East, 1860–1914', *The Historical Journal*, n.29, 1986, pp.109–35.

Canizzo, Jeanne, 'David Livingstone Collects' in *David Livingstone and the Victorian Encounter with Africa* (London; National Portrait Gallery, 1996).

Carazzi, M., *La Società Geografica Italiana e l'esplorazione coloniale in Arrica (1867–1900)* (Florence: La Nuova Italia, 1978).

Claval, Paul, 'Playing with Mirrors: The British Empire According to Albert Demangéon' in Anne Godlewska and Neil Smith (eds), *Geography and Empire* (Oxford: Blackwell, 1994, pp.228–43).

Chipman, J., *French Power in Africa* (Oxford: Basil Blackwell, 1989).

Cohen, W. B., *The French Encounter with Africans: White Responses to Blacks, 1530–1980* (Cincinnati: Indiana University Press, 1980).

De Hemtinne, A., 'Les moyens pour engager les jeunes voués à l'enseignement s'expatrier ...' *Les Actes du Congrès International d'Expansion Economique Mondiale. Section V. Expansion civilisatrice vers les pays neufs*, Mons, 1905, pp.1–15.

Démangéon, Albert, *L'Empire britannique. Etude de géographie coloniale* (Paris: Armand Colin, 1923).

Domergue-Cloarec, Danièle, 'Explorations et conquête: l'exemple du Haut-Cavally, 1896–1900 (Côte d'Ivoire)' in Michel Bruneau and Daniel Dory (eds), *Géographies des colonisations XV°–XX° siècles* (Paris: Éditions L'Harmattan, 1994, pp.411–20).

Driver, Felix, 'Henry Morton Stanley and His Critics: Geography, Exploration and Empire', *Past and Present*, n.133, November 1991, pp.134–64.

Dubois, Marcel, 'Leçon d'ouverture du cours de géographie coloniale', *Annales de Géographie*, v.10, 1894, pp.121–37.

Dunbar, Gary S., ' "The Compass Follows the Flag": The French Scientific Mission to Mexico, 1864–7' *Annals of the Association of American Geographers*, n.78, 1988, pp.229–40.

Eagleton, T., F. Jameson and E. Said, *Nationalism, Colonialism and Literature* (Minneapolis: University of Minnesota Press, 1990).

Emerit, M., 'Les Explorateurs Saint Simoniens en Afrique orientale et sur les routes des Indes', *Revue Africaine,* v.87, 1943, pp.92–116.

—— 'L'idée de colonisation dans les socialismes français', *L'Age Nouveau,* v.24, 1967, pp.103–15.

—— 'Diplomates et explorateurs saint-simoniens', *Revue d'Histoire Moderne et Contemporaine,* v.22, 1975, pp.397–415.

Gambi, Lucio, 'Geography and Imperialism in Italy: From the Unity of the Nation to the "New" Roman Empire' in Anne Godlewska and Neil Smith (eds), *Geography and Empire* (Oxford: Blackwell, 1994, pp.74–91).

Ganiage, J., *L'Expansion coloniale de la France sous la Troisième République 1871–1914* (Paris: Payot, 1968).

Garnier, Francis, *Voyage d'exploration en Indo-Chine,* 1873.

Giblin, B., 'Elisée Reclus and Colonisation' in P. Girot and E. Kofman (eds), *International Geopolitical Analysis: a selection from Herodote* (London: Croom Helm, 1989).

Girardet, Raoul, *L'Idée coloniale en France de 1871 à 1962* (Paris: La Table Ronde, 1972).

Godlewska, Anne, 'Napoleon's Geographers: Imperialists or Soldiers of Modernity?' in Anne Godlewska and Neil Smith (eds), *Geography and Empire* (Oxford: Blackwell, 1994, pp.31–53).

—— and Neil Smith (eds), *Geography and Empire* (Oxford: Blackwell, 1994).

Guillaume, Pierre, *Le Monde colonial XIX°–XX° siècle* (Paris: Armand Colin, 1994).

Hardy, G., *Géographie et colonisation* (Paris: Éditions Gallimard, 1933).

—— *La Politique coloniale et le partage de la terre aux XIX° et XX° siècles* (Paris: Albin Lichel, 1937).

Heffernan, Michael J., 'Militant Geographers: the French Geographical Movement and the Forms of French Imperialism, 1870 to 1920' in Anne Godlewska and Neil Smith (eds), *Geography and Empire* (Oxford: Blackwell, 1994, pp.92–114).

Hudson, Brian, 'The New Geography and the New Imperialism: 1870–1918', *Antipode,* n.9, 1977, pp.12–19.

Juhe-Beaulaton, Dominique, 'Environnement et exploration géographique de l'ex-Dahomey (Rép. du Bénin) à la veille de la conquête coloniale' in Michel Bruneau and Daniel Dory (eds), *Géographies des colonisations XV°–XX° siècles* (Paris: Éditions L'Harmattan, 1994, pp.289–314).

Kereny, A., M. *La società d'esplorazione commerciale in Africa e la politica coloniale (1879–1914)* (Florence: La Nuova Italia, 1978).

Lacoste, Yves, 'Géographie coloniale et géographie académique: approche épistémologique' in Michel Bruneau and Daniel Dory (eds), *Géographies des colonisations XV°–XX° siècles* (Paris: Éditions L'Harmattan, 1994, pp.345–8).

Laffey, J. F., 'Roots of French Imperialism in the Nineteenth Century: the Case of Lyons', *French Historical Studies,* n.6, 1969, pp.78–92.

—— 'Municipal Imperialism in Nineteenth Century France', *Historical Reflections/Réflexions Historiques,* n.1, 1974, pp.81–114.

—— 'Municipal Imperialism in Decline: the Lyons Chamber of Commerce, 1925–1938', *French Historical Studies,* n.9, 1975, pp.329–53.

—— 'The Lyons Chamber of Commerce and Indochina During the Third Republic', *Canadian Journal of History,* n.10, 1975, pp.325–48.

Lejeune, Dominique, *Les Sociétés de géographie en France et l'expansion coloniale au XIXe siècle* (Paris: Albin Michel, 1993).

Liauzu, Claude, 'Elisée Reclus et l'expansion européenne en méditerranée' in Michel Bruneau and Daniel Dory (eds), *Géographies des colonisations XV°–XX° siècles* (Paris: Editions L'Harmattan, 1994, pp.129–35).

Marseille, Jacques *,Empire colonial et capitalisme français. Histoire d'un divorce* (Paris: Albin Michel, 1984, reissued 1989).

MacKay, Donald Vernon, 'Colonialism in the French Geographical Movement 1871–1881', *Geographical Review,* n.33, 1943, pp.214–32.

Maharaux, Alain, 'La géographie et le tracé des espaces coloniaux et postcoloniaux' in Michel Bruneau and Daniel Dory (eds), *Géographies des colonisations XV°–XX° siècles* (Paris: Éditions L'Harmattan, 1994, pp.349–67).

Mainardi, Patricia, *Art and Politics of the Second Empire. The Universal Expositions of 1855 and 1867* (New Haven: Yale University Press, 1987).

Mignon, Jean-Marie, 'Terres de mission. La géographie du saint-siège en Afrique noire francophone' in Michel Bruneau and Daniel Dory (eds), *Géographies des colonisations XV°–XX° siècles* (Paris: Éditions L'Harmattan, 1994, pp.369–81).

Morsy, M. (ed.), *Les Saint-Simoniens et l'Orient: vers la modernité* (Paris: Edisud, 1989).

Nicolai, Henri, 'Les géographes belges et le Congo' in Michel Bruneau and Daniel Dory (eds), *Géographies des colonisations XV°–XX° siècles* (Paris: Éditions L'Harmattan, 1994, pp.51–65).

Nordman, C. and J.-P. Raison (eds), *Sciences de l'homme et conquête coloniale: constitution et usages des humanités en Afrique (XIXe et XXe siècle)* (Paris: Presses de l'École Normale Supérieure, 1980).

Persell, S. M., *The French Colonial Lobby 1889–1938* (Stanford: Hoover Institute Press, 1983).

Pourtier, Roland, 'Territoire et identité nationale en Afrique centrale. La fonction de la géographie dans le mouvement colonisation/décolonisation' in Michel Bruneau and Daniel Dory (eds), *Géographies des colonisations XV°–XX° siècles* (Paris: Éditions L'Harmattan, 1994, pp.329–41).

Said, Edward W., *Orientalism. Western Conceptions of the Orient* (London: Routledge & Kegan Paul, 1978).

—— *The World, the Text and the Critic* (Cambridge, MA: Harvard University Press, 1983).

—— 'Orientalism Reconsidered' in F. Barker et al. (eds), *Europe and its Others* (Colchester: University of Essex, 1985).

—— 'Representing the Colonised: Anthropology's Interlocutors', *Critical Inquiry*, n.15, pp.205–25.

—— *Culture and Imperialism* (London: Chatto & Windus, 1992).

Schneider, William H., 'Geographical Reform and Municipal Imperialism in France, 1870–1880' in John M. MacKenzie (ed.), *Imperialism and the Natural World* (Manchester: Manchester University Press, 1990, pp.80–117).

Soubeyron, Olivier, 'Imperialism and Colonialism versus Disciplinarity in French Geography' in Anne Godlewska and Neil Smith (eds), *Geography and Empire* (Oxford: Blackwell, 1994, pp.244–64).

—— 'La géographie coloniale au risque de la modernité' in Michel Bruneau and Daniel Dory (eds), *Géographies des colonisations XV°–XX° siècles* (Paris: Éditions L'Harmattan, 1994, pp.193–213).

Spurr, David, *The Rhetoric of Empire: Colonial Discourse in Journalism, Travel Writing and Imperial Administration* (Durham, NC: Duke University Press, 1993).

Suret-Canale, Jean 'Les Géographes français face à la colonisation: l'exemple de Pierre Gourou' in Michel Bruneau and Daniel Dory (eds), *Géographies des colonisations XV°–XX° siècles* (Paris: Éditions L'Harmattan, 1994, pp.155–69).

Ethnography and sociology

Adamowicz, Elza, '"Un masque peut en masquer (ou démasquer) un autre" Le Masque et le surréalisme' in C. W. Thompson (ed.), *L'Autre et le sacré: surréalisme, cinéma, ethnologie* (Paris: Éditions L'Harmattan, 1995, pp.73–9).

Ansart, Pierre, *Sociologie de Saint-Simon* (Paris: Presse Universitaires de France, 1970).

Arroyo, Eduardo, *Panama Al Brown, 1902–1951* (Paris: J.-C. Lattès, 1982).

Atkinson, P., *The Ethnographic Imagination: Textual Constructions of Reality* (London: Routledge, 1990).

Azoulay, L., 'L'ère nouvelle des sons et des bruits', *Bulletins et Mémoires de la Société d'Anthropologie de Paris*, n.1, 1900, pp.172–8.

—— 'Sur la constitution d'un musée phonographique', *Bulletins et Mémoires de la Société d'Anthropologie de Paris*, n.1, 1900, pp.222–6.

Bataille, Georges, 'Poussière', *Documents*, n.5, 1929.

Boas, Franz, *Anthropology and Modern Life* (New York: W. W. Norton, 1928).

Bourdieu, Pierre, *La Distinction, critique sociale du jugement* (Paris: Editions de Minuit, 1979).

Breton, Phillippe, *L'Utopie de la communication,* (Paris: La Découverte, 1992).

Caillois, Roger, *L'Homme et le sacré* (Paris: Gallimard-Idées, 1972).

Carp, Ivan and Stephen D. Lavine (eds), *Exhibiting Cultures: the Poetic and the Politics of Museum Display* (Washington, DC: Smithsonian Institution Press, 1991).

Chambers, Ian, *Migrancy, Culture, Identity* (London: Routledge, 1994).

Chénieux-Gendron, Jacqueline, 'L'altérité et ses modèles dans l'oeuvre de Georges Bataille, André Breton, René Daumal' in C. W. Thompson (ed.),

L'Autre et le sacré: surréalisme, cinéma, ethnologie (Paris: Éditions L'Harmattan, 1995, pp.37–50).

Clifford, James, 'On Ethnographic Surrealism', *Comparative Studies in History,* v.XXIII, n.4, 1981, pp.534–64.

—— *The Predicament of Culture: twentieth-century ethnography, literature and art* (Cambridge MA: Harvard University Press, 1988).

—— and George E. Marcus, *Writing Culture: the Poetics and Politics of Ethnography* (Berkeley: University of California Press, 1986).

Comte, Auguste, *Système de politique positive* (Paris: Baillière,1854).

Deliss, Clementine, 'L'épiderme de la culture' in C. W. Thompson (ed.), *L'Autre et le sacré: surréalisme, cinéma, ethnologie* (Paris: Éditions L'Harmattan, 1995, pp.113–27).

Dias, Nélia, *Le Musée d'ethnographie du Trocadéro (1878–1908). Anthropologie et muséologie en France* (Paris: CNRS, 1991).

Douglas, Mary, 'Réflexions sur le renard pâle et deux anthropologies: à propos du surréalisme et de l'anthropologie française' in C. W. Thompson (ed.), *L'Autre et le sacré: surréalisme, cinéma, ethnologie* (Paris: Éditions L'Harmattan, 1995, pp.199–218).

Durkheim, Émile, *Les Formes élémentaires de la vie religieuse* (Paris: Presses Universitaires de France, 1960 [1912]).

Geertz, Clifford, *Works and Lives. The Anthropologist as Author* (Stanford: Stanford University Press, 1988).

Griaule, Marcel, *Méthode de l'ethnographie* (Paris: Presses Universitaires de France, 1957).

Hand, Sean, 'Hors de soi: politique, possession et présence dans l'ethnographie surréaliste de Michel Leiris' in C. W. Thompson (ed.), *L'Autre et le sacré: surréalisme, cinéma, ethnologie* (Paris: Éditions L'Harmattan, 1995, pp.185–95).

Heusch, Luc de, 'Pierre Mabille, Michel Leiris anthropologues' in C. W. Thompson (ed.), *L'Autre et le sacré: surréalisme, cinéma, ethnologie* (Paris: Éditions L'Harmattan, 1995 pp.397–405).

Hinsley, Curtis M., 'The World as Marketplace: Commodification of the Exotic at the World's Colombian Exposition, 1893, in Ivan Carp, and Stephen D.

Lavine (eds), *Exhibiting Cultures: the Poetic and the Politics of Museum Display* (Washington, DC: Smithsonian Institution Press, 1991).

Hockings, P. (ed.), *Principles of Visual Anthropology* (The Hague: Mouton, 1975).

Hollier, Denis, *Le Collège de Sociologie,* (Paris: Éditions Gallimard, 1979).

—— 'La valeur d'usage de l'impossible' préface à la collection complète de *Documents* (Paris: Jean-Michel Place, 1991, pp. VII–XXIV).

—— 'La valeur d'usage de l'impossible' in *Les Dépossédés* (Paris: Éditions de Minuit, 1993).

Jamin, Jean, 'A la recherche des paradis perdus: à propos de la Mission Dakar–Djibouti' in Jacques Hainard and Roland Kaehr (eds), *Collections passion: exposition du 5 juin au 28 décembre* (Neuchâtel: Musée d'ethnographie, 1982).

—— 'L'Ethnologie mode d'inemploi. De quelques rapports de l'ethnologie avec le malaise dans la civilisation' in Jacques Hainard and Roland Kaehr (eds), *Le mal et la douleur* (Neuchâtel: Musée d'Ethnographie, 1986, pp.45–79).

—— Du Musée de l'Homme considéré comme un laboratoire de représentations' (unpublished ms.) 5–6 December 1986.

—— 'De l'humaine condition de *Minotaure*' in *Regards sur Minotaure* (Henève: Musée d'Art et d'Histoire, 1987).

—— '*Documents* et le reste. De l'anthropologie dans les bas-fonds', *La Revue des revues,* n.18, 1994, pp.15–24.

Johnson, Chris, 'Lévi-Strauss et la logique du sacré' in C. W. Thompson (ed.), *L'Autre et le sacré: surréalisme, cinéma, ethnologie* (Paris: Éditions L'Harmattan, 1995, pp.249–59).

Kirschenblatt-Gimblett, Barbara, 'Objects of ethnography', in Ivan Carp and Stephen D. Lavine (eds), *Exhibiting Cultures: the Poetic and the Politics of Museum Display* (Washington, DC: Smithsonian Institution Press, 1991).

Kristeva, Julia, *Etrangers à nous-mêmes* (Paris: Fayard, 1988).

Lala, Marie-Christine, 'Au miroir de la tauromachie' in C. W. Thompson (ed.), *L'Autre et le sacré: surréalisme, cinéma, ethnologie* (Paris: Éditions L'Harmattan, 1995, pp.151–60).

Lechte, John, 'Bataille, L'Autre et le sacré' in C. W. Thompson (ed.), *L'Autre et le sacré: surréalisme, cinéma, ethnologie* (Paris: Éditions L'Harmattan, 1995, pp.129–50).

Leclerc, G., *Anthropologie et colonialisme: essai sur l'histoire de l'Africanisme* (Paris: Éditions du Seuil, 1972).

Lecoq, Dominique, 'L'oeil de l'ethnologue sous la dent de l'écrivain' in D. Lecoq and J. L .Lory, *Écrits d'ailleurs. Georges Bataille et les ethnologues* (Paris: Éditions de la Maison des Sciences de l'Homme, 1987, pp.111, 114).

Leiris, Michel, *L'Afrique fantôme* (Paris: Éditions Gallimard, 1934).

—— *Miroir de la tauromachie* (Paris: GLM, 1938; reissued Montpellier: Fata Morgana, 1980).

—— *L'Âge d'homme* (Paris: Éditions Gallimard, 1939; reissued Gallimard, 1973).

—— *Frêle bruit* (Paris: Éditions Gallimard, 1976).

—— *Miroir de l'Afrique* (Paris: Éditions Gallimard, 1993).

—— 'De Bataille l'impossible l'impossible *Documents*' in *Brisées* (Paris: Éditions Gallimard, 1992, pp.288–99).

—— 'L'ethnographe devant le colonialisme' in *Brisées* (Paris: Éditions Gallimard, 1992; originally printed in *Les Temps Modernes,* 6, n.58, August 1950).

—— *Zébrage* (Paris: Éditions Gallimard,1992).

—— *C'est-à-dire* (Paris: Jean-Michel Place, 1992).

—— and J. Delange, *Afrique noire, la création plastique* (Paris: Éditions Gallimard, 1967).

Lepenies, Wolf, *Between Literature and Science: the Rise of Sociology* (Cambridge : Cambridge University Press, 1988).

Lèvy-Bruhl, Lucien, *La Morale et la science des moeurs* (Paris: 1903).

—— *La Mentalité primitive* (Paris: Félix Alcan, Paris,1925).

Lourdou, Philippe, 'Mettre en circulation des objets inquiétants: ethnographie et surréalisme' in C. W. Thompson (ed.), *L'Autre et le sacré: surréalisme, cinéma, ethnologie* (Paris: Éditions L'Harmattan, 1995, pp.307–14).

Massey, Doreen, *Space, Place and Gender* (Minneapolis: University of Minnesota Press, 1994).

Maubon, Catherine, 'Michel Leiris: Des notions de "crise" et de "rupture" au "sacré dans la vie quotidienne"' in C. W. Thompson (ed.), *L'Autre et le sacré:*

surréalisme, cinéma, ethnologie (Paris: Éditions L'Harmattan, 1995, pp.161–84).

Mauss, Marcel, *Les techniques du corps*.

Métraux, Alfred, 'La comédie rituelle dans la possession', *Diogène*, n.11, 1955, pp.26–49.

Minotaure, n.2, printemps 1933 (an entire issue devoted to the Mission Dakar–Djibouti).

Natali, Johanna, Marco Mozzati and Jacques Perriault, *Les Fonds de vues sur verre du Musée pédagogique. Premier inventaire des `notices explicatives*, INRP (roneote), Paris, octobre 1978.

Parsinnen, Carol Ann, 'Social Explorers and Social Scientists: the Dark Continent of Victorian Ethnography' in Jay Ruby (ed.), *A Crack in the Mirror* (Philadelphia: University of Pennsylvania Press, 1982).

Pratt, Mary Louise, 'Fieldwork in Common Places' in James Clifford and George E. Marcus, *Writing Culture: the Poetics and Politics of Ethnography* (Berkeley: University of California Press, 1986).

Revue de géographie humaine et d'ethnologie, n.2, 1948, p.107.

Richman, Michèle, 'Anthropology and Modernism in France: from Durkheim to the *Collège de Sociologie*' in Marc Manganaro (ed.), *Modernist Anthropology* (Princeton: Princeton University Press, 1990).

—— 'L'altérité sacrée chez Durkheim' in C. W. Thompson (ed.), *L'Autre et le sacré: surréalisme, cinéma, ethnologie* (Paris: Éditions L'Harmattan, 1995, pp.21–33).

Rivet, Paul, 'Ce que sera le Musée de l'Homme', *L'Oeuvre*, 14 juin, 1936.

—— and Georges-Henri Rivière, 'La Réorganisation du Musée d'ethnographie du Trocadéro', *Bulletin du Musée national d'histoire naturelle*, 2° série nn. 2, 5, juin 1930.

—— P. Lester and Georges-Henri Rivière, 'Le Laboratoire d'Anthropologie du Musée', *Archives du Musée national d'histoire naturelle*, 12, n.2, juin 1935.

Rivière, Georges Henri, 'A propos de l'art nègre', *Le Figaro artistique*, juillet–août 1931, pp.81–3.

Schaeffner, André et André Coeuroy, *Le Jazz* (Paris: Claude Aveline, 1926; reissued by Jean-Michel Place, 1988).

Schaeffner, André, 'Le jazz', *Revue musicale*, 1 novembre 1927, pp.72–6.

—— 'Des instruments de musique dans un musée d'ethnographie', *Documents,* n.5, 1929, pp.133ff.

Sheringham, Michael, 'Du surréel à l'infra-ordinaire: avatars du quotidien dans le surréalisme, l'ethnographie et le postmodernisme de Georges Perec' in C. W. Thompson (ed.), *L'Autre et le sacré: surréalisme, cinéma, ethnologie* (Paris: Éditions L'Harmattan, 1995, pp.219–36).

Syrotinski, Michael, 'Paulhan, Caillois et l'autre du sacré' in C. W. Thompson (ed.), *L'Autre et le sacré: surréalisme, cinéma, ethnologie* (Paris: Éditions L'Harmattan, 1995, pp.237–47).

Thompson, C.W., 'Du Sacré comme puissance au sacré comme jeu' in C. W. Thompson (ed.), *L'Autre et le sacré: surréalisme, cinéma, ethnologie* (Paris: Éditions L'Harmattan, 1995, pp.7–19).

Thornton, Robert, 'Narrative Ethnography in Africa, 1850–1920: The Creation and Capture of an Appropriate Domain for Anthropology', *Man* (NS), v.18, n.38, 1983.

Geography

Andrews, Howard F., 'The Durkheimians and human geography: some contextual problems in the sociology of knowledge', *Transactions, Institute of British Geographers* (NS), n.9, 1984, pp.315–26.

—— 'The Early Life of Paul Vidal de la Blache and the Makings of Modern Geography', *Transactions, Institute of British Geographers* (NS), n.11, 1986, pp.174–82.

—— 'A French view of geography teaching in Britain in 1871', *Geographical Journal,* n.152, 1986, pp.225–31.

—— 'Les premiers cours de géographie de Paul Vidal de la Blache', *Annales de géographie,* v.95, n.529, 1986, pp.341–67.

Berdoulay, Vincent, 'The Vidal–Durkheim Debate' in David Ley and Marwyn Samuels (eds), *Humanistic Geography: Prospects and Problems* (London: Croom Helm, 1978, pp.77–90).

—— 'French Possibilism as a Form of Neo-Kantian Philosophy', *Proceedings of the Association of American Geographers,* n.8, 1976, pp.176–9.

—— 'The Contextual Approach' in D. R. Stoddart (ed.), *Geography, Ideology and Social Concern* (Oxford: Blackwell, 1981, pp.8–16).

—— *La Formation de l'école française de géographie (1870–1914)* (Paris: CTHS 1981 [Bibliotheque Nationale]).

—— *Les Mots et les Lieux: la dynamique du discours géographique* (Paris: Éditions du Centre Nationale de Recherche Scientifique, 1988).

—— and Olivier Soubeyran, 'Lamarck, Darwin, Vidal: aux fondements naturalistes de la géographie humaine', *Annales de géographie,* nn.561–62, 1991, pp.617–34.

Bird, Jon et al. (eds), *Mapping the Futures* (London: Routledge, 1993).

Blachère, Jean-Claude, 'Géographie physique de l'Éden chez André Breton', *Mélusine,* n.7, 1985, pp.100–17.

Boas, Franz, 'The Study of Geography', *Science,* n.9, 1887, pp.587–9.

Bouillet, Marie-Nicolas, *Dictionnaire universel d'histoire et de géographie* (Paris: 1842).

Broc, Numa, 'Histoire de la géographie et nationalisme en France sous la IIIe République (1871–1914)', *L'Information Historique,* n.32, 1970, pp.21–6.

—— 'L'Etablissement de la géographie et nationalisme en France: diffusion, institutions, projets 1870–90', *Annales de Géographie,* n.83, 1974, pp.545–68.

—— 'La Géographie française face à la science allemande (1870–1914)', *Annales de Géographie,* n.86, 1975, pp.71–94.

—— *La Géographie des philosophes. Géographes et voyageurs français au XVIIIe siècle* (Paris: Éditions Ophrys, 1975).

—— 'La pensée géographique en France au XIXe siècle: continuité ou rupture?', *Revue Géographique des Pyrenées et du Sud–Ouest,* n.47, 1976, pp.225–47.

—— 'La géographie française face à la science allemande (1870–1914)', *Annales de Géographie,* v.86, n.473, 1977, pp.71–94.

Buttimer, Anne, *Society and Milieu in the French Geographic Tradition* (Chicago: Rand McNally, 1971).

——'Charism and Context: The Challenge of *La Géographie Humaine*' in David Ley and Marwyn Samuels (eds), *Humanistic Geography: Prospects and Problems* (London: Croom Helm, 1978, pp.58–76).

Carriere, B., 'Le Transsharien: histoire et géographie d'une entreprise inachevée', *Acta Geographica,* n.74, 1988, pp.23–38.

Claval, Paul, *Essai sur l'evolution de la géographie humaine* (Paris: Les Belles Lettres, 1964).

—— 'La naissance de la géographie humaine' in *La Pensée géographique contemporaine (Mélanges offerts à A. Meynier)* (Sainte Breiuc: Presse Universitaires de Bretagne, 1972, pp.355–76).

—— and J. P. Nardy, *Pour le cinquantenaire de la mort de Paul Vidal de la Blache* (Paris: Les Belles Lettres, 1968).

Conrad, Joseph, 'Geography and Some Explorers' in *Last Essays* (London: Dent 1926, pp.1–31).

Cordonnier, Christophe, 'Preface' in Paul Vidal de la Blache, *Principes de géographie humaine* (Paris: UTZ, 1995).

Demangeon, Albert, 'Géographie politique', *Annales de Géographie,* v.41, 1932, pp.22–31).

De Martonne, E., 'La vie des peuples du Haut-Nil I', *Annales de Géographie* v.24, 1896, pp.506–21.

—— 'La vie des peuples du Haut-Nil II', *Annales de Géographie,* v.25, 1897, pp.61–70.

Dubois, Marcel, 'Géographie et géographes, à propos d'une thèse', *Le Correspondant,* v.86, n.255, 1914, pp.833–63.

Dunbar, Gary S., *Élisée Reclus. Historian of Nature* (Hamden: Archon Books, 1978).

—— 'Élisée Reclus, an Anarchist in Geography' in David R. Stoddart (ed.), *Geography, Ideology and Social Concern* (Oxford: Blackwell, 1981, pp.154–64).

Febvre, Lucien, *La Terre et l'évolution humaine:introduction géographique à l'histoire* (Paris: La Renaissance du Livre, 1922).

—— *A Geographical Introduction to History* (trans.: E. G. Mountford and J. H. Paxton) (London: Kegan, Paul, Trench, Trubner, 1932).

Fierro, A., *La Société de Géographie de Paris (1826–1946)* (Geneva/Paris: Librairie Droz/Librairie H Campion, 1983).

Fleure, Herbert John, 'Régions Humaines', *Annales de Géographie,* n.26, 1917, pp.161–74.

Flory, T., *Le Mouvement régionaliste francais: sources et développement* (Paris: Presses Universitaires de France, 1966).

Foncin, Pierre, 'La France extérieure', *Annales de Géographie,* v.1, 1891, pp.1–9.

George, H. B., *The Relations of Geography and History* (Oxford: Oxford University Press, 1901).

Godlewska, Anne, 'Tradition, Crisis, and the New Paradigms in the Rise of the Modern French Discipline of Geography, 1760–1850', *Annals of the Association of American Geographers,* n.79, 1989, pp.192–213.

Gourou, Pierre, *Les Paysans du delta tonkinois. Etude de géographie humaine* (Paris: Éditions d'Art et d'Histoire, 1936).

—— *Pour une géographie humaine* (Paris: Flammarion, 1973).

Guiomar, J.-Y., 'Le Tableau de la géographie de la France de Vidal de la Blache' in P. Nora (ed.), *Les Lieux de memoire: La Nation* (Paris: Éditions Gallimard, 1986).

Heffernan, Michael J., 'The Limits of Utopia: Henri Duveyrier and the Exploration of the Sahara in the Nineteenth Century', *Geographical Journal,* n.155, 1989, pp.342–52.

—— 'Bringing the Desert to Bloom: French Ambitions in the Sahara Desert During the Late Nineteenth Century – the Strange Case of "la mer interieure"' in D. E. Cosgrove and G. E. Petts (eds), *Water, Engineering and Landscape: water control and landscape formation in the modern period* (London: Belhaven Press, 1990, pp.94–114).

—— 'From Knowledge to Power: The Geography of Geographical Knowledge in Late Nineteenth-Century France', Paper presented at the Annual Conference of the Association of American Geographers, Toronto, April 1990.

Hugon, Anne, *The Exploration of Africa* (London: Thames and Hudson, 1993).

Konvitz, Josef, *Cartography in France, 1660–1848: Science, Engineering and Statecraft* (Chicago: University of Chicago Press, 1987).

Lejeune, Dominique, 'La Société de Géographie de Paris: un aspect de l'histoire sociale française', *Revue d'Histoire Moderne et Contemporaine,* v.29, 1982, pp.141–63.

Levasseur, Émile, *L'Étude de l'enseignement de la géographie* (Paris: 1872).

Livingstone, David N., *The Geographical Tradition* (Oxford: Blackwell, 1992).

Lukermann, Fred, 'The "Calcul des Probabilités" and the École Française de Géographie', *Canadian Geographer,* n.9, 1965, pp.128–37.

Malte-Brun, Conrad, *Précis de géographie universelle ...* (Paris: Chez Fr. Buisson, 1810–29).

—— (ed.), *Annales des voyages et de l'histoire ...* (Paris: Chez Fr. Buisson, 1807).

Malte-Brun, Victor A., 'Aperçu de l'état de nos connaissances géographiques', *Bulletin de la Société de la Géographie de Paris,* 1875, pp.561–5.

May, J. A., *Kant's Concept of Geography and its Relation to Recent Geographical Thought* (Toronto: University of Toronto, Department of Geography Research Publications, 1970).

Meynier, Andre, *Histoire de la pensée géographique en France (1872–1969)* (Paris: Presses Universitaires de France, 1969).

Naef, Weston, *Era of Exploration* (New York: The Metropolitan Museum of Art, 1975).

Perret, 'M. Dubois, Un grand géographe', *Le Correspondant,* v.88, n.265, Novembre 1916, pp.476–501.

Pinchèmel, P., M.-C. Robic and J.-L. Tissier, *Deux siècles de géographie française* (Paris: Bibliothèque Nationale, 1984).

Poirier, Louis, 'L'Évolution de la géographie humaine', *Critique,* 8, n.9, janvier–février 1947.

Rhein, Catherine, 'La Géographie: discipline scolaire et/ou science sociale?, 1860–1920', *Revue française de sociologie,* n.23, 1982.

Sarrazin, H., *Elisée Reclus ou la passion du monde* (Paris: La Découverte, 1985).

Schirmer, H., 'La France et les voies de penetration au Soudan', *Annales de Géographie,* v.1, 1891, pp.9–32.

—— 'La géographie de l'Afrique', *Annales de Géographie*, v.1, 1891, pp.57–67.

—— 'La géographie de l'Afrique', *Annales de Géographie,* v.2, 1892, pp.185–96.

Soubeyran, Olivier, 'Dubois, Gallois, Vidal: filiations et ruptures' in Paul Claval (ed.), *L'Histoire de la géographie française au XIX° et au début du XXe siecle* (Paris: CNRS, 1992).

Soja, Edward, *Postmodern Geographies* (London: Verso, 1989).

Vallaux, C., *Les sciences géographiques* (Paris: Félix Alcan, 1925 [?]).

Vidal de la Blache, Paul Marie-Joseph, 'L'École Normale', *Revue internationale de l'enseignement,* 8, 1884.

—— *Autour de la France. Pays et nations d'Europe* (Paris: De la Grave, 1889).

—— 'Le principe de la géographie générale', *Annales de Géographie*, n.5, 1896, pp.129–41.

—— 'Leçon de l'ouverture du cours de géographie', *Annales de Géographie*, n.38, 1899, pp.97–109.

—— 'La géographie humaine, ses rapports avec la géographie de la vie', *Revue de Synthese Historique*, n.7, 1903, pp.219–40.

—— *Tableau de la géographie de la France* (1903) (Paris: Éditions de la Table Ronde, 1994).

—— 'Les Pays de France', *La Réforme sociale*, n.48, 1–16 septembre 1904.

—— 'Rapports de la sociologie, avec la géographie', *Revue Internationale de Sociologie*, n.12, 1904, pp.309–13.

—— 'Les Bourses de voyage autour du monde' in *Congrès international d'exposition économique mondiale*, Mons mars 1905, section 1.

—— 'Régions françaises', *Revue de Paris*, v.5, n.17, 15 décembre 1910.

—— 'Les genres de vie dans la géographie humaine', *Annales de la Géographie*, n.20, 1911, pp.193–212, 289–304.

—— 'Des caractères distinctifs de la géographie', *Annales de Géographie*, n.22, 1913, pp.290–99.

—— *La France de l'Est (Lorraine-Alsace)* (Paris:Armand Colin, 1917).

—— 'Nécrologie de Pierre Foncin', *Annales de Géographie*, n.139, 1917, pp.67–9.

—— *Principes de géographie humaine* (Paris: Armand Colin, 1922).

—— *Principles of Human Geography* (trans: Millicent Todd Bingham) (London: Constable and Company, 1926).

History

Barthes, Roland, 'Le discours de l'histoire' (1967) in Roland Barthes, *Essais critiques IV: Le bruissement de la langue* (Paris: Aux Éditions de Seuil, 1984 pp.153–66).

Beltran, Alain and Pascal Griset, *La Croissance économique de la France, 1815–1914* (Paris: Armand Colin, 1988).

Benjamin, Walter in *Paris, capitale du XIX° siècle* (Paris: Éditions du Cerf, 1989).

Berstein, Serge and Pierre Milza, *Histoire de la France au XX° siècle*, vol. I: 1900–1930 (Brussels: Éditions Complexe, 1990).

Bloch, Marc, *Apologie pour l'histoire, ou Le métier d'historien* (Paris: Armand Colin,1961).

Blumberg, Hans, *The Legitimacy of the Modern Age* (Cambridge, MA: MIT Press, 1983).

Bourdieu, Pierre, Robert Chartier and Robert Darnton, 'Dialogue à propos de l'histoire culturelle', *Actes de la recherche en sciences sociales,* n.59, 1985, pp.86–93.

Braudel, Fernand and Ernest Labrousse (eds), *Histoire économique et sociale de la France*, vols III and IV (Paris: Presses Universitaires de France, 1976–82).

Certeau, Michel de, *L'écriture de l'Histoire* (Paris: Éditions Gallimard, 1975).

—— *La culture au pluriel* (Paris: Bourgois, 1980).

—— *Hétérologies: Discourse on the Other* (Manchester: Manchester University Press, 1986).

—— *L'invention au quotidien: 1. arts de faire* (Paris: Éditions Gallimard, 1990).

Charbit, Y., *Du malthusianisme au populationisme: les économistes français et la population, 1840–1970* (Paris: Presses Universitaires de France, 1981, pp.185–92).

Chevalier, Michel, *Le Système mediterranéen* (Paris: Le Globe, 1832).

Christin, Anne-Marie, 'L'Écrit et le visible: le dix-neuvième siècle français' in *L'Éspace et la lettre* (Paris: Cahier Jussieu, 1977, pp.163–92).

—— (ed.), *Écritures: Systèmes idéographiques et pratiques expressives,* Actes du colloque international de l'Université de Paris, Le Sycomore, 1982.

—— (ed.), *Écritures 2,* Le Sycomore, 1985.

Clark, Linda L., *Social Darwinism in France* (Birmingham Ala.: University of Alabama Press, 1984).

Clark, T. N., *Prophets and Patrons: The French University and the Emergence of the Social Sciences* (Cambridge, MA: Harvard University Press, 1973).

Conry, Y., *L'Introduction du darwinisme en France en XIXe siècle* (Paris: J Vrin, 1974).

Crosland, Maurice P., *Science in France in the Revolutionary Era* (Cambridge, MA: Harvard University Press, 1969).

Elwitt, S. J., *The Making of the Third Republic: Class and Politics in France, 1868–1884* (Baton Rouge: Louisiana State University Press, 1975).

Elwitt, S. J. *The Third Republic: Bourgeois Reform in France, 1880–1914* (Baton Rouge: Louisiana State University Press, 1985).

Febvre, Lucien, *Combats pour l'histoire* (Paris: Armand Colin, 1965).

Fourcy, A., *Histoire de l'École Polytechnique* (Paris: Eugene Bellin, 1987).

Hartog, Françoise, *The Mirror of Herodotus: The Representation of the Other in the Writing of History* (Berkeley: University of California Press, 1988).

Judt, Tony, *Past Imperfect. French Intellectuals 1944–1968* (Berkeley: University of California Press, 1992).

Lefranc, Abel, *Histoire du Collège de France* (Paris: Hachette, 1893).

Lejeune, Dominique, *La France de la Belle Époque 1896–1914* (Paris: Armand Colin, 1991).

—— *La France des débuts de la IIe République 1870–1896* (Paris: Armand Colin, 1994).

Manuel, Frank E., *The Prophets of Paris* (Cambridge, MA: Harvard University Press, 1962).

Novak, Barbara, *Nature and Culture* (New York: Oxford University Press, 1980).

Ory, Pascal, *L'Aventure culturelle française, 1945–1968* (Paris: Flammarion, 1989).

Outram, Dorinda, 'Politics and Vocation: French Science, 1793–1830', *British Journal for the History of Science,* n.13, 1980, pp.27–43.

Rabinow, P., *French Modern* (Cambridge, MA: MIT Press, 1989).

Rajan, Gita and Radhika Mohanram, *Postcolonial Discourse and Changing Cultural Contexts: Theory and Criticism* (Westport: Greenwood, 1995).

Roger, Jacques, *Les Sciences de la vie dans la pensée française du XVIII° siècle* (Paris: Armand Colin, 1963).

Rollet, Henri, *L'Action sociale des catholiques en France, 1871–1901* (Paris: Boivin, 1947).

Literature

Baudelaire, Charles, *La Vie antérieure.*

Conrad, Joseph, *Heart of Darkness.*

—— *The Mirror of the Sea.*

—— *A Personal Record.*

De Maupassant, Guy, 'Le Roman' in *Pierre et Jean*.

Dezon-Jones, Elyane, Introduction to *Du côté de chez Swann* (Paris: Librairie Générale Française, 1992).

Doumet, Christian, *Passage des oiseaux pihis* (Cognac: Le temps qu'il fait, 1996).

Éluard, Paul, *Les Dessous d'une vie ou la pyramide humaine* (Marseille: Les Cahiers du Sud, 1926).

Genette, Gerard, *Figures III* (Paris: Éditions du Seuil, 1972).

Hergé, *Tintin au Congo,* (Tournai: Éditions Casterman, 1930).

Hugo, Victor, *Travailleurs de la mer*.

—— *Les Orientales*.

Malraux, André, *La Tentation de l'Occident* (1926) (Paris: Bernard Grasset, 1996).

Péret, Benjamin, *Anthologie de l'amour sublime* (Paris: Albin Michel, 1956).

—— *L'Anthologie des mythes, légendes et contes populaires d'Alérique*.

Proust, Marcel, *Du côté de chez Swann*.

Roussel, Raymond, *Impressions de l'Afrique* (1910) (Paris: Jean Jaques Pauvert,1963).

Valéry, Paul, *Variété, 1924, Regard sur le monde actuel* (Paris: Éditions Gallimard, 1945).

Van Lier, H., 'Tintin ou la collecte du Monde' in *Le Musée imaginaire du Tintin* (Tournai: Éditons Casterman, 1980).

Verne, Jules, *Voyages extraordinaires: Mondes connus et inconnus*.

—— *Cinq semaines en ballon*.

—— *De la Terre à la Lune*.

—— *Géographie illustré de la France et de ses colonies*.

—— *Enfants du capitaine Grant*.

—— *Histoire des grands voyageurs*.

Zola, Émile, *Le ventre de Paris*.

Philosophy, aesthetics and social theory

Adorno, Theodor and Max Horkheimer, 'La production industrielle de biens culturels' in *La Dialectique de la raison* (Paris: Éditions Gallimard, 1983, pp.129–76).

Bachelard, Gaston, *L'Air et les songes* (Paris: 1962).

—— *Poetics of Space* (Boston: Beacon Press, 1964).

—— *On Poetic Imagination and Reverie. Selections from the Work of Gaston Bachelard* (Indianapolis: Bobbs-Merrill, 1971).

Barthes, Roland, 'L'effet du réel' (1968) in Roland Barthes, *Essais critiques IV: Le bruissement de la langue* (Paris: Éditions du Seuil, 1984, pp.167–74).

—— 'Déliberation', *Tel Quel,* n.82, Winter 1979, pp.8–18.

Bataille, Georges, *L'Érotisme* (Paris: Minuit, 1957).

Baudrillard, Jean, *Simulacra and Simulations* (New York: Semiotext(e), 1983).

Benjamin, Walter, *Charles Baudelaire: A Lyric Poet in the Era of High Capitalism* (London: Verso, 1983).

Carter, P. and D. Malouf, 'Spatial History', *Textual Practice,* n.3, 1989, pp.173–83.

Davies, Howard, *Sartre and Les Temps Modernes* (Cambridge: Cambridge University Press, 1987).

Dreyfus, Hubert L. and Paul Rabinow, *Michel Foucault: Beyond Structuralism and Hermeneutics* (Chicago: University of Chicago Press, 1983).

Foucault, Michel, *Les Mots et les choses: une archéologie des sciences humaines* (Paris: Éditions Gallimard, 1966).

—— *L'Archéologie du savoir* (Paris: Éditions Gallimard, 1969 [translated as *The Archaeology of Knowledge,* New York: Harper and Row, 1976]).

Freud, Sigmund, 'L'inquiétante étrangeté' in *Essais de psychanalyse appliquée* (Paris: Éditions Gallimard, 1933).

Giddens, Anthony, *The Consequences of Modernity* (Stanford: Stanford University Press, 1990).

Habermas, Jurgen, *The Philosophical Discourse of Modernity: Twelve Lectures* (Cambridge, MA: MIT Press, 1987).

Hall, Stuart et al. (eds), *Modernity: An Introduction to Modern Societies* (Oxford: Blackwell, 1996).

Harvey, David, *The Condition of Post-Modernity* (Oxford: Blackwell, 1989).

Jameson, Fredric, 'Questions à Michel Foucault sur la géographie', *Hérodote,* v.I, janvier–mars 1976.

—— *Postmodernism or the Cultural Logic of Late Capitalism* (Durham, NC: Duke University Press, 1991).

Mattelart, Armand, 'Les nouveaux scénarios de la communication mondiale', *Le Monde Diplomatique,* v.42, n.487, août 1995, p.24.

—— 'Une éternelle promesse: les paradis de la communication', *Le Monde Diplomatique,* v.42, n.500, novembre 1995, pp.4–5.

—— and Michèle Mattelart, *Histoire des théories de la communication* (Paris: La Découverte, 1995).

Merleau-Ponty, Maurice, *L'Oeil et l'Esprit* (Paris: Éditions Gallimard, 1964).

Ricoeur, Paul, *Temps et Récit,* 3 vol, (Paris: Éditions du Seuil, 1983–5).

Photography and painting

Anderson, Patricia, *The Printed Image and the Transformation of Popular Culture, 1790–1860* (Oxford: Clarendon Press, 1991).

Artforum, Autumn 1984–Spring 1985 (a debate on the 1984 exhibit on primitivism in twentieth-century art).

Banta, Melissa and Curtis Hinsley, *From Site to Sight: Anthropology, Photography and the Power of Imagery* (Cambridge, MA: Peabody Museum Press, 1986).

Barringer, Tim, 'Fabricating Africa: Livingstone and the Visual Image 1850–1974' in *David Livingstone and the Victorian Encounter with Africa* (London: National Portrait Gallery, 1996).

Barthes, Roland, *La chambre claire* (Paris: Éditions du Seuil, 1980 [translated as *La Camera Lucida,* New York: Farrar, Straus & Giroux, 1981]).

Beers, Burton F., *China in Old Photographs, 1860–1910* (New York: Charles Scribner & Sons, 1978).

Benjamin, Walter, 'Petite histoire de la photographie' in *Essais 1: 1922–1934* (Paris: Denoël, 1971–83).

Bensusan, A., *Silver Images: History of Photography in Africa* (Cape Town: Howard Timmins, 1966).

Berger, John, *Ways of Seeing* (London: Penguin, 1972).

Bernard, Denis and André Gunthert, *L'Instant rêvé. Albert Londe* (Nîmes: Jacqueline Chambon, 1993).

Bernier, R. R., 'The Subject and Painting: Monet's "Language of the Sketch"', *Art History,* v.12, n.3, September 1989, pp.298–321.

Berthier, Philippe, 'Des Images sur les mots, des mots sur les images: A propos de Baudelaire et Delacroix', *Revue d'histoire littéraire de la France,* v.80, n.6, 1980, pp.900–15.

Boulouch, Nathalie, *La Photographie autochrome en France (1904–1931)* (Thèse en histoire de l'art), Université de Paris I Panthéon-Sorbonne, 1994.

Bourdieu, Pierre, *Un Art moyen. Essai sur les usages sociaux de la Photographie* (Paris: Éditions de Minuit, 1965).

Brassaï, 'The Three Faces of Paris', *Architectural Digest,* n.54, March 1954.

Breton, André, 'Préface' in Karel Kupka, *Un Art à l'état brut. Peintures et sculptures des aborigènes d'Australie* (Lausanne: Éditions Claire Fontaine, 1962).

Burgin, Victor, 'Photographic Practice and Art Theory' in Victor Burgin (ed.) *Thinking Photography* (London: Macmillan, 1982).

Busy, Léon, 'L'autochromie en voyage de France au Tonkin', *Photo-Gazette,* n.9, 1912, pp.177–8.

Cagan, Steve, *Photography's Contribution to the 'Western' Vision of the Colonized 'Other',* Paper presented at the Center for Historical Analysis, Rutgers University, 10 April 1990.

Cardinal, Roger, 'Soluble City: The Surrealist Perception of Paris', *Architectural Design,* v.48, nn.2–3, 1978.

Charles Marville, Photographs of Paris 1852–1878 (Paris: The French Institute/Alliance Française, 1981).

Clark, T. J., *The Painting of Modern Life: Paris in the Art of Manet and his Followers* (New York: Knopf, 1985).

Courtellement, G., *Le Pionnier photographe de Mahomet* (Nîmes: Lacour, 1994).

Crary, Jonathan, *Techniques of the Observer. On Vision and Modernity in the Nineteenth Century* (Cambridge, MA: MIT Press, 1992).

Demours, Pierre, 'Une exposition d'Art plastique Nègre', *La Patrie,* 31 janvier 1927.

Didi-Huberman, Georges, *Invention de l'hystérie, Charcot et l'iconographie photographique de la Salpêtrière* (Paris: Macula, 1982).

Fabian, Rainer and Hans-Christian Adam, *Masters of Early Travel Photography* (New York: Vendome Press, 1983).

Falconer, John, 'Ethnographical Photography in India: 1850–1900', *The Photographic Collector,* v.5, n.1, 1984, pp.16–46.

—— *A Vision of the Past: A History of Early Photography in Singapore and Malaya, The Photographs of G R Lambert & Co, 1880–1910* (Singapore: Times Editions, 1987).

Gage, J., *Colour and culture. Practice and Meaning from Antiquity to Abstraction* (London: Thames & Hudson, 1993).

Galassi, Peter, *Before Photography* (New York: The Museum of Modern Art, 1981).

Gernsheim, Helmut and Alison Gernsheim, *L. J. M. Daguerre: The History of the Diorama and the Daguerreotype* (New York: Dover, 1968).

Gervais-Courtellement, Jules, 'La photographie des couleurs renovatrice des arts et des sciences', *La Fotografia artistica*, n.4, 1912, pp.53–5.

Gimon, Gilbert, 'Jules Itier, Daguerreotypist', *History of Photography*, v.5, n.3, July 1981, pp.225–44.

Gombrich, Ernst, 'Image and Word in Twentieth-Century Art', *Word and Image*, v.1, n.30, 1985, pp.213–41.

Goodrich, L. Carrington and Nigel Cameron, *The Face of China as Seen by Photographers and Travelers, 1860–1912* (Millerton: Aperture, 1978).

Graybill, Florence Curtis and Victor Boesen, *Edward Sheriff Curtis. Visions of a Vanishing Race* (New York: Thomas Y. Crowell, 1976).

Green, David, 'Classified Subjects – Photography and Anthropology: the Technology of Power', *Ten–8*, n.14, 1984, pp.3–37.

Hambourg, Maria Morris, 'Eugene Atget, 1857–1927: The Structure of the Work' (unpublished PhD dissertation), Columbia University, 1980.

Hambourg, Maria Morris and John Szarkowski, *The Work of Atget: Volume 1, Old France* (New York: Museum of Modern Art, 1981).

Hodeir, Catherine, Michel Pierre and Sylvaine Leprun, 'Les expositions coloniales. Discours et images' in Nicolas Bancel, Pascal Blanchard and Laurent Gervereau, *Images et colonies. Iconographie et propagande coloniale sur l'Afrique française de 1880 à 1962* (Paris: BDIC [Nanterre] and ACHAC [Paris], 1993, pp.129–39).

Horstmann & Godfrey Ltd, *Old Photographs of Chinese Cities: Hong Kong, Macau, Canton, Amoy, Shanghai and Peking, 1865–1912* (Hong Kong: Horstmann & Godfrey, 1995).

Hunter, Jefferson, *Image and Text* (Cambridge, MA: Harvard University Press, 1988).

Ishaghpour, Youssef, *Aux origines de l'art moderne* (Paris: La Différence, 1989).

Japonisme, Catalogue de l'exposition présentée au Grand Palais du 17 mai au 15 août 1988 (Paris: Éditions de la Réunion des Musées Nationaux, 1988).

Kerchache, Jacques, Jean–Louis Paudrat and Lucien Stephan, *L'Art Africain* (Paris: Mazenod, 1988).

Krauss, Rosalind, 'A Note on Photography and the Simulacra', *October 31,* 1981.

—— 'Photography's Discursive Spaces' in Rosalind Krauss (ed.), *The Originality of the Avant-Garde and Other Modernist Myths* (Cambridge, MA: MIT Press, 1985).

Lai, Edwin K., 'The Beginnings of Hong Kong Photography' in Asia Society Galleries, *Picturing Hong Kong: Photography 1855–1910* (New York: Asia Society Galleries and George Braziller, 1997).

Lee, Carmen Shawy, *John Thomson: A Photographic Vision of the Far East (1860–1872)* (M. Litt. thesis), St Antony's College, Oxford, 1985.

Lee, Rensselaer, *Ut pictura poesis: The Humanistic Theory of Painting* (New York: W. W. Norton, 1967).

Lindquist-Cock, Elisabeth, *Influence of Photography on American Landscape Painting* (New York: Garland Press, 1977).

Lucas, Christopher J. (ed.), *James Ricalton's Photographs of China during the Boxer Rebellion: His Illustrated Travelogue of 1900* (New York: Edward Mellen Press, 1990).

Melly, George, *Paris and the Surrealists* (London: Thames & Hudson, 1991).

Merleau-Ponty, Maurice, *Le Visible et l'invisible* (Paris: Éditions Gallimard, 1964).

Metz, Christian, 'Photography and Fetish', *October 34,* 1985, pp.81–90.

Michaels, Barbara, 'An Introduction to the Dating and Organisation of Eugene Atget's Photographs', *The Art Bulletin,* v.LXI, September, 1979.

Moholy-Nagy, L., *Peinture–Photographie–Film et autres écrits sur la photographie* (Nîmes: J. Chambon, 1993).

Morris, Frances (ed), *Paris Post War: Art and Existentialism 1945–1955* (London: Tate Gallery, 1993).

Newhall, Beaumont, *The History of Photography* (New York: Museum of Modern Art, 1993).

Park, Roy, '*Ut pictura poesis*: The Nineteenth Century Aftermath', *Journal of Aesthetics and Art Criticism*, v.28, n.2, Winter 1969, pp.155–64.

Peltre, Christine, *L'Atelier du voyage: Les peintres en Orient au XIXe siècle* (Mayenne: Le Promeneur, 1995).

Pinney, Christopher, 'Underneath the Banyan Tree: William Crooke and Photographic Depictions of Caste' in Elizabeth Edwards (ed.), *Anthropology and Photography 1860–1920* (New Haven: Yale University Press. 1992).

—— 'The Parallel Histories of Anthropology and Photography' in Elizabeth Edwards (ed.), *Anthropology and Photography, 1860–1920* (New Haven: Yale University Press, 1992, pp.74–95).

Rouillé, A., *La Photographie en France. Textes et controverses: une anthologie* (Paris: Macula, 1989).

Rubin, William (ed.), '*Primitivism*' *in Twentieth Century Art* (Boston: Little Brown, 1984).

Ryan, James, R., 'Imperial Landscapes: Photography, Geography and British Overseas Exploration, 1858–1872' in Morag Bell, Robin Butline and Michael Heffernan (eds), *Geography and Imperialism, 1820–1940* (Manchester: Manchester University Press, 1995).

Sagne, Jean, *Delacroix et la photographie* (Paris: Herscher, 1982).

Schiff, R., *Cézanne and the End of Impressionism. A Study of the Theory, Technique and Critical Evaluation of Modern Art* (Chicago: University of Chicago Press, 1984).

Scott, David, *Pictorialist Poetics: Painting and the Visual Arts in the Nineteenth Century* (Cambridge: Cambridge University Press, 1988).

Sekula, Allan, 'On the Invention of Photographic Meaning' in Victor Burgin (ed.), *Thinking Photography* (London: Macmillan, 1982).

Smith, Bernard, *European Vision and the South Pacific* (New Haven: Yale University Press, 1985).

Sobieszek, Robert, 'Photography and the Theory of Realism in the Second Empire: A Reexamination of a Relationship' in Van Deren Coke (ed.), *One Hundred Years of Photographic History* (Albuquerque: University of New Mexico Press, 1975, pp.145–59).

Sontag, Susan, *On Photography* (Harmondsworth: Penguin, 1979).

Spencer, Frank, 'Some Notes on the Attempt to Apply Photography to Anthropometry during the Second Half of the Nineteenth Century' in Elizabeth Edwards (ed.), *Anthropology and Photography, 1860–1920* (New Haven: Yale University Press, 1992).

Stapp, William F., 'Souvenirs of Asia: Photography in the Far East, 1840–1920', *Image,* v.37, nos. 3–4 Fall–Winter 1994.

Sternberg, Jacques and Pierre Chapelet, *Le Tour du monde en 300 gravures* (Paris: Planète collection 'Redécouvertes', 1972).

Street, Brian, 'British Popular Anthropology: Exhibiting and Photographing the Other' in Elizabeth Edwards (ed.), *Anthropology and Photography, 1860–1920* (New Haven: Yale University Press, 1992).

Tagg, John, 'The Currency of the Photograph' in Victor Burgin (ed.), *Thinking Photography* (London: Macmillan, 1982, pp.110–41).

—— *The Burden of Representation: Essays on Photographies and Histories* (London: Macmillan, 1988).

Thomson, John, *Illustrations of China and Its People: A Series of 200 Photographs with Letterpress Description of the Places and People Represented,* 4 vols (London: Sampson Low, Marston & Searle, 1873–4. Reprinted as *China and Its People in Early Photographs* [New York: Dover, 1982]).

—— *Thomson's China: Travels and Adventures of a Nineteenth-Century Photographer,* Introduction by Judith Balmer (Hong Kong: Oxford University Press, 1993).

Tomas, David, 'The Ritual of Photography', *Semiotica,* v.40, ns1–2, 1982, pp.1–25.

—— 'Toward an Anthropology of Sight: Ritual Performance and the Photographic Process', *Semiotica,* v.68, nos. 3–4, 1988, pp.245–70.

Travel and exploration

Allégret, Elie, *La Mission du Cameroun* (Paris: Société des missions évangéliques, 1924).

Allégret, Marc, *Carnets du Congo: voyage avec André Gide* (Paris: CNRS Éditions, 1993).

Autour du Monde (Paris: Félix Alcan, 1925).

Baudelaire, Charles, *Invitation au voyage.*

Berchet, Jean-Claude, *Le Voyage en Orient. Anthologie des voyageurs français dans le Levant au XIX° siècle* (Paris: 1985).

Bruno, G., (pseudonym of Mme A. Fouillée), *Le Tour de France par deux enfants* (Paris: E. Belin, 1877).

Calvino, Italo, *Collezione di sabbia* (Milano: Garzanti, 1984).

Carre, J.-M., *Voyageurs et écrivains français en Egypte* (Cairo: Imprimerie de l'Institut Français d'Archéologie Orientale, 1956).

Céline, Louis Ferdinand, *Lettres et Premiers Écrits d'Afrique 1916–1917* (Paris: Éditions Gallimard, *Cahiers Céline* n.4, 1978).

Christy, Cuthbert, *Big Game and Pygmies. Experiences of a Naturalist in Central Africa Forests in Quest of the Okapi* (London: Macmillan, 1924).

Claudel, Paul, *Connaissance de l'Est* (1900) (Paris: Éditions Gallimard, 1974).

Cook, James, *The Explorations of Captain James Cook in the Pacific as Told by Selections of his Own Journals, 1768–1769* (New York: Dover, 1971).

Durosay, Daniel, 'Le livre et les cartes. L'espace du voyage et la conscience du livre dans le *Voyage au Congo*', *Littérales,* n.3, 'L'espace optique du livre', Centre de Recherches du Département de Français de l'Université de Paris-X-Nanterre, juin 1988, pp.55, 73–4.

Flaubert, Gustave, *Voyage en Orient.*

Gervais-Courtellement, Jules, *Mon voyage à la Mecque* (Paris: Hachette, 1896).

—— 'Visions d'Orient', *L'Illustration,* 26 novembre 1910, p.374.

Gide, André, 'Les villages des tribus Massas', *L'Illustration,* 5 mars 1927, pp.236–7.

—— *Voyage au Congo* and *Le Retour de Tchad* (Paris: Éditions Gallimard, 1927).

Guigne, de, 'Réflexions sur les anciennes observations astronomiques des chinois, et sur l'état de leur empire dans les temps les plus recules', *Annales des Voyages,* v.8, pp.145–89.

Jeanneret, Michel, Introduction to Gerard de Nerval, *Voyage en orient,* v.I, (Paris: Flammarion, 1980, pp.15–41).

Johnson, M., *Safari. Récit de la brousse africaine* (Paris: Stock, 1931).

—— *Gongorilla* (Paris: Société parisienne d'édition, 1933).

Itier, Jules, *Journal d'un voyage en Chine, 1843, 1844, 1845, 1846,* 3 vols (Paris: Dauvin et Fontaine, 1848).

Lamartine, Alphonse, *Voyage en Orient*

Lanfant, Marie-Françoise et al. (eds), *International Tourism: Identity and Change* (Thousand Oaks: Sage, 1995).

Le Hérissé, René, *Voyage au Dahomey et à la Côte d'Ivoire* (Paris: H. Charles-Lavauzelle, 1903).

Livingstone, David, *Missionary Travels and Researches in South Africa* (London: John Murray, 1857).

—— and Charles Livingstone, *Narrative of an Expedition to the Zambesi and its Tributaries; and of the Discovery of the Lakes Shirwa and Nyassa, 1858–1864* (London: John Murray, 1865).

London, Charmian, *Journal de bord du 'Snark'* [*The Log of the 'Snark'*, 1915] (Paris: UGE 10–18, 1979).

Londres, Albert, *Terre d'ébène* (Paris: Albin Michel, 1929).

Loti, Pierre, *Suprêmes visions d'Orient* (Paris: Calman-Levy, 1921).

—— *Voyages (1872–1913)* (Paris: Robert Laffont, 1991).

MacCannell, Dean, *The Tourist, a New Theory of the Leisure Class* (New York: Schocken, 1976).

Maclaren, I. S., 'Exploration/Travel Literature and the Evolution of the Author', *International Journal of Canadian Studies/Revue Internationale d'Etudes Canadiennes,* n.5, 1992.

McClintock, F. Leopold, *The Voyage of the 'Fox' in the Arctic Seas* (London: John Murray, 1859).

Martin, Claude, 'Préface' to Pierre Loti, *Voyages (1872–1913)* (Paris: Robert Laffont, 1991).

Maupassant, Guy de, *De Tunis à Kairouan.*

Monk, Williams (ed.), *Dr Livingstone's Cambridge Lectures* (Cambridge: Deighton Bell, 1858).

National Portrait Gallery, *David Livingstone and the Victorian Encounter with Africa* (London: National Portrait Gallery, 1996).

Nerval, Gerard de, *Voyage en orient,* v.I (Paris: Flammarion, 1980).

Ozouf, M. and J. Ozouf, 'Le Tour de France par deux enfants' in P. Nora (ed.),

Les Lieux de Mémoire, v.2, 'La République' (Paris: Éditions Gallimard, 1986, pp.291–321).

Ponting, Herbert, *The Great White South* (London: Duckworth, 1923).

Poulaine, R., *Étapes africaines, Voyage autour du Congo* éd. de la *Nouvelle Revue Critique*, coll. 'La vie aujourd'hui', n.12, 1930.

Pratt, Mary Louise, *Imperial Eyes: Travel Writing and Trans-culturation* (London: Routledge, 1992).

Robertson, George et al. (eds), *Travellers' Tales: Narratives of Home and Displacement* (London: Routledge, 1994).

Roosevelt, Theodore, *African Game Trails* (London: 1910).

—— *Through the Brazilian Wilderness*, 1911(?).

Rousset, Jean, 'Pour une poétique du journal intime' in Joseph P. Strelka (ed.), *Literary Theory and Criticism. Festschrift presented to René Wellek in Honor of his Eightieth Birthday*, v.2, (New York: Peter Lang, 1984, pp.1215–28).

Salisbury, Edward A. and Merian C. Cooper, *The Sea Gypsy* (New York: G. P. Putnam & Sons, 1924).

Seabrook, William, *Jungle Ways* (London: George G. Harrap, 1931).

Sédat-Jobe, *L'Experience africaine d'André Gide 1925–1926*.

Speke, John Hanning, *Journal of the Discovery of the Source of the Nile* (London: William Blackwood, 1863).

Stanley, Henry Morton, *How I Found Livingstone ...* (London: Sampson and Low, 1872).

—— *Through the Dark Continent* (London: Sampson and Low, 1880).

—— 'Central Africa and the Congo Basin; or, The Importance of the Scientific Study of Geography', *Journal of the Manchester Geographical Society*, n.1, 1885.

—— *In Darkest Africa* (1890).

Stone, I., *Jack London, l'aventurier des mers* (Paris: Stock, 1970).

Urry, John, *The Tourist Gaze* (Newbury Park: Sage, 1990).

—— *Consuming Places* (London: Routledge, 1995).

Youngs, Tim, *Travellers in Africa: British Travelogues, 1850–1900* (Manchester: Manchester University Press, 1994).

Wallace, A. R., *Malay Archipelago*.

Acknowledgments

Many people have assisted me with this book, directly and indirectly.

Above all I want to thank Peter Stambler. He read each chapter, made suggestions, helped me to think and gave me encouragement.

I am especially grateful to David Johnston, Geoffrey Nowell-Smith, Bill Routt and my editor Rob White.

I wish to thank Patricia McMurray for her careful editing and Nigel Harkness who checked my translations from French.

I would like also to thank Zygmunt Baranski, Carmen Cheng and Stephanie Eschenlohr.

I am grateful for the help I was given by the Musée Albert Kahn and in particular I wish to thank Gilles Baud Berthier, Marie Mattera Corneloup, Sophie Couëtoux, Monique Demeillers and Martine Espalieu-Ruby.

Lam Shuk Foon would lie on the couch in the sitting room in my flat in Hong Kong reading sections of the book that I had written that day while I prepared dinner in the kitchen. She would come into the kitchen, a smile on her face, a slight giggle of pleasure, her head tilted, and I knew it was ok.

Index